THE BETTER PART
The Life of Teresa Demjanovich

THE MACMILLAN COMPANY
NEW YORK · CHICAGO
DALLAS · ATLANTA · SAN FRANCISCO

**THE MACMILLAN COMPANY
OF CANADA, LIMITED**
TORONTO

SISTER MIRIAM TERESA

(Taken from a charcoal sketch)

THE BETTER PART

The Life of Teresa Demjanovich

BY

THEODORE MAYNARD

THE MACMILLAN COMPANY · NEW YORK

1952

B
D

Nihil obstat

JOHN M. A. FEARNS, S.T.D.

CENSOR LIBRORUM

Imprimatur

✠ FRANCIS CARDINAL SPELLMAN

ARCHBISHOP OF NEW YORK

October 29, 1952.

The nihil obstat and imprimatur are official
declarations that a book or pamphlet is free of
doctrinal or moral error. No implication is contained therein that those who have granted the
nihil obstat and imprimatur agree with the con-
tents, opinions or statements expressed.

To Edith Donovan

CONTENTS

INTRODUCTION   1

1. BACKGROUND OF BAYONNE   11

2. TERESA'S CHILDHOOD   24

3. FAMILY AND SCHOOL LIFE   45

4. ADOLESCENCE   56

5. INTERLUDE   66

6. AT ST. ELIZABETH'S   75

7. FIRST TEACHING   99

8. THE PROBLEM OF VOCATION   106

9. THE SISTERS OF CHARITY   117

10. TAKING THE HABIT   127

11. THE PRIVATE VOWS   143

12. FLEDGLING INSTRUCTRESS   153

13. INFLUENCE—CONSCIOUS AND UNCONSCIOUS   163

14. MISUNDERSTANDINGS   188

15. THE CONFERENCES   203

16. OTHER WRITINGS   218

17. DEEPENING SPIRITUAL LIFE   230

18. SIGNALS FOR DEPARTURE   244

19. AFTERWARDS   261

THE BETTER PART
The Life of Theresa Demjanovich

Introduction

ONLY a few months after Teresa Demjanovich's death I began to teach at the college from which three or four years earlier she had graduated. That I did not hear of her at the time is easily explainable: the posthumous volume of her conferences, *Greater Perfection,* with which her fame began, was not published until late in 1928, and the first of the biographies dealing with her, eight years after that. Moreover, most of the Sisters with whom I had closest contact had had little contact with her. This was true even of the dean of the college of her time (and mine), Sister Marie José, who, as its president, died on November 11, 1951. Though this was less true of the librarian of the same period, who now, as Mother Benita, is the superior-general of the Sisters of Charity of New Jersey, somehow Teresa's name never came up in our conversations. So also with the college chaplain, Monsignor Lalor McLaughlin, who taught a course in philosophy which she attended. Recently I have consulted all these about her, together with a number of Sisters whose acquaintance was not made before but who were among her college professors or prefects; and naturally there are a good many of Teresa's classmates still alive, or those who were novices with her.

Without pretending that I have interviewed all who knew Teresa, I have seen a good many of them, and probably from the rest I would only have heard much the same story. But of course I went to see her two surviving and older sisters, Miss Mary Demjanovich and Mrs. Paul McLaughlin; and her brother Charles, known to everybody as Father Charles, has often come to my home and has provided me with all the documents bearing upon his sister's cause for beatification (running to about 1,200 pages), some of very great value. Unfortunately, though I several times met Teresa's spiritual director, Father Benedict Bradley, when I was a guest at St. Mary's Abbey in Newark, he never mentioned her, nor was there any reason why he should have done so to me—unless he had possessed the gift of prophecy, which would have informed him that I was to be her biographer. He died, nearing eighty, at the end of 1945.

This may seem to be a serious gap in my knowledge, yet it is probably of little consequence in view of the fact that he preserved all of Teresa's long letters to him, as well as some other papers. It goes without saying that the seal of the confessional would have debarred him from imparting more than is to be found in these documents and in several detailed statements he wrote regarding Teresa after her death in 1927. These constitute the necessary basis of this book, in which Father Benedict appears as one of the main characters. Now that I have studied these documents, there are a few points about which I would like to ask him further questions; but as most of these questions can be (and have been) put by me to other people who were close to Teresa, that Father Benedict is no longer here to answer them is of little vital consequence.

Names have already been mentioned, and I propose mentioning a good many more. When Sister Zita wrote Teresa's biography in 1936, she (or her superiors) considered it advisable to have everybody, so far as possible, anonymous, even Sister Zita signing her book merely "By a Sister of Charity." It is now recognised in her community that veils of this sort diminish the authenticity of any historical or biographical work; I have been able to persuade my informants to lay aside their personal reticence, to this extent, for the sake of substantiating more definitely what they have in their power to relate.

This does not mean that every statement recorded here has necessarily to be taken at its face value. Not for an instant do I doubt the perfect sincerity of those whom I have consulted, but there is sometimes a considerable difference between objective and subjective accuracy; and it soon became evident that now and then there were minor discrepancies in several of the accounts with which I was furnished. This being the case, I did not feel that I was called upon to sit in judgment upon the evidence, even had this been desirable or possible. After all, I was not conducting even the most informal court of enquiry. In the rare instances when I had some mental reservation about particular points, I could not but recognise the honesty of my informants. The caution I have occasionally had to exercise does not imply scepticism. I have put down everything as faithfully as I am able to present it; the reader himself must draw his own conclusions.

My function should be understood as I understand it. For I have noticed now and then a disposition to ask whether or not I believe that Teresa was a saint. As a matter of fact I do incline to that belief, but it is not for me to take up any definite attitude; whatever private opinion I have is held with a loose hand, as this is a matter upon which only ecclesiastical authorities have any right to speak. They will do so only after long investigation, and though this has begun, nobody can anticipate the decision that will be reached. Father Benedict Bradley did, it is true, say roundly from the start that Teresa would eventually be canonized, but even he, who knew far more about her than anybody else, was really only saying that in his opinion she ought to be canonized. I write these words on All Saints' Day, when not only those formally registered as saints are honored but also "the host that no man can number," few of whose names are known on earth. Presumably Teresa Demjanovich is among them; and as the process for her beatification is now in its preliminary stage, it may well be that it will be carried through to success. Further than that it is not safe to go.

It rather amused me (but edified me too) that one Sister, consulted in a group, seized an opportunity to whisper to my wife, "Will Dr. Maynard drop the project if he is not convinced?" This was apparently said hopefully—as the Sister in question is not herself among Teresa's partizans—but also, I trust, indicated her confidence in my integrity. A misunderstanding is also indicated: to write this book I do not feel that I have to be "convinced" that Teresa was a saint but merely that she was somebody worth writing about. It is not my business to prove or disprove anything that does not fall within my province. However, I intend to be absolutely candid, and probably shall be too much so to please all who read me.

Yet I do not look for many objections on this score. For what struck me powerfully was the freedom with which Teresa was discussed by those who knew her, among whom there was a considerable difference of opinion. Even when this discussion took place in a group, those with reservations about her did not show the slightest hesitation in saying precisely what they thought, without the slightest fear of offending those present who held a contrary view. This was all the more remarkable because in these groups were those in a high position and therefore capable of making their displeasure felt. It was clear that there was something like the situation that existed when Teresa was in college and, later, in the novitiate; some loved her almost to the point of adoration, while others—even when they respected her character and admired her gifts—were not attracted by her personality.

A more delicate matter has to be gone into. There was a good deal of misunderstanding on the part of Sister Mary

Ellen, the novice-mistress who had Teresa in charge, and much of this was unintentionally caused by Father Benedict Bradley under whose direction she came. Basically this conflict (if that is not too hard a word) was between those who exalted the contemplative life and those who held—it must be admitted with some reason—that Sisters of Charity are called to the active mode. What cannot be denied is that St. Vincent de Paul, in gathering his Daughters, thought of them as strong girls who would do the rough work necessary in his charitable enterprises but of whom not much more was demanded than that they be moderately pious. He definitely did not want them to be nuns; therefore instead of being given a religious habit they wore a kind of uniform, that of peasant girls of the seventeenth century. As for vows, they were permitted to take none until towards the end of his life, and then only for a twelve-month period. This situation will have to be examined in greater detail later, in order to place it in its historical background. It is enough for the moment to say that many of the older members of the community—and some of the younger ones too—considered that Teresa was out of place among them and that she should have joined the Carmelites instead. This was Sister Mary Ellen's view, and she must not be blamed for holding it.

Teresa, however—and here we touch the very core of her life—regarded herself as having a mission to infuse the Marthas around her with the spirit of Mary; indeed, she believed herself to be commissioned in this by Christ Himself, though such claims were never advanced by her and though this was a secret that remained unknown except to her spiritual director. Only after her death was the meaning of her life disclosed, though the trend of her spirituality could not be completely concealed, and was sometimes resented by those who had another theory as to the vocation of a Sister of Charity. Its full disclosure resulted in her fame.

Finally, as to Father Benedict Bradley, he was the spiritual director not only of the novices but of the professed Sisters. Among them were those who sometimes complained that he was trying to transform them into Benedictine contemplatives. The charge had this much justification: without in the least wishing to change the character of the Sisters' distinctive vocation, he did believe that a greater degree of contemplation would not be incompatible with it. But he would not have ventured so far as he did had he not felt certain that Teresa was inspired by God.

In some respects he may not always have been well advised in his dealings with her. What the documentary evidence to be presented shows is that, in seeking to develop Teresa's inner life, he put her in a position in which she had to endure an immense amount of suffering. To the extent that he may have unwittingly brought this about he was sorry; but he dared not be "disobedient to the heavenly vision," and he knew that a treasure had been committed to him. Of the thorny problems that arose as a consequence, I do not have the presumption to offer any definite solution. If in touching upon them I indicate the direction to which I incline, I must not be understood to be making any positive assertions. At the same time to be absolutely noncommittal would also be colorless; it is only through candor (not devoid, I hope, of charity) that the truth can be arrived at about all concerned.

A Daily Thought from Sister Miriam Teresa, selected and arranged by Sister Mary Gertrude Quinlan, and published in 1948, offers gems of spirituality gleaned from Sister Teresa's writing. Some of these selections, taken from letters and other sources, had not been published previously.

The most important, and virtually the only, documentary source for Teresa Demjanovich's life is the collection of papers made for presentation to the Holy See. The originals are in the Chancery Office at Paterson, New Jersey. An autobiography, which she undertook at Father Benedict's suggestion but which was cut short by illness after she had written a few pages, is printed in full by Sister Zita. Father Benedict drew upon it when making his long statements about Teresa.

In addition to those already mentioned as having supplied information, I should set beside Sister Zita's biography a little book published in 1946 under the title of *An American Teresa*. Its author, Margaret Conklin, while drawing upon Sister Zita, is able to tell us things about which Sister Zita, as she was not at college with Teresa, could only know by hearsay. Teresa's closest friend at that time, Agatha Spinella, was able to supplement Miss Conklin. I have interviewed a number of other college friends, and her college professors (some of whom changed their role to that of disciple); I have also made a point of consulting those who are hardly to be called friends, in the sense that their attitude is somewhat critical or sceptical, as I wanted to know what they thought about it all. None of those I encountered can be described as antagonistic towards Teresa (though one or two may have been antagonistic at one time); rather they were cool and aloof. In any event I was not so much interested in opinions but in facts.

Of printed sources the two most important are Teresa's two posthumously published books, *Greater Perfection*, and her poems, *The Seventieth Week*. While her verses do not, in my judgment, have much literary merit, they often throw a good deal of light upon her life and character; and, after all, that was primarily the purpose of their publication. To these must be coupled the biographies to which reference has already been made.

In the way of subsidiary printed sources I have made use of Sister Mary Agnes Sharkey's three volumes *The Sisters of Charity of New Jersey* (1933) and Sister Mary Catharine's anonymously published pamphlet *Elizabeth Seton and St. Elizabeth's*. It was written some time after 1947 and exhibits wonderful verve and brilliance and humour. On the Constitutions, I have before me the *Regulations of the Society of the Sisters of Charity of the Diocese of Newark, New Jersey* (Convent Station, N.J., 1925), and also their *Directory and Praiseworthy Customs.*

The Bulletin of the Sister Miriam Teresa League of Prayer, issued quarterly since 1946, contains a number of details not obtainable elsewhere. There is a chapter on Teresa in the latest edition of *Sanctity in America* (1945) by the Most Reverend Amleto Giovanni Cicognani, the Apostolic Delegate to the United States. And a pamphlet biography by the Vincentian Father Joseph P. Donovan, *Will Sister Miriam Teresa Make the Grade?* (1948) should be mentioned despite its unfortunate title. A further useful guide has been *Canonical Legislation Concerning Religious: Authorized English Translation* (Westminster, Md., 1948).

With regard to the Catholic Church of the Eastern Rite, to which Teresa never ceased to belong, though since adolescence her actual association was with the Latin Rite, I have consulted Donald Attwater's *The Christian Churches of the East,* published in two volumes in 1946–1947, and some information was gleaned from the compilation *Byzantine Slavonic Rite Catholic Diocese of Pittsburgh, Silver Jubilee 1924–49,* presumably brought out in 1949 in Pittsburgh. This provides data on all the parishes of the diocese, the great majority of which are in Pennsylvania, but with others in New Jersey, New York, Connecticut, Massachusetts, Ohio, Michigan, West Virginia, Indiana, Illinois, and Minnesota. But as Teresa never went beyond the confines of New Jersey, except for an occasional trip to New York City and a single excursion to Philadelphia, the book, fascinating though it is, was useful, so far as she was concerned, only for the general picture it presents of one of the Eastern Rite Catholic Churches in operation in the United States. On the same subject are the excellent booklets *The Eastern Catholic Church* by John Callok (1937); *Eastern Catholics* by Clement C. Englert, C.SS.R (1940), and the same author's *A Comparison of the Roman and Byzantine Mass* (1947).

Revelatory of Teresa's versatility is the college yearbook *The Elizabethan* for 1923, of which she was the art editor but of which most of the letterpress was also by her. As for her reading in the field of spirituality, she had, since her college days, been saturated in the Bible, and upon this and the Liturgy of the Church she most frequently draws in her own writing. We know also that she had read St. Teresa of Ávila and St. Thérèse of Lisieux, though their influence upon her is not very apparent. One discerns more of Abbot Marmion's *Christ the Ideal of the Monk* (1926) and its classical predecessor, *Christ the Life of the Soul* (1924). Of still greater immediate effect were the following: *How to Walk Before God* by T. F. Vaubert, S.J. (1910), *A Catechism of the Vows* by Peter Cotel, S.J., *The Little Secret* by Cassian Karg, O.M. Cap., and *The Degrees of the Spiritual Life* (1907) by the Abbé Saudreau, especially Volume II.

To all those who have supplied information it is perhaps unnecessary to make thanks in each individual case, for their names occur in the text. But at least Mother Benita must be thanked at this point, as except for her it would not have been possible for me to have written this book. And Sister Zita and Sister Anne Lucille gave invaluable help and were our hostesses when my wife and I were staying at St. Elizabeth's, seeing to it that we were made comfortable and arranging a rapid-fire succession of interviews. At these interviews my wife, who was always present, was so adroit in extracting what she knew I needed to know that it probably seemed to some of those who came to see us that she and not I was doing the interviewing.

Finally, a very special word of thanks is due to Sister Zita. Because of her sympathetic understanding of Teresa, she was selected to write her biography, and did an excellent piece of work. In view of this it would have been understandable had she slightly resented the fact that I, as a layman, should have been asked to write this book. It would have been all too possible for her, while giving ostensible support, actually to have held back. Instead she has given without stint. It is a pleasure to record that, while working together, we have become friends.

CHAPTER ONE

ↄ৵৶

Background of Bayonne

BAYONNE is not among the more attractive of the larger
cities of New Jersey, slight as is the beauty of most of the
principal centres of the state. Some of the smaller places, such
as Morristown and Princeton and Montclair, are as charming
as anything one could hope to find, and there are delightful
villages in the hills and along the coast resorts which, if somewhat garish, are redeemed by the grandeur of the ocean. But
on the flat stretch between Newark and Camden, whatever
evidences of prosperity may be seen, utilitarianism is close to
being at its ugliest. Though with growing wealth there has
come about some effort to improve the aspect of the crowded
industrial centres, those of the well-to-do who are able to live
elsewhere almost inevitably leave the spot from which they
derive their wealth and, except for recognising the advantages
of imposing stores and hotels and public buildings, show little
interest for improving squalor, so long as it is not too naked.

Bayonne, however, reveals to the most casual eye—and this
is no doubt true of other such places—evidences of having
been considerably improved during the past fifty years; but
it is also at once evident upon what it lives—refineries for oil
and gasoline and their by-products. For this it is suited by

having nine miles of dock space, which is used for loading coal as well as oil, but thus only adding to the grime and stench which, try as the city may, cannot be much disguised. Nor are there, except in the more select quarters, any very serious efforts to cope with so difficult a task. For the rest the teeming population has to manage as best it can, supplying longshoremen and hands for the refineries and the factories of chemicals, margarine, and so forth.

Bayonne, though so directly serving New York City—giving service as well to all parts of the Eastern States—was until recently cut off from nearly all the cities surrounding it. It lies at the tip of a long narrow peninsula, which is only three-quarters of a mile wide at Bayonne, lying between New York and Newark Bay, into which the Hackensack River enters a little to the north. Farther up between the Hackensack and the Hudson are a number of pleasant suburbs, but as one comes south, past West New York and Union City and Hoboken, the peninsula begins and, with it, great dreariness. Because Bayonne is at the tip of this peninsula, it was the most isolated spot there—or was at one time—being separated from Newark by marshes and from Staten Island by the Kill van Kull, the narrow strip of water lying between. To get anywhere except to Jersey City used therefore to be so great an undertaking that few of the inhabitants of Bayonne had much incentive to travel beyond their familiar drab streets. However, with the disabilities went some advantages; a series of compact little societies grew up there—Irishmen, Poles, Italians, Ukrainians, and so forth—held together all the more firmly by their isolation. It was to one of these European-born groups that Teresa Demjanovich's father and mother, surrounded by their children and a number of relatives who had come out to join them, definitely belonged. Indeed, it was to associate with their own racial group that they had settled in Bayonne.

The situation has of course considerably changed; the children of the immigrants grew up as Americans, and sometimes felt vaguely ashamed of their origins. Being Americans, they need to get around, and the automobile offers them a means of escape from their surroundings, which many of them, having got on in the world, prefer to leave for ever. Fifty years ago, for this purpose, there was only the Central Railroad of New Jersey, but this, while carrying passengers, was built mainly for freight; now, in addition to the cars, there are buses and a bridge to Staten Island and ferries from this point or that, though not from Bayonne itself. Of the city as it was in Teresa's childhood, it might almost be said that once deposited there one had no choice but to stay. The prospect does not strike one as delightful, but to most who went there it had its compensations.

If the young Ruthenian immigrant Alexander Demjanovich and his bride Johanna Szuchy settled there nearly seventy years ago, after a brief stay in New York City, it was not that Alexander should work in the refineries—though to that he came in the end—but that the place was cheap to live in and, more important, that so many fellow Ruthenians were already there. Yet the term may be misleading, for that of Czech or Ruthenians is usually considered equivalent to that of Ukrainian or "Little Russian," and these are to be found in Russia, Poland, and the present Czechoslovakia, which was then part of the Austro-Hungarian Empire. But however indistinct the lines of racial cleavage may be to most of us, they were perfectly clear to the various racial groups themselves, who, in fact, often brought some of their old animosities with them to the New World. Probably the most accurate term to use is Rusins.

Yet from what one hears of the young couple, their decision to move to Bayonne was not so much to find the companionship of their kind—for they were, if not unsociable, content with one another—but because in New York it was difficult, if not impossible, at that time to find a Catholic church of the

Eastern Rite to which they belonged, whereas Bayonne did contain one in which Mass was said in the Old Slovak to which they were accustomed. To people so pious as they were this was a great consideration. In New York they could assist only at a Mass said in Latin, with which they were not familiar. They understood that, despite the surface differences in the ritual, the Holy Sacrifice was essentially the same, but the liturgical language and actions were somewhat bewildering, and the Latin Rite may have seemed to them cold, as it was certainly less ornate than their own. Besides, they could not have felt much at their ease among Irish and German Catholics.

There had been a time when Bayonne, which was originally a Dutch settlement, had been largely inhabited by Irish families, and some of these are still to be found there. But the Irish were rapidly rising in the world, and when they remained in Bayonne they obtained better houses than those relegated to the newer immigrants pouring in from Russia, Central Europe, the Balkans, and Italy. The Poles, often a bit belligerent, were strenuously of the Latin Rite, nor was it forgotten by such people as the Ukrainians and the Ruthenians that in Poland, when they had the chance, they tried to turn Greek Catholics into Roman Catholics, in flat contravention of the Catholic spirit and the declared policy of the Holy See. However, in Bayonne they were not numerous enough to create much difficulty; a more serious danger came from the Orthodox Church, indistinguishable from the Eastern Catholics in liturgy and well-nigh indistinguishable in doctrine. The divergencies between them were not very sharply understood by an unlearned people, with the result that there was a good deal of passing back and forth between the two bodies, with the more powerful drag exerted by those of the Orthodox Church.

The Demjanovich family never for an instant wavered in their Catholic loyalty, little as they may have known of the complex history of the great schisms that separated Russia and Greece from the Roman obedience, and much as it may have been to their social advantage to leave a part of the Catholic Church so little understood by their fellow Catholics for one whose position was recognized and respected. That they stood firm in the crisis that eventually occurred is greatly to their credit.

They had come from Bardejov (or Bartfeld) on the southern slopes of the Carpathians. From that district, as it is now under Communist domination, uncounted thousands have been mysteriously drawn behind the Iron Curtain—no doubt because of their Christian fealty—to sweat and die in Russian slave camps. (All this was of course undreamed of in those days.) Bardejov was a beautiful spot and was moreover of notable prosperity of a quiet sort, as it was a centre where custom-built shoes were manufactured. Smart Austrian officers and affluent Hungarian nobles kept the place well supplied with orders.

Under such circumstances it seems slightly odd that Alexander should have left his native soil. We may presume that he had heard—as what European had not?—that the streets of the United States were paved with gold. Though he was not doing badly in Bardejov, he was led to believe that a man of his special skill could in a short time glean a small fortune among the millionaires of New York. He was not in the least avaricious, nor was he—as soon appeared—a very good businessman, but it was natural enough that he thought of improving his position. As with so many—perhaps the majority —of the immigrants, there was no intention of permanent Americanization but rather of quickly making in this country enough money to make them affluent according to the standard of living in the land of their birth when they should return there. His visit with Johanna to the United States has been represented as a honeymoon trip—and so it was, if it be considered chronologically—but it seems much more likely that his motives were what I have suggested.

Moreover, there is no reason to doubt that he would have returned to Bardejov—for he soon discovered that the United States were not exactly paved with gold—had he not received word that his mother in that little Carpathian town was dead. There was now much less inducement for him to leave America—perhaps all the less because he had so little to show for his labors—so he decided to invest what money he had saved while working at his trade in New York (he may have brought some money with him too) in a store of his own in Bayonne. Though from the material aspect he might have done better to have invested his money in New York, it may be that he did not have quite enough money for that. In any case he wanted a place where he could attend Mass according to the Eastern Rite; Bayonne seemed to him suitable both as a place of residence and business.

The section he chose had formerly been known as Irishtown, though most, if not all, the Irish had, by the time he went there, gone elsewhere. The name it still bears—derived I do not know how but suggesting to my ear something out of J. M. Barrie—is Constable Hook. It was about the most noisome part of the city, full of huge oil tanks, whose odors were not as yet under much control, with other odors blowing across from adjoining paint and soap factories, and with a good deal of soot in the air. In those days the industry of oil refining was not very refined. Today, while the huge towering tanks still assault the eye, they do not assault the nostrils to the extent that they did when the Demjanoviches had to close all the windows when the wind blew in their direction. It was in Constable Hook that they took a square, unprepossessing box of a house at 217 East 22nd Street, living in close quarters behind the shoe store Alexander opened. It had the advantage of costing very little and of having a church of the Eastern Rite hardly a step away.

Children were born in fairly rapid succession, two of them dying in infancy but five of them surviving, as three of them still survive. Alexander must have been thought of as a family leader to have been able to persuade several of his relatives to join him at Bayonne. Either that, or he must have painted Bayonne as a more desirable place than many would now consider it. Possibly they needed little urging, for they had the same idea of the material advantages to be found in America that had lured Alexander from the beautiful Carpathians and the friendly communal life they had enjoyed at Bardejov. When they arrived, the house on East 22nd Street came to be regarded as the fortress of the clan, where on Sundays they could foregather for talk and companionship.

Unluckily for Alexander, his shoe business did not prosper. He should have understood (but evidently did not) that there would be only the very slightest demand for custom-built shoes in a place like Bayonne. Even the well-to-do managers of the refineries and factories bought ready-made shoes with only a few of them aware that those built by a skilled craftsman wore so well that their higher cost made them, in the long run, an economy. The mass of the people—those living from hand to mouth—could not afford such economies. In order to keep going at all, Alexander had to offer cheap factory-made footwear (it was still the day of high shoes or what the English call boots), and though he did now and then obtain an order for custom-built shoes, such orders did little more than satisfy his pride in craftsmanship; they did not begin to provide for the needs of his increasing family.

Even in Bayonne he might have done better than he did, had he established himself in a better location. Who except poorly paid workmen ever went to Constable Hook? In a smart store on the Boulevard things might have been different, but he was off in a hole in an insalubrious section; there he found that it is not invariably true that he who makes a better mousetrap will find a path trampled to his door. He came rather near to being caught in a rattrap himself.

His greatest drawback was that he was not insistent enough about being paid promptly. He gave credit too readily to friends or the friends of friends, until the day came when he found himself saddled with bad debts to the extent of $600, a large sum for him to carry. Even then perhaps he might have adopted a strict cash-and-carry policy and got "tough" with his debtors, but probably he recognized that he did not have the heart to carry it out. What could he do when a poor, well meaning woman promised to pay the following week for her child's badly needed shoes? So rather than go into the ignominy of bankruptcy, after nearly twenty years of struggle with an unprofitable shoe store, he decided to close up shutters and try something else.

One surmises that the fact that he was so good a craftsman at his own trade gave him an insight into other crafts. At any rate that is what happened: Bayonne needed coopers for its oil, men whose work had to be perfect, with its cunning adjustment of stave to stave so that no drop could ever escape from the barrel. It may be that he had already had some experience of such work at Bardejov, for in the Europe from which he had come a rigid specialization was not the rule. Perhaps during periods when orders for custom-built shoes were slack, he had been obliged to master a second craft upon which he could fall back when necessary. Be that as it may, he found employment as a cooper, and it was as a cooper that he earned his living for the next sixteen years.

The refineries did not pay high wages, but because Alexander was a skilled man he was put in charge of the most delicate process of cooperage. The wages he received were good for those days—about $20 a week, perhaps equivalent to four times as much today, especially when we remember that cars and television sets were as yet unknown and that life was not cluttered up with the gadgets that everybody now seems to think indispensable. As we never hear of his being out of work, being not only highly skilled but sober, conscientious, and reliable, he did not do at all badly, though one may still wonder how it came about that he was able to bring up his children so well. This must have been largely due to Johanna's ability to stretch pennies and to the fact that the older children got jobs as soon as they were out of high school and contributed to the family budget. The household had few amenities and no elegances, but it was never in want, and it may be said that the Demjanoviches tended to rise a bit above their social class. Even from the material point of view this must be considered a family blessed by God. Most of all was it blessed in its admirable father and mother, to whom the worship of God and the keeping of His commandments were of paramount importance. To be exact in the performance of all religious duties and to work hard and live frugally may strike some people as dull. But they were all happy and respected and prosperous, in a quiet fashion.

They were in no sense to be pitied, unless it be that poverty in a Europe to which a sturdy peasantry gave its tone—even a poverty greater than the Demjanoviches ever knew—does not involve ugliness, whereas in such a town as Bayonne, though it may offer more opportunities for advancement than occur in Bardejov, the externals of living are often drab. The odious phrase "gracious living" means simply opulent living. This the Demjanoviches lacked; their grace, like that of the King's Daughter, was within.

When Alexander first settled in Bayonne, the automobile had not been invented, so there was no need for gasoline. While this limited their radius, no hardship was imposed upon a family content with their own home. By the time Alexander drifted into cooperage, the car was beginning to be used, adding to Bayonne's prosperity, and he lived to see the land being covered with a host of Model-T's. Before that, however, lubricants had been needed for machinery,

and kerosene oil still gave the kind of illumination that most
families used, though gas and electricity were in the better-
class houses. Even so, many old-fashioned people insisted that
a kerosene lamp gave a light easier on the eyes than any
other. So even in this respect there is no need to pity a family
because it did not enjoy all the conveniences of what we are
accustomed to consider civilization.

It was into this milieu that Teresa, the youngest of the
Demjanovich children, was born on March 26, 1901. She
was baptized at home five days later by Father Theodorus
Stephan, the curate of the parish, this fact seeming to indicate
a desire on the part of the parents that their baby be
christened at once with Johanna present. Such a desire must
have been urgent, for the child could have been carried to
the church, which was less than a block away; and a domi-
ciliary baptism meant that the full ritual of the Eastern Rite
had to be somewhat modified. One may suppose that this was
a rather special concession made to devout and important
parishioners, for there was no apparent reason why the
baptism could not have been put off for another week, by
which time Johanna would have been able to walk to church.

Some have imagined that the name Teresa was conferred
because of the family devotion to St. Teresa of Ávila, but for
this there is not a particle of evidence. These simple people,
who venerate a large number of saints of their own rite, of
some of whom most people in this country have never heard,
would in their turn in all likelihood never have heard of St.
Teresa. In view of the baptismal certificate, a copy of which
lies before me, the explanation of the name is simple. The
child's godmother was her father's sister-in-law, and as she
was a Teresa it was part of good manners to give that name
to the new-made Christian. Uncle Heinrich Hoffman acted
as godfather.

Most Eastern Rite Catholics—though this is not generally
true of the Ruthenians—baptize by immersion. In other re-

spects the ritual followed differs from the Roman in that it is
—as is true of other sacraments—at once elaborate and administered in a deprecatory instead of an assertive form. Thus
the priest says, "The servant of God [whose name he then
mentions] is baptized in the name of the Father, Amen. And
of the Son, Amen. And of the Holy Ghost, Amen." After this
come three exorcisms and the renunciation of Satan made
by the sponsors and the anointing of the child—done twice—
on the forehead, chest, back, ears, hands, and feet. Then the
Nicene Creed is said. At the end of the baptism the thirty-
first psalm is intoned three times by the priest while he puts
the baptismal robe on the child. The ceremony is long and
includes, as is characteristic of the Eastern Rite, several
litanies and prayers not found in the Roman Rite. But essentially, of course, it is the same as that of the Western
Church.

A feature of the Eastern Rite is that confirmation comes
immediately after baptism and that this is administered by
any priest and not necessarily by a bishop. Again there are
anointings on the forehead, eyes, nostrils, mouth, ears, chest,
hands, and feet, at each anointing the words, "The seal of
the gift of the Holy Ghost, Amen," being said. The great
passage on baptism addressed to the Romans by St. Paul (6:
3–11) about being buried with Christ as a pledge of being
made free from the dominion of sin and rising with Him
from the dead is then read, as well as Matthew 28: 16–20,
where Christ commissioned his disciples to go and teach and
baptize all nations. The ceremony concludes with another
litany.

Confirmation immediately after baptism will seem less
strange to members of the Western Church if they reflect that
many Councils and Fathers emphasized that confirmation is
the consummation of baptism. Eastern Catholics, instead of
waiting for the child's later development, arm him forthwith
as Christ's soldier. Teresa herself, when writing a fragmentary

biography twenty-six years later, calls the day of her baptism and confirmation "the real beginning of my life, the life of the spirit." In a letter written shortly before that time to her spiritual director, she says: "The sweetest of all graces vouch-safed to me was, not when Jesus called me His spouse, nor when the Holy Ghost inebriated me with the torrents of His love, but when the Father revealed Himself to me, and I realized what it meant to be a child of God." So clear and in-tense a perception of what happened on March 31, 1901, is rare among Christians, however full a theoretical admission is made that baptism is indispensable for admission to the Kingdom, a grafting into the Vine, our adoption as co-heirs with Christ.

Two years before this there had been another christening and confirmation, when Teresa's brother Charles—whom Teresa used jestingly to call her twin, and whom many peo-ple took to be actually so, noticing how close was the bond between them—was made a Christian. Whether or not this took place in the church, as is customary, or at home, as in Teresa's case, I do not know. What needs to be recorded is that there was a christening party afterwards for relatives and friends and that Alexander, stirred by uneasy forebodings about the future, broke down and sobbed, "Who is going to bring up the baby?" The gloom does not seem to have been at all called for; though no doubt he was in financial diffi-culties, brought about by people who did not pay him what they owed, he was not quite forty at the time, and Johanna was about the same age. Moreover, they both still had good health, and Alexander, though a poor businessman, was not without some measure of resourcefulness. But the one photo-graph I have seen of him suggests that he was not only gentle and refined but, perhaps for that very reason, subject to moods of melancholy.

It is pleasant to be able to record that this momentary de-pression—or any recurring fits of depression that may have come upon him—was needless. He lived long enough to see five of his children grown up, and several of them holding good positions, so that he was able to retire. Indeed, the baby who had drawn forth his sudden tears was ordained a priest two years before Alexander died. As for Teresa, she had graduated from college and, after a year and a half at home, was on the point of becoming a Sister of Charity. Her entering the novitiate at St. Elizabeth's had to be postponed for a week because of her father's funeral.

CHAPTER TWO

෨෨

Teresa's Childhood

THERE are two stock phrases that come into many of the briefer biographical notices of the saints: "She was born of noble but devout parents"; "He came from a poor but honest family." Even in the case of the saints about whom we have more detailed information, the same is in general true. Now and then one comes across one who had formerly been a notorious sinner—but usually with his sins greatly exaggerated, or going not much further than the "wildness" of youth. But for one of these there must be a hundred who were well brought up, in many instances carefully trained by a notably religious father and mother. There is more joy in heaven over one repentant sinner, Our Lord remarked in a sardonic way, than over ninety and nine who need no repentance. But He was referring primarily to those of the pharisaical breed who, of all people, have most cause to repent. The historical fact is that sanctity is usually nurtured in youth. Even St. Paul, who called himself the chief of sinners, was an outstandingly religious man in his own way—a persecutor of the Church, but one who sincerely believed that he was in this capacity doing God a service. The first thing to seize about Teresa is that she was an exemplary child, trained in an exemplary family, however little any of them would have thought of themselves (or of Teresa) as being more than an ordinarily faithful Christian.

Though, as was natural, the greater part of Teresa's religious upbringing was in the hands of her mother, she tells us that her father himself took over her instruction when she was being prepared for her First Communion—which is certainly rather unusual, especially in the case of a girl. He did not feel that he should neglect anything so very important, sure though he was that his wife would attend to it properly. Father and mother were equally particular that all their children assist at Mass regularly and attend to their other religious duties. These were most punctiliously carried out, for the fasts of the Eastern Catholic Church are many and severe, and the great feasts of the Church were in that household of purely religious significance. Yet Santa Claus came to fill their children's stockings, and there were Christmas presents, if no Christmas tree, that charming German custom that Queen Victoria's Prince Consort was the first to introduce to the English-speaking world. There were no Easter bunnies, however; and though the Easter eggs for their breakfast were gaily painted they were first taken in a basket to church, together with ham and home-made cheese and a cake called *pascha,* to be blessed by the priest. Human merrymaking was not excluded, for these were no sour-faced puritans, but they never lost sight of the great facts: Christ had been born; Christ had risen from the tomb. In the main it was a spiritual joy that radiated their hearts.

A strict obedience was exacted by the parents, and had to be shown to all those in authority, as for all elders deference and respect were demanded. Moreover, though there was nothing of a grim "sabbatarianism" there was also nothing of that too comfortable laxity often to be found among Latin peoples. Sundays and holydays were set apart for the worship of God, but in the afternoons there were social gatherings at the Demjanovich home. These were rather sedate affairs as a rule, consisting of little except quiet conversation, except when some music was provided by a relative or a guest.

Alexander was a model Christian father, never sitting down to his six o'clock supper—even when it was ready and on the table—until the Angelus had been rung. Family prayers said in common were the rule and—surely this must be an almost unique circumstance—Mary the eldest daughter read the Martyrology aloud every night before the family retired, using the Old Slovak translation. What we do not hear of as being said was the Rosary, as in Irish families of the more pious sort, for this was a devotion which at that time (as now) was not in general use among Catholics of the Eastern Rite.

Teresa wrote in her fragmentary autobiography that, though her parents had early taught her the Our Father and the Hail Mary and to make the sign of the cross, "up to the time of my First Communion the knowledge acquired from others in matters of religion was rather limited." This, however, needs some qualification. As she attended only public schools—the only parochial school being some distance away, and doubtless too crowded with children of the parish to have room for outsiders—she, like all the children belonging to the Eastern Rite, went to the church for two hours a day after school to attend a course given by a lay teacher. Perhaps this teacher attempted little more than to give them lessons in the intricate chant used at Mass, in which the whole congregation joined, for had they received instruction in doctrine for two hours a day even a poor teacher would surely have taught them a good deal. But Teresa's phrase "from others" should be carefully noted; it implies that she was already blessed by infused knowledge of divine things, about which she elsewhere has something more specific to say, though without indicating what form it took. Father Benedict, her spiritual director when she was in the novitiate, corroborates the same point most emphatically, but from statements made to him by Teresa herself.

A family legend—perhaps not to be taken too seriously—is that when she first started to walk as a baby, she used to be lured on by a book. There need be no question about the fact itself, but we all know how those looking back upon such incidents are prone to discover in them a significance that never existed. If this is taken only as an indication of such intellectual curiosity as an infant can show, well and good; but we must not be asked to believe that she was showing a precocious interest in books. She might have been just as much enticed to make her first steps at the sight of a coloured rubber ball. Sir Edmund Gosse in his delightful *Father and Son* relates that he had been told that the first word he ever spoke was "book," and he did become one of the most bookish of men, though he read no prophecy of his future propensities in the incident. Nor must we read any prophecy as to Teresa's future in the story about the book.

What is much more to the point, and much more surprising, is that Teresa believed that she attained the age of reason before she was three. For proof she offers the fact that she distinctly remembered the burning of the church nearby, which sight she gazed at with tiny face flattened against the windowpane while the firemen worked in vain to save the structure. It was into her father's shoe store that helpers from the parish carried such of the sacred vessels and plate as they were able to save from the flames. She recalls, too, how from the kitchen in the living quarters at the rear her mother served the people with coffee to warm them against the winter cold.

There need be no doubt that Teresa had a remarkable memory. But other children have had infantile memories almost as good. My own, for that matter, goes back, however capriciously, to incidents that happened in India when I was three. Yet I am sure that this does not prove that I had reached the age of reason by then, and I can see no reason for supposing that Teresa's memory, even if it was phenomenal, demonstrates that a power of judging morally between right and wrong was developed in her at that time. What she may be thinking of was that she had already discovered that little naughtinesses were liable to be punished with a slap; but babies in arms discover as much, or even puppies. Here I profess some rational scepticism, based upon a fairly extensive knowledge of babies and small children.

This nevertheless is offered by Teresa as "the first noteworthy proof of my attainment of the age of reason," and she goes on to say that she remembers her first sin but does not say just when it happened. "It was," she tells us, "an act of disobedience, followed by a lie." We may be sure that it was not anything serious, for her spiritual director was able to say after her death: "I doubt whether in all her life she had ever committed a deliberate venial sin. Of one thing I am certain—that she had never committed a mortal sin." And Father Benedict was in the best position to judge.

Teresa was not permitted to make her First Confession and Communion before she was twelve. This was the usual age in the Western Church until Pope Pius X urged that an earlier age was desirable, and in 1910 the Sacred Congregation of Rites said that from the age of discretion there existed the obligation of satisfying the precept of Holy Communion. Catholics of the Eastern Rite, however, without intending to flout the Pope's recommendations—which, after all, were not mandatory—tended to cling to their own ways. Holy Communion was received in those days only once a year, at Easter. Then the faithful received the Sacrament under both species. Ordinary and not unleavened bread is used, and this, having been divided into small pieces at the commencement of Mass, is put after the Consecration into the chalice of the Precious Blood. At the Communion the Sacred Host is placed into the mouth of the communicants with a golden spoon. Communion is received standing, not kneeling. In St. John the Baptist Church, however, the communicants knelt.*

There is much in which Catholics of the Eastern Rites differ in their practices from the Western Church, that is, the Catholic Church as most of us know it. Thus on certain occasions, especially Easter, as we have seen, food is carried to the church to be blessed by the priest. In the early Church there was the *agape,* the love feast that preceded the Mass. This custom is alluded to both by St. Jude and by St. Paul, and Tertullian described it in some detail as he knew it at the end of the second century. But as these love feasts became occasions of disorder, they were eventually forbidden. What the Eastern Rites retain is no more than a vestige of them, just as another vestige may be found in the *pain bénit* distributed in France at the end of Mass.

In other ways the Eastern Rites appear (usually only superficially) different from those to which we are accustomed. Statues are virtually non-existent, their place being taken by a profusion of ikons, many of them, naturally enough, representations of the saints of the East, but also including many of the saints venerated universally. Our Lady and St. Joseph and St. Anne are specially honoured, but one gets the impression that the great archangelic figures receive, I will not say more attention than most of the saints, but more attention than the West usually gives them. The plaques of the Stations of the Cross are not often seen. And when side altars are set up, they are normally enclosed by a screen, as is the high altar—about which more in a moment. Only recently has there been any devotion to the Sacred Heart, though as it is

---

*The reformers of the sixteenth century made a great ado in demanding the cup for the laity, so much that it was made to seem part and parcel of their revolt and therefore was resisted. Yet at that very time the Eastern Rites not only permitted Communion in both kinds but were forbidden to make any change. The Holy See was obliged to take the position it did because of attacks upon the full doctrine of the Real Presence.

only in recent centuries that this has come to have prominent place in the Western Church, Catholics of the East can hardly be expected to know much about it. Their tendency is conservative, and they do not wish to be mistaken for Catholics of the Latin Rite, though in our time a Latin tendency has operated. This is somewhat to the distress of priests of the old school. They wish to preserve their own liturgy (in which the Holy See gives them full support) and are reluctant to encourage what might be called "extraliturgical" devotions. Though devotion to the Sacred Heart is not of course to be classed among these, in the Eastern Church it has its equivalent in the devotion to the Good Shepherd, very frequently seen in ikons or stained glass.

One would look in vain for the familiar figures of St. Anthony of Padua and the Little Flower; but St. Peter and St. Paul and John the Baptist and Catherine of Alexandria and Helena, the mother of the Emperor Constantine (and according to an amusing tradition the daughter of Old King Cole), and of course a number of saints about whom members of the Western Church hear little, are special favourites. But it must be remembered that there are a great many local or national saints in the countries of Western Europe who fall into the same category. The glorious fact is that there are so many canonized saints that the vast majority of them can, for most people, be no more than a name in the Martyrology. What may be said of the ikons is that, not being articles of mass production, they usually reach a higher level of artistic taste than do most of the plaster statues seen in the West. As Catholics of the Eastern Rite are rarely well-to-do, one must conclude that they give generously and enthusiastically towards the support of their religion.

They are, indeed, drawn upon rather heavily in other ways, for though they do not often have to maintain parochial schools or, so far as I am aware, back any extensive foreign missionary work of their own, they are called upon to support a married priesthood and of course the children of such marriages. One might suppose that they might grumble at this burden, but apparently they do not, for, while they are prepared to admit that a celibate clergy is more ascetic, their own married priests are, so they believe, more fatherly.

Here we touch what has contributed most to their being misunderstood in a country in which Catholic priests—all except those of their own rite—are vowed to celibacy. We too easily forget that this is merely a disciplinary regulation and that the Pope could, if he wished, at any moment dispense the secular clergy from this obligation, extremely unlikely though it is that he would do anything of the kind. But because of what has come close to being a scandal—and is unquestionably an embarrassment—the Holy See, under some prompting from the American hierarchy, has followed up an earlier prohibition of marriage to priests of the Eastern Rite in America with a ban, issued in 1929, which is absolute. Such priests as are already married are left undisturbed, but not even priests who are married abroad—as is still perfectly permissible—are allowed to exercise their sacred functions should they come to the United States.

The matter calls for a little further explanation. Eastern Rite priests in countries where celibacy is not enjoined do not marry as priests. If they wish to marry, they must do so before ordination to the sub-diaconate, and no priest is allowed to marry a second time should his wife die. Moreover, bishops are always chosen from among celibates—as is true also of the Orthodox dissidents—so that they come from the religious orders or are widowers. The result is that while clerical marriage is for the moment tolerated in the United States (within these limitations), it is now doomed to extinction. But of course there are monks and nuns—those of the Order of St. Basil, and of some of the other religious orders, in particular the Franciscans and Redemptorists, but also including Jesuits—belonging to the Eastern Rite. A married

clergy cannot be other than confusing, if not actually incomprehensible, to the average American Catholic. This only
means that the average American Catholic does not know
much Church history, for the law about celibacy was not
definitely promulgated until the eleventh century, and after
that many bishops more or less winked at the existence of
married men among their priests, believing that the disciplinary rule could not be immediately enforced.

We stumble here across a prejudice which, like all prejudices, is unreasonable and ignorant. What, however, must be
added is that, unfortunate as prejudices in this matter may
be, a married priesthood is not of the essence of the Eastern
Rite any more than celibacy is of the essence of clerical life
in the West. As for the Rite itself and the variety of liturgical
languages, the Holy See has been at considerable pains to pro-
tect them, going so far as to forbid a Catholic to change his
Rite without explicit permission from Rome in each individual case. Nevertheless, Catholics are perfectly free to receive the sacraments from priests of any Rite and, in order
to quicken the sense of unity, Western Catholics are encouraged to attend an Eastern Mass now and then, and to receive Holy Communion (under both species) when they do
so.

The point is stressed because Teresa, owing to circumstances which will be related in due course, became in effect
a member of the Latin Rite, to which she never received
any formal transference, such as was given her brother
Charles when he entered the seminary at Seton Hall in South
Orange. She therefore remained all her life technically a
member of the Greek Catholic Church. Because of this she
may have a subsidiary mission in being a connecting link
between the two divisions of the Church, something of considerable importance in view of Rome's hope that the Eastern Catholics—sometimes vulgarly, incorrectly, and even
slightingly termed "Uniats"—will yet prove to be a means of

reuniting to the Holy See those who broke off from its obedience in the great schisms of the Middle Ages. Though it goes without saying that, if Teresa is ever canonized, it will be because of her heroic sanctity, it would be a great thing for the Church if beatification were decreed for one who never ceased to belong to the Eastern Rite.

Another point should be made: one may discern in Teresa the mark that her early religious associations put upon her. This may have accounted for her fervour, or at least its special manifestations, for it helps to explain why at college, and even in the novitiate of the Sisters of Charity, many looked upon her as something of an outsider. They saw that she was different from themselves; and while it would be too much to claim that this was solely due to her upbringing, one cannot but feel that her upbringing had a good deal to do with it. The intensity of piety she had acquired during her "sojourn in the East" she carried with her to the West. Much of this must of course be credited to the saintly family into which she was born, but their sanctity was developed by their Eastern Catholicism. They seem indeed to have had no strong interests outside their home and their church. Their church was almost as much their home as their domicile; indeed, their household at 217 East 22nd Street might be described as an extension of the church. Teresa's earliest friend was Elizabeth Szabo, the daughter of the priest. The two girls were in and out of each other's house all the time.

Coming to the liturgy, it must be remembered that Latin as the language of the Western Church came rather late, for even in Rome itself Mass was said in Greek until the third century, the first appearance of Latin occurring (so it is said) in North Africa. There are still about sixteen languages (I have heard the number placed as high as nearly thirty, but certainly there are at least sixteen) in which Mass is regularly said. Moreover, even among Catholics who use Latin there are a number of liturgical divergencies. Milan has what is

called the Ambrosian Rite (and it was to this that Pope Pius
XI belonged), and other rites that are Latin but not Roman
are to be found in France and Spain. Finally, some of the
religious orders—for example the Cistercians, the Carthu-
sians, and the Dominicans—do not observe the Roman usage,
slight as may be their departures from it. The Church wishes
to preserve such variations, which in no way affect the essence
of uniformity, as this is centred in obedience to the Holy See.
They—and we may include the existence of a married clergy
—should be looked upon as the multicolored flowers in Our
Father's garden.

For practical purposes no doubt the Latin Mass with which
we are familiar is to be preferred in a busy city parish, where
a new crowded congregation has to be provided for every
hour, with sometimes a Mass being said in the basement or
the school auditorium while it is also being said in the main
edifice. But that is just as it happens; it is not by design.
Broadly it may be said that while the Latin Mass has its own
austere beauty and grandeur, that of the Eastern Rite is in
some respects more elaborate, richer, and more poetical, as
in some of its features it is also more ancient.

While the Eastern Catholic Church is the open door
through which it is hoped the Orthodox Church may return
to Catholic unity, the liturgical identity of the two bodies is
also a door through which Eastern Catholics, when they are
looked upon with a doubtful eye by their fellows of the West,
are tempted to escape to a communion in which they might
have less to explain. Therefore the schisms that have been
of frequent recurrence in America are hardly to be wondered
at. What is never to be forgotten is the loyalty to Rome
shown by Eastern Catholics in spite of the not very handsome
treatment given them by some of the Latin Rite. Lost though
they must often have felt themselves to be, it is remarkable
how well, upon the whole, they have understood that their
isolation is more apparent than real, and that they are as

thoroughly Catholic as those who have now and then spoken and acted as though they were slightly under a cloud. This at least must be said of them: their religious zeal is a good deal higher than that of the Orthodox dissidents—a larger body than they are in this country but of whom only a small proportion make much effort to practice their religion.

Among American families of the Eastern Rite, the Demjanoviches stand out for their piety and their undeviating Catholicism. On Saturday Johanna always cooked enough for Sunday, except for what had to be heated up. It was Alexander who cooked the Sunday breakfast, not because he was less punctilious than his wife, but so as to give her a complete rest on that day. Similarly, before any of the great feasts of the Church enough food was cooked in advance, for these were occasions when the worship of God was not to be interrupted. And if the family observance of Sundays and holy days was notable, so also was its observance of the fasts, which in the Eastern Church are stricter than is customary among us. It has often been remarked that in general tone the East is more ascetic than the West, except in the matter of clerical celibacy. It is not a question of singling out this or that practice, but of the pervading spirit. Here, too, may be found a further explanation of Teresa.

It is unquestionable that Catholics of this sort are, taken as a group, more unworldly than others. Or if "unworldly" is not quite the word to use, "submissive" would not be far off the mark. Perhaps this is because everywhere they have been able to maintain themselves only with difficulty—in the Ukraine and the Balkans and the Near East against the dominant Orthodox Church, and in Poland against Catholics of the Latin Rite who brought pressure on them to turn *Roman* Catholics. While this last factor tends to make them a bit thin-skinned (which is not surprising), it exists side by side with great humility. This shows itself, for example, in the deprecative form used in the administering of the sacraments. Even in confession the priest does not say to the penitent, as with us, "I absolve thee," but, "May God, through me a sinner, forgive thee." There is something very sweet and touching about it.

The reverse of the medal is that the Churches of the East incline to an extravagance no longer followed by the Churches of the West. This no doubt comes about because of their historical circumstances. They had their rise in parts of the world in which the monks of the Desert are still remembered. Though their monastic lawgiver, St. Basil, aimed at moderating the excesses of those who had gone before, St. Benedict, when later he drew up the rule that came to be accepted as the norm for monks, had further to modify St. Basil. To this day on the promontory of Athos, where nobody lives but monks, no woman is allowed to set her foot. Though their *lauras* have been respectfully treated by the conquering Turks, a Byzantine mood prevails. The East, whether in communion with Rome or not, is accustomed to bow to secular authority, and knows little of the struggle that went on for centuries in the West between Emperor and Pope. Even in the case of such bodies—and they are relatively small ones—as have returned to the Roman obedience* (for only the Melkites of the patriarchate of Antioch can claim, rather dubiously, never to have fallen into schism), they remain stamped, to some extent, by the experience they have undergone.

The touchiness that has been mentioned is sometimes perhaps more in evidence than the humility, though that is never far away. Nobody can blame even the meekest of people for resenting the attitude only too often assumed by their fellow Catholics; so in the United States they take a mild revenge (which may take a different form elsewhere) by saying, among

---

*Catholics of the Eastern Rite number rather less than ten million, as against a nominal fifteen times more for the Orthodox Church, and more than thirty times as many Western Catholics.

themselves, that American Roman Catholics have a formal and businesslike religion, a criticism which is not unjust, though it leaves much out of account. Though West and East do not differ a hair's breadth in doctrine, the East is so very liturgical that it is not hard to understand why its Catholics should comment, a little disdainfully, on the accumulation of devotions now found in the West. Individuals among them may practice some of these, but they are not introduced into church services under the guise of perpetual novenas and the like. The clergy would be afraid that the quiet serenity of their people would be broken by such distractions.

While there are no doubt some gains in this, there are also some losses. They lose, for instance, a good deal by not having the Rosary in general use; on the other hand they benefit immensely from the fact that it is not said while attending Mass, or the Divine Service, the term they ordinarily use. At this the worshippers are never merely present, or hear it said for them, but take an active part. The whole congregation makes the responses—at least in the main parts of the Holy Sacrifice—singing, as does the celebrant, in their uniquely beautiful chant. The litanies, which form so prominent a part of it, are known to all; so also are the great liturgical hymns, in which everybody joins.

The congregation stands, though pews are now coming into use, and there is much bowing, though no genuflecting as we know it. In the bowing the body is bent almost at right angles and the outstretched hands almost sweep the floor, as a token of the completest obeisance. The sign of the cross frequently occurs, made from right to left and not, as with us, from left to right. The first two fingers are pressed together to symbolize the two natures in Our Lord, and these two fingers are pressed against the ball of the thumb to acknowledge the Blessed Trinity.

Such symbolism runs throughout all that is done, and Mass is made the more mysterious by being sung—it is always a

Missa cantata—behind a screen, known as the *eikonostasis*, whose doors are closed except at certain great moments. The worshippers therefore only catch glimpses of the altar. In some pre-Reformation churches in England there may be found a rood screen, and this has been introduced into some Catholic churches of the "Pugin-Gothic" type. But this rood screen is rarely, if ever, found in more recently built churches, and modern ecclesiastical architecture tries, so far as possible, to avoid many pillars so that everybody may see the officiating priests and the Victim, when elevated after consecration. In the Eastern Rite it is otherwise.* The *eikonostasis* is needed by the elaborate ritual; the screen is crowded with ikons, up to perhaps fifty of them, symbolizing the participation in the Holy Sacrifice of all those pictured there, representing the whole host of heaven.

Normally such a Mass calls for the assistance of a deacon, or a priest taking the deacon's part, as he stands at the main door of the *eikonostasis,* where his function is of great importance, for he is the link between priest and people, directing them, leading them. In the United States, however, where the clergy of the Eastern Rite are few, in many cases the cantor, who is also the server, has to substitute for the deacon. The Catholics of the East have never lost sight of what has been somewhat obscured in the West since the Reformation—that the laity are, all of them, of the "Kingly Priesthood," as St. Paul calls it, and offer Mass in conjunction with the priest consecrated to the sacerdotal office. The Divine Service is one of profound impressiveness and beauty.

In all Masses the priest, as he approaches the supreme moment, stands with outstretched arms while he reads the

---

*I have kept speaking of the Eastern *Rite*. But it must be understood that there are many such rites, only very slightly differing from one another in liturgy, though each one that uses its own distinctive liturgical language may be reckoned a rite. In the United States the only one of these rites that is not to be found is the Coptic.

wonderful prayer: "O King of Glory, to serve Thee is something great and awesome even for the powers of heaven. Yet through Thine unspeakable love for men, Thou hast given us the ministry of this unbloody Sacrifice. And Thou only, O Lord our God, dost reign in heaven and earth, Thou Who sittest upon the throne of the cherubim, the Lord of the seraphim, who only art holy. And so I ask Thee, Thou only and gracious Lord, to look down upon me a sinner and to cleanse my soul and my heart." Meanwhile the people chant the *Cherubikon:* "Let us, who mystically represent the cherubim and who sing to the life-giving Trinity the thrice-holy hymn, let us now put aside all earthly cares, that we may receive the King of all things Who comes escorted by unseen armies of angels. Alleluia, Alleluia, Alleluia."

Yet sublime as all this is, with the officiating priest seated at intervals on a throne similar to that of a bishop, and with incense far more lavishly used than it is among us, the Divine Service is of course essentially the same as the Mass in the Western Church. Being sung, it takes longer than a Latin Low Mass (or even than a High Mass), though not a great deal longer. And the Office, if chanted, similarly takes longer than that of the Roman usage. But as the whole day's liturgy is regarded as a single thing, there is what seems to us the strange rule that if, for some reason a priest does not sing Mass on a particular day, he is absolved from the saying of that day's office. Nor is he ever strictly bound to say more of the Office than he conveniently can. Confronted with these differences, we should never forget the words of Benedict XV: "The Church of Jesus Christ is neither Latin nor Greek nor Slav, but Catholic. Accordingly she makes no difference between her children, and Greeks, Latins, Slavs and members of all other nations are equal in the eyes of the Apostolic See."

The Blessed Sacrament is sometimes reserved, as with us, in a tabernacle, but as often as not in a hanging pyx, something common in the West during the Middle Ages. But though the

Real Presence is known to hallow the church at all times, it is not among Eastern Catholics the subject of veneration outside Mass to the same extent as it is to Catholics of the Latin Rite. Such services as Benediction, or the Forty Hours' Devotion, if they occur at all, are considered innovations, and visits to the Blessed Sacrament, though they do take place, are not a prominent feature among Catholics of the Eastern Rite. The East is more medieval in its religious tone than is the West.

It is unnecessary to dilate upon such trifles as the fact that few priests of the Eastern Rite now wear full (often they were very glorious) beards, though these still adorn their dissident brethren. In the United States the clergy are now clean-shaven, presumably so as not to add to the feeling that people have of their being "foreign." But their vestments are different, again a greater elaborateness being the rule. The main point, however, is that whatever the surface differences, whether great or small, the clergy of the Eastern Rite are *Catholic* priests, holding the same faith as all other Catholics, offering the same Mass, dispensing the same sacraments, acknowledging the same centre of unity. If the matter has been dealt with here at some length, it has not been merely to expatiate about an unfamiliar liturgy and what may seem some strange practices, but in the belief that Teresa Demjanovich is not to be fully understood except in relation to this source of her spiritual formation.

Had Teresa remained in the Greek Catholic Church—technically she never left it, though from her adolescence on all her associations were with the Latin Rite—she might have become a saint, but she would not have been able to fulfill her distinctive mission there. The reference is not to what she may be able to accomplish in increasing the sense of unity between East and West—for that never seems to have crossed her mind—but rather to what she was able to do in showing the religious community she joined, and through them other communities, and even people living in the world, that the active life need not exclude the contemplative spirit.

Since her childhood, according to the spiritual director she encountered while she was in the novitiate, she had been accorded many extraordinary mystical favours, which would have made her even then—though of this she did not have the least suspicion—what Thomas Merton has called a "masked mystic." There are so many of these, according to Abbot Butler, the historian of Western mysticism, that they make up the majority of those who ascend the heights of contemplation. Teresa herself declared that Christ was Himself her teacher, which would indicate that she had little, if any, ordinary spiritual direction while still actively associated with the Catholic group into which she had been born. Its sacraments, however, were mightily efficacious, and the liturgical spirit so characteristic of the Eastern Rite permeated her. If she remembered what happened to her before she was three, we cannot but conclude that she always had in vivid memory what was her daily experience until she was fifteen.

Father Benedict Bradley was astounded when she told him of what she had gone through, yet every member of her family has been most emphatic in saying that none of them had any idea of what was occurring in her interior life. Her brother Charles, close confidant though he was, while knowing that she had some idea of entering a convent, did not suspect that she was aiming at sainthood, except in the sense that all Christians aim at it. At college she was simply known as a good pious girl, perhaps a shade more pious than the other girls but nothing out of the ordinary in this respect, even by those who set her down as a bit "queer."

Teresa herself, while enjoying an exceptionally close union with God, seems to have imagined that all those around her possessed the same privileges. Perhaps under the circumstances—allowing for her natural disposition—this was as well; it permitted her to make progress in spirituality in mat-

ter-of-fact obscurity until the time when an expert in the
spiritual life was found to direct her. Her intensity and
fervour were fostered by her early upbringing, which was
fortunate, as it was also fortunate that she was protected all
this while by supposing that there was nothing out of the
way about her. Under so lucky an illusion her humility and
simplicity were saved; without them, instead of any growth
in holiness, she might have become an insufferable prig.

In one of the conferences she wrote when she was in the
novitiate, and which will be examined in some detail at the
proper place, she offers a comment that may be useful to form
a bridge between the natural and supernatural as found in
her during these early years. There she says: "This is a point
we often overlook in the lives of the saints. And it is not
always our fault either. The fault is often the biographer's. So
many biographers seem so engrossed in impressing their
readers with the authentic and genuinely supernatural sanctity of the saints, that the human element is so far omitted
or obscured or distorted that the mere man is apparently no
longer human. While humanity admires, it is at the same
time repelled." Because much of what we hear about Teresa
as her life unfolded concerns her spiritual experiences, it is
a pleasure to see her as the very normal child that everybody
took her to be. Thus her brother Charles tells me how he and
Teresa used to creep downstairs very early in the morning,
before the nearby refineries and factories had begun their
day's operations, to play outside. But softly as they might tip-
toe, their mother would sometimes hear them and call from
her bed, "Is that you, kids?" Whereupon the "kids" would
keep silence and stand stock-still on the landing until they
were sure that it was safe to go downstairs. There they used
to dress and then creep quietly out to play baseball together
in the yard, batting the ball to each other. Presumably Teresa's
eyesight was still fairly good and so did not interfere with
her batting and fielding. Once, when she was on a team play-

ing against Charles, she tried to put him out as he was sliding for the brick that was used as a base, and he hurt his head on it badly. On that occasion, the game ended abruptly.

The reading of the two younger children was supervised by Mary, who, being fourteen years older than Teresa and twelve years older than Charles, probably seemed in their eyes to be tottering on the verge of extreme old age. Mary had several qualifications to play the part of a second mother to them. Johanna knew little English, so that it was her schoolteacher daughter who examined every book that Charles took home from the Public Library on Avenue C and 31st Street. Those that Mary approved of were read together by her little brother and sister as they sat in the same armchair, Teresa often on Charles's knee. Page by page they went, nodding to one another when ready to go on to the next.

Their father and mother knew German and Hungarian as well as Slovak, but usually, so as not to get the children confused, they used Slovak, except when they were saying something they did not want the children to understand, or when relatives and friends dropped in who were more familiar with Hungarian or German. Outside their home the children used English, as did their friends. When visitors called, the effect was often to drive Teresa and Charles to the porch. When Alexander Szuchy, Johanna's nephew, brought his fiddle he would play. As it was sometimes an Hungarian czardas or an air to which somebody would sing, the children preferred what they understood, the songs they learned at school, of the "My Old Kentucky Home" and "Take Me Out to the Ball Game" type.

Uncles who visited were Constance (it was shortened to "Stanzi") and Tony. A favourite visitor with the children was a cousin Teddy Kubeck, for he was a teller of the kind of stories they relished about giant-killers and Robin Hood. To tell them these, he would seat them, when they were small, one on each of his knees. Alexander and Johanna seem to have been rather too sombre for that. The only relaxation either of them seems to have had was on these sedate Sunday afternoons.

Alexander's shoe store kept the family going for a while and, after that, his cooperage job with its small but regular wages. His was the story of so many other immigrants: by frugality and industry a good deal was accomplished, so that the lot of all his children was bettered. Every one of them did well, all the better, it may be surmised, because "doing well" was not primarily thought of as making much money. Food, though plain, was sufficient; their clothes inexpensive, and in the case of the womenfolk mostly made by themselves; but it may have pained them to have been obliged to put up with the kind of house furnishings which were all they could afford. The decorations on their walls were holy pictures, but of a less insipid sort than is usually seen, for they were ikons, and had been imported from a Christian country where even popular representations of art are not without dignity.

What must be understood is that Teresa's early childhood was passed in a foreign enclave, and that the great majority of those whom she knew when she started going to school were the children of immigrants. She had had as yet no contact with the main stream of Catholic life in America, if we understand by that the life as lived by the Irish and Germans. Until she went to St. Elizabeth's College she did not know any Sisters well, for the Sisters of St. Basil had no establishment anywhere near; though she was acquainted with the Sisters of St. Joseph at St. Vincent's, Bayonne.

✒︎

CHAPTER THREE

Family and School Life

In the case of children brought up so carefully as those of the Demjanovich family, attendance at the public schools did none of them any harm. Moreover, the secularization of such schools had not been carried so far at that time as has happened since. Possibly something may have been lost that no parochial school was available, but it could not have been a great deal, and was all the less so because many of the public-school teachers were Catholics. And for children belonging to the Eastern Rite there were a daily two hours of instruction in church after school was let out.

We have been told that Mary Demjanovich prepared her little sister for the grade school to the extent of getting her through the kindergarten part of it at home. On the other hand, Mrs. Grace Coyle Nugent, who taught her when she went to the Lincoln School, has told me that Teresa was in Miss Frances Feehan's kindergarten class. What is probably the truth is that Mary gave her some preliminary instruction and that this enabled her to advance rapidly; to say more than this would obviously be to say too much.

Mary Demjanovich was herself not really a trained kinder-

garten teacher. Under the system then existing, she had gone
no further than to graduate from high school, after which,
with a year in a normal school and a year as supply teacher,
she was considered qualified. She was so efficient a person that
Anna Herbert, when she was appointed assistant supervisor
of the thirteen public schools of Bayonne, took Mary as her
secretary. Miss Herbert has told me that Mary was perfection
itself in her work, needing no direction as to what to do next
but being quite able to act on her own responsibility, and
never making a mistake. She supervised Teresa's reading and
gave her some help with her homework, and so laid the
foundation of her brilliant scholastic record. As her brother
Charles had put it, Teresa entered school when she was four
and a half, because she was too bright a child, and too eager
to learn, to be kept out until the usual age. After over forty
years Mrs. Grace Nugent is able to say that only two children
taught by her stand out in her memory, Teresa and another,
and of these two Teresa was the better.

At Number 5 School Teresa did well, usually being the
head of her class; but because the school did not have the
seventh and eighth grades she completed her grammar-school
course at the Lincoln School, which was where Mrs. Nugent
knew her, teaching her during the year in which she graduated. It was charming to note Charles's solicitude; always he
carried his sister's satchel of books, and would come into the
classroom with them after she had demurely seated herself
with her little pinafore carefully spread out. It was from this
school that she graduated in January, 1913, half a year ahead
of her class, when she was getting on towards twelve.

Her brother Charles, who was two years older than she was,
had graduated in June, 1911, from the same school, a year
and a half ahead of her, receiving a bicycle as a graduation
present from his brother John. From then on he carried
Teresa to and from the Bayonne High School on his handle
bars. She was his constant companion, still reading sitting

side by side the books he borrowed from the Public Library, with Mary still supervising and telling him to take back anything that she did not consider worth spending time upon.

Teresa had never been, even when a small child, much given to the ways of little girls. When one Christmas she received a gift that all the family imagined would delight her— a doll in a pram—she thanked the giver but pushed the carriage into a corner of the living room and never touched it again. But for baseball she continued to show a great fondness—in part probably because this kept her always close to her beloved "twin," for whom her name was the inexplicable "Swallops," as his for her was "Shrimp." Similarly, her indifference to dolls was based on the fact that "Swallops" could not be expected to have much interest in them. Such indifference could, of course, indicate a deficiency in normal maternal instincts were it not that many girls who are not attracted by marriage yet find an outlet for their love of children in active works of charity. That she had, even at this time, a vague idea of the religious life, and in its contemplative form, was learned later. But as for her lack of interest in dolls, it was in all likelihood part of her somewhat masculine cast of mind that appeared later. It is only a matter of the shade of a degree, but I think I can discern it, though I would not wish to insist on it too strongly. What I have in mind is something intellectual, but it corresponded to her strongly built and very erect body, her carriage, and the way she had of laughing uproariously, bending down towards the ground in her mirth.

Except for this indifference to dolls, she was looked upon as perfectly normal, and though she was beginning to have a suspicion that she might be in some way set apart, she did not show it, nor was it observed by others. There seemed to be nothing in the least odd about the girl who sat with Charles and his friends on the porch steps singing "Carry me back to Old Virginny" and "The Old Oaken Bucket," or played cards with her cousin Wilma, who was about ten years her senior, when on Sunday afternoon her relatives were talking in Hungarian or German inside the house. They stopped only when Alexander Szuchy brought out his fiddle and the rest of the company sang folk songs to his merry or melancholy airs.

Perhaps it was because Teresa had so much to do at home —no hands were allowed to be idle in that busy household— and spent so much time in church that few confidences were exchanged among the members of the family. Though closely attached to one another, and very affectionate, they were not at all demonstrative. Not even Teresa and Charles knew much of what was passing in the other's mind. But Charles may have had some inkling of Teresa's secret ambition, for when he decided in the middle of his high-school course to study for the priesthood he gave her a life of her famous namesake of Ávila.

Teresa might have told him more than she did, had Charles told her of his intention to become a priest. But this he did not know himself until he was halfway through the commercial course he had chosen at the high school. It meant that when he entered the college department at Seton Hall in South Orange, he would have to take special courses in Latin before he could be admitted to the seminary. Seton Hall was not an expensive college, and the fees were considerably reduced for "Church students"—otherwise Charles could not have afforded to go there at all. As it was, he had to be helped by other members of his family.

Johanna was overjoyed, and so was Teresa. Indeed, it may be surmised that this decision of his helped to clarify her own thoughts, which until then had not taken a very sharp shape; though quite apart from what Charles did, undoubtedly to a girl of her type would sooner or later have come a perception of what was to be her vocation. During her first two years of high school—the two years he was there with her—she was constantly thinking about Charles, with joy and pride as to the purpose he had avowed but with some pain in anticipation of the separation so soon to come.

Sister Zita says that it was often a wonder to her that Teresa was not spoiled. In most families, of course, this would have been a real danger for the youngest child. But Sister Zita knew Teresa only when they were fellow novices, and never saw the Demjanovich household. It was one in which nobody would have been spoiled. Their reticence and reserve made their feelings all the more intense, but each of them followed a lonely path, keeping close-lipped counsel. Above all this was true of Teresa; she was of too solitary a nature to invite much petting or spoiling. Even to Charles, even to her mother she did not unbosom herself.

But though this was the case, the amusements—such as they were—of all were found in the family circle. Frugality had grown to be a settled habit, though as Mary and John and Anne were all supporting themselves and contributing to the family budget, the circumstances of the group had become easier. Yet the elder children joined with their parents in seeing to it that nothing was wasted. There was no going out to parties and dances, and the clothes they wore—many of the dresses of Johanna and the girls were made by themselves —were far from being costly. Frugality, however, was never felt to be a deprivation, and was not as a rule so much as noticed. All this was excellent discipline for them all, but in particular for Teresa; undistracted by outside activities, she was left all the more free to develop her intellectual and spiritual life. The family in which she grew up might almost be described as a novitiate for a novitiate. If the elder son and the two elder girls never showed any such inclination as Charles had just announced, and which Teresa already cherished in secret, this may have been because they accepted as their primary duty that of helping to shoulder the general burden. It was from this generosity that Charles and Teresa, by being so much younger, benefited.

A most intimate relationship with the local church and its succession of pastors continued. Father Mihalyi had been there when it was burned down. When it was rebuilt on the same spot, a new rectory was built by its side, and was occupied by a new priest, Father Szabo. The Demjanoviches now had the chance to rent the old rectory, 89 Avenue H. As their backyard and that of the priest's adjoined each other, this was very convenient for Teresa and her friend Elizabeth Szabo. It was there that Teresa's family remained until Teresa was entering into her senior year at high school.

They would no doubt have continued to reside there except for an occurrence they had not foreseen, for though the old rectory was somewhat shabby it was a good deal roomier than their quarters behind the now abandoned shoe store had been. But in 1916 one of the schisms that are not infrequent in parishes of the Eastern Rite took place. Many of these schisms are all too understandable, as when in 1891 a priest in Minnesota organized a new parish but was refused recognition by the local bishop—not for some time yet did Catholics of the Eastern Rite have their own bishops—because of his being a married man. The upshot was that he and his flock took refuge under the Orthodox aegis. At Bayonne the schism was of more obscure origin; all that can safely be said of what lay behind it is that the parishioners were of several racial groups and that these sometimes brought with them to the New World the sectional animosities of the Old. What made the schism possible was the trustee system, which had caused so much havoc during the earlier part of the previous century in America and which still continues in some quarters. The committee that controlled the finances was able to stop the priest's salary and to put a Russian Orthodox priest in his place. The priest so rudely ousted was a Father Thegze, Father Szabo having been transferred to another charge. He might have been able to control the situation by his personal force; but when conflicts of this sort arise and are carried into a court of law the decision is in most instances in favor of the trustees, who can claim that technical right is on their side.

A portion of the congregation remained loyal to Father Thegze and the Holy See, and they managed to buy an old Lutheran church on East 25th Street, which then became known as the Ukrainian Catholic Church, as most of those who stood by the priest were Ukrainians. But with them went some Ruthenians, the Demjanoviches among them. Alterations were made in a not very suitable building, the chief of these being the erection of an altar and an *eikonostasis*. The healing of the schism some years later came about in a curious way. The Standard Oil Company bought the site on which the church of the schism and its rectory stood, paying a good enough price to permit the building on East 26th Street of a large and solid brick church, which the cornerstone, laid in 1920, describes as the Greek Catholic Church of St. John the Baptist. The people of this parish, one gathers, object to being described as Ukrainians and insist that they are Rusins.

Donald Attwater gives in his two-volume work on the Eastern Churches an account of a rather general schism that occurred among the Rusins at the end of the First World War, when part of the Carpathian Mountains ceased to be part of Hungary and became Czechoslovakia. The Rusins, he tells us, were racially and culturally conscious of their affinities with the northern Slavs, and they resented the policy of the local Catholic authorities, which they suspected was directed towards turning them into Magyars or Slovaks. Moreover, their clergy, who had been for the most part trained in Hungarian seminaries, were somewhat out of touch with their flocks. What happened in Bayonne seems to have been an anticipation of what was brewing elsewhere; the schism in

Europe resulted in over a hundred thousand Rusins going over to the Orthodox Church.*

This helps to explain the situation, but beyond that it does not concern us. However, the schism had its effect upon the Demjanovich family. Because the schismatics were in control, and now legally owned the house the Demjanoviches occupied, the family received notice that they would have to vacate their home if they would not throw in their lot with the majority. Therefore they moved to the Pamrapo section of Bayonne, buying on 15 East 44th Street a narrow grey clapboard house with steps leading up to a high patch of porch with gingerbread trim. The street has brick pavements and few trees, and the rest of the houses on the block are brick. Though their new home was not very prepossessing, it was a considerable improvement on the cramped quarters behind the shoe store or even the old rectory. Both these houses have now gone, the whole of that part of Constable Hook having been taken over by the oil refineries. Only the East 44th Street house remains, now done over in brown shingle and with the porch painted a cream that is almost yellow.

The moving from one house to another—or rather, the moving from Constable Hook to the Pamrapo district—affected Teresa's story in an unexpected way. When the family moved to 15 East 44th Street, it was a good twenty blocks away from the Eastern Rite church, and after that it was only Alexander Demjanovich (but sometimes Johanna as well) who took the long walk there and back, the children finding it more convenient to attend the church of St. Vincent de Paul in the next street, which of course was of the Latin Rite. It need hardly be said that they were perfectly free to go there, but not even Charles until some years later received, upon beginning his studies in the seminary at South Orange (he was as yet only midway through his college

---

The Christian Churches of the East, I, 89–90.

course), formal permission to transfer his Rite. To the other members of the family such permission would have been refused; indeed, their request for this would probably not so much as have been presented at Rome by the bishop of Newark, for there was no valid reason why such a transfer should be made. Their canonical status therefore remained what it had been, though for practical purposes this made little difference.

There were obvious advantages of another sort for the family in settling where they did. While the Pamrapo section of Bayonne was not completely devoid of the odors prevalent in Constable Hook, at least they were so much less oppressive as not to be very noticeable. No longer was it necessary to keep the windows closed whenever the wind was blowing from the direction of the oil refineries and paint factories—or only when the wind was exceptionally strong. One fancies that Mary Demjanovich, who was at this time getting on towards thirty and who was in a good position, was able to be emphatic, and that in this she was supported by John and Anne. Charles and Teresa, who as yet counted for less in the family council, would have been of the same opinion, and their mother, uncomplaining for so long, was undoubtedly glad to be able to live elsewhere. Constable Hook had been chosen in the first instance because it was cheap, and near an Eastern Rite church. But that church had forced a schism; and though a house nearer the remodeled Lutheran church could presumably have been found, it would have been in, or very near, Constable Hook, and from that everybody thought they now had a good chance to escape.

Father Charles has told me that he entered the seminary shortly before this move, but presumably he had for some years made up his mind to apply to Rome to be transferred to the jurisdiction of the bishop of Newark. This had nothing to do with the attendance of the children at St. Vincent's, which was merely a matter of convenience; but that in turn may have had something—a good deal—to do with Teresa's vocation. One may imagine that, had she applied for admission to one of the religious orders of the Western Church, she would at once have been met with the objection, "As you are of the Eastern Rite, you should join the Sisters of St. Basil."* But nebulous as her notions were, at least she had never once thought of the Sisters. It may, however, have crossed her mind (though I doubt whether it did) that if she applied to the Carmelites, of whom she was already thinking, her application would be all the stronger if it was endorsed by Father (now Monsignor) Dolan, the pastor of St. Vincent's.

We know very little of what was going on in Teresa's head, and it is more than likely that, while she had a fairly clear idea as to her vocation, she was not at all clear as to how it could be effected. It was her habit (as it was the habit of all the members of the family) to keep her own counsel, and this was accentuated in her by her knowledge that her father —good pious man though he was—would find it hard to part from her. Why trouble him until her plans were more definite? Even to her mother and Charles she spoke only in the very general terms that she was able, at that stage, to use.

As for her sisters and her elder brother and her father, they believed that she should go to college after she had graduated from high school and become a teacher. As they were already trying to devise ways and means to effect this, they would not

---

*One may guess that when she joined the Sisters of Charity, it never occurred to anybody to enquire what her canonical status might be. When she did apply there, eleven years after this date, she had been for that whole period attending St. Vincent's Church and had graduated at St. Elizabeth's College and had taught (if it be permissible to anticipate) for a year afterwards at one of the Sisters' academies. It would have been assumed that she was of the Latin Rite, as in effect (though not technically) she was. Not everybody is very well up in the niceties of canon law (and neither am I), but I imagine that, as a Sister of Charity, who at that time took vows only for a twelve months' period, at the expiration of which time she was free to depart, the Holy See might not have seen adequate reason for transferring her from the Eastern to the Western Church.

have been at all enthusiastic about a convent for her, had they known that that was her objective. Moreover, Johanna was by this time in rather poor health, so much so that even going to college had to be postponed for Teresa, so that she could stay at home and help her mother. Had she seriously proposed going into a convent at that time, there would have been (and rightly) strong reason to protest. If objections were not raised, this was not merely because Teresa's plans were not as yet formulated but because she was a Demjanovich—and all the Demjanoviches were so closely knit as to be willing to place immediate duties above personal desires, above everything else except the ascertained will of God.

We may see here, as is commonly true in human affairs, especially where a group is involved, a complex of motives. But on the main issue all were agreed; even Charles would have agreed that Teresa was needed at home. In such cases, where good will is shown all round, a providential outcome may be perceived in the end. For Teresa the move into St. Vincent's parish was momentous, simple and natural and inevitable as at the time it seemed to be.

CHAPTER FOUR

✎

Adolescence

ALREADY—but especially at the conclusion of the preceding chapter—I have run somewhat ahead of my story by alluding to things that had not yet occurred, and sometimes even to things that had not so much as been envisaged. As to this I make the plea that, except in cases of historical figures whose lives can be presented in orderly chronological progression, one is often obliged to interpret what is to happen later by what happens earlier, and vice versa. This is particularly true in the life of one about whose inner workings we know a good deal but about the precise dates of the various stages of whose development we know hardly anything. I am, after all, an old hand at biography, and I confess that Teresa's biography is not an easy one to write; I am presenting it in the only way that seems feasible to me. Lest anyone get alarmed, I think I may announce that from now on it will go forward in a rather more orderly fashion—though I cannot guarantee that "flash-backs" and "fore-views" will be altogether excluded.

In one of the several accounts that Father Benedict Bradley has left us of Teresa's early years—derived from what Teresa herself had told him—we learn that the priest of the reconstituted parish after the schism in 1916 did not oppose the practice of daily Communion, though he cannot be said to have actively encouraged it and though it had to be asked for every time. This overjoyed Teresa, but brought on her, and also the priest, a good deal of criticism, so much was frequent Communion at variance with the practice of the Eastern Rite at that time. It was therefore a good deal of a relief that, when the Demjanovich family moved into St. Vincent's parish, Teresa could be a daily communicant without arousing any adverse comment.

Charles Demjanovich had entered Seton Hall college in 1915 and had obtained a considerable reduction in his fees on the ground that he was intending to enter the priesthood. This greatly pleased his mother, who had prayed that this vocation should be given him and who had been bitterly disappointed when at high school he had taken a commercial course. Though she and her husband kept up, at some inconvenience, their attendance at the Ukrainian Catholic Church on East 25th Street, they made no objection when their children showed that they preferred to go to St. Vincent's.

The objection has sometimes been raised that Teresa by virtually, though not technically, changing her Rite had infringed canon law in such a way as to militate against her chances of beatification. The objection is invalid if for no other reason than that the Sisters of Charity of St. Elizabeth, at Convent, New Jersey, at that time were not canonically established. But apart from this technicality, she acted in good faith, and she could not be expected to know much about such matters. The responsibility lay upon her superiors in the convent, but ultimately upon the bishop of the diocese. If Bishop O'Connor considered the question he may have decided that in her case there was no need to ask the Holy See for a permit to transfer. The fact that both Western and

Eastern Catholicism now claim her may bring them to closer understanding.

The parting from Charles brought Teresa all, and even more, of the pain she had anticipated when she first knew of it; but it also brought compensating joy. Of such joy she had sore need after being separated from her hitherto inseparable companion. During her last year of high school, the journey there and back had to be made disconsolately alone. Since Father Szabo had been given an appointment elsewhere and had left Bayonne in 1912, taking with him his daughter Elizabeth, we do not hear of Teresa's having any very intimate friend until during her senior year at high school she was drawn to a Jewish girl, possibly because she was a neighbour in the section of the city to which the Demjanoviches moved.* After that there were apparently no other close friends until Teresa met, at St. Vincent's a few years later, Alice Pratt and Aileen Flynn. This friendship with a young Jewess is interesting for several reasons; one is that it could only have made Teresa all the more aware that the Church is the true Israel. At the same time she could hardly forget that the Jews once had the character of the Chosen People. Therefore she could not be, as unfortunately Christians sometimes are, antagonistic to Jews.

In a passage quoted by Sister Zita in her biography, Mary Demjanovich writes that keenly though Teresa felt her loss of Charles, there was "no outburst of grief . . . only a more than ordinary quietness for several months. Like the other members of the family, she was filled with interior joy at the thought that her brother had been called by the Lord to become one of His anointed." Mary also wrote: "The only thing noticeable about her piety was the recollected way in which she walked to her place after receiving her Lord and Master.

---

*I would give her name if I knew it, but Father Charles Demjanovich, no doubt because he was at Seton Hall at this time, cannot supply information on the point.

One day a friend was speaking of her to some girls, one of whom could not recall Teresa. After some further remarks she said, 'Oh, I know now. She's the girl who walks down to her place so slowly after Holy Communion.' " Teresa was undoubtedly completely unaware of this behaviour of hers, for she always disliked any form of singularity. But as nobody ever seems to have commented on it to her, she kept the practice up to the end of her life.

It cannot be said too emphatically that she was extremely reticent about what was going on in her mind. But though she did not speak even to those closest to her, she did reveal in some of the poems she had begun to write what her thoughts and feelings were. Thus in a four-stanza piece entitled "To My Spouse" she begins:

> My Beloved One is a great King's son,
> The Son of the King of Kings.
> To become His bride I must put aside
> All thoughts of earthly things.

She was only seventeen when she wrote that, and the expression is trite; but it is apparent that she was already thinking of entering a convent, and it may be gathered from her tone that the idea is one that had not recently come to her but must have been occupying her secret thoughts for a long while.

The same is true of the opening of another set of verses, "Loneliness," written the previous year, of which her brother, who edited her poems, remarks that her melancholy "was hidden completely and effectually from those who knew her jovial disposition." Again the lines are, as poetry, not very good—indeed several of the lines limp—but they ring true in sentiment:

> My heart is heavy with the weight of woe
> And pain that has oppressed it. All, all

Is dark within me, and the thoughts that flit
And fly about are deepest gloom. The ghosts
Of other sorrow-laden days are with me,
Yet there is no one who can comfort me
Or cheer my aching heart. Alone
Am I! Heartsick! Alone with my sad thoughts
And grieving heart! My soul still quakes with fear
At my forebodings. Sorrowing, I weep.

Had Teresa left it there, one might have suspected some exaggeration, for certainly she shows that she does not know how to handle what she has to say. But this leads to the thought of One

Who in an olive garden years ago
Was bathed in sweat of blood for love of me;

and with this she is consoled.

She was not much given to any kind of writing in those days, except for an occasional letter to her brother, who while he was in his college course could come home from South Orange for week ends now and then and who spent all his vacations at Bayonne. The poems from which quotations have been made must have been among the few early "attempts at verse," as she calls them, that she sent to Father Benedict when she was in the novitiate. She explained: "I have never been in the habit of writing—not even letters. The first of the enclosed is the third 'poem' (?) I ever wrote, the first of all being a class assignment during my third year high, and the second, a class song. All I ever wrote before I came to college is here. . . . I realise only now how much they reveal." The first of the poems to which she refers is "Hope in Exile," opening:

The night is long, and weary is the way
To Thee, my God, Who art my only stay
Along the darksome road from day to day.

These lines she tells him had been published and therefore must be those accepted (though not until she was in college) by the *Messenger of the Sacred Heart*. Teresa did not take herself very seriously as a poet, and there is no need for us to do so. If I quote any of her verse, it is only because of any biographical interest it may possess, or because, as she put it, it was often "revealing." It is clear that in her loneliness she threw herself upon God for consolation and that this period was a definite stage in the development of her spiritual life.

What we do not hear about is the very thing that we might have expected to hear—that she had taken a private vow of chastity. This might have been all the more to have been expected because of the fact that the Demjanoviches were not a marrying family. The only one of the children who ever did marry was Anne, some years after Teresa's death. While Monsignor Thomas H. McLaughlin, later the bishop of Paterson, was rector of the seminary, Mrs. Paul McLaughlin, his sister-in-law, was ill and needed a nurse. Because Anne was one, Father Charles suggested her. Some time after her patient's death she became the second Mrs. McLaughlin. Of the other members of the family, John died when he was forty-one, still a bachelor, and Mary, the eldest of the family, has never married.

A private vow of such great importance should not be taken, needless to say, without the permission of one's confessor and would today not be regarded as prudent except under such circumstances. Ordinarily a spiritual director would allow it to be made only for a stated period, lest enthusiasm or a mood of depression lead one into something subsequently perceived to be rash. Teresa's good sense prevented this, though later, when she was in the novitiate of a congregation that did not allow Sisters to take anything but annual vows, she took a series of private vows that were explicitly intended to bind her in perpetuity, though in every instance not until her spiritual director had given his consent.

At this time, as she was not sure of her path, she prudently refrained from binding herself to anything.

At home Teresa was kept busy, for as she arrived home from school earlier than her sisters did from their jobs, upon her fell the duty of helping her mother prepare the family supper. This was all the more necessary now, for Johanna was not in very good health. Though Mary and Anne helped with the washing up, or made it their special duty, Teresa still had many household chores to perform before she could settle down to her homework for school.

Somehow Teresa managed to find time to make most of her own dresses, as well as dresses for her mother and sisters, and even while she was talking to others her fingers were usually busy with knitting. It is evident that no minute of her day could have been wasted. Though she would not perhaps immediately strike one as being a typical housewife, she was conscientious in this respect, as in everything else; and whether or not she was notably proficient, she did at this time more than her fair share, as later she came to shoulder almost the whole of what had to be done. She used to say that she found such work restful; she could do it without taxing a mind sufficiently active in other ways.

As though this and her school work were not enough, Teresa took up, now or a little later, the playing of the piano. Her sister Mary, who tells of this, assures us that, though she was self-taught, she played with the touch of an artist and that her memory was so good that "after playing a selection of several pages a few times, she could sit down and play it without the music." Teresa's family wanted her to take lessons, but she refused, saying that she would have no time for practice, so that it was not until she was twenty-one that she consented to receive instruction.

I confess to being a little sceptical about Teresa's musical gifts. She never would play, if she could help it, in the presence of others, which seems to indicate that she knew that she was not very good. But a number of reasons for doubt will occur to anybody who knows even a little about music. However, perhaps all that her sister meant to convey was that Teresa learned to execute a few simple pieces. Because she did have a remarkable memory and great powers of concentration, it could be that she performed to the satisfaction of not very exacting critics.

It might also be unfair to carry these comments still further and to say that, though she could not sing very well, she insisted on joining the choir at St. Vincent's, as she did later at St. Elizabeth's, for the singing of few church choirs is good. One with a poor voice may still have a perfect sense of pitch, though such a person usually refrains from singing, for he cannot help hearing himself. But Teresa was apparently unaware that she had a strange voice—"squeaky" is what so many people have called it, and I gather that it was a bit scratchy as well and that in the higher registers it was liable to get slightly off key—so that I conclude that her piano-playing was a feat of memory and a demonstration of her doggedness. It helped to beguile her loneliness, and that was probably the reason for her taking it up, and also the reason for writing bits of verse now and then.

The class assignment in versemaking, belonging to her third year in high school, has not been preserved. But one surmises that it was so superior to the other compositions turned in that for that reason she was selected to write the class song for the graduation exercises in January, 1917. What she produced is no worse than nine out of ten such things, and may be better than the majority; but though her brother printed it in the posthumous collection he made of her verse, I will refrain. It is enough to remark that it was written to be sung to the tune of "Love's Old Sweet Song," a limitation that hardly left her much room for the attainment of real poetry.

What matters a good deal more is that Teresa was chosen

to deliver the salutatorian's address. Miss Anna Herbert, who was at that time assistant superintendent of schools for Bayonne, informs me that perhaps the obstacle that prevented Teresa's being made valedictorian was that her sister Mary had been valedictorian twelve years earlier. As Mary was now Miss Herbert's secretary, there might have been people to suspect some "pull" on her sister's part. Even those who would not have entertained such a suspicion might have thought that the Demjanoviches were getting too strong a hold on high-school honors. If Miss Herbert attended the graduation exercises, it was not for Teresa's sake (for she had no intimate acquaintance with the Demjanovich family), nor did she go because her secretary's sister was graduating. Her attendance was due merely to her thinking that it was incumbent upon her office.

She remembers that the address was on Japan, and from another source I got the information that the subject was Japanese drama. It is the kind of topic that a serious-minded young student *would* take, and, as is the way with such students, we may be sure that Teresa spoke with gravity and confidence, though necessarily on the basis of rather meagre knowledge. However, we may also be sure that, limited though Teresa's reading may have been—perhaps a book or two borrowed from the public library and an article in an encyclopedia—she knew more than any of those present and therefore impressed her audience, especially since she kept going for ten minutes without using any notes. Miss Herbert had with her her father, the contractor who had built what was at that time the tallest smokestack in the world. He was so struck with the performance that, turning to his daughter at the close of the salutatorian's speech, he said in a most solemn tone, "You will hear from that girl some day." The world did hear about her, though perhaps in the very last way that those there looked for.

A juvenile address of this sort might scarcely be worth mentioning were it not for one fact: it hinted, in its choice of subject, at something of greater importance. Teresa in college was to show an interest in dramatics, and while this too is common enough, I cannot but think it helps to explain why what were probably the two best items in her volume of poems were verse plays, and in them it is possible to trace some influence of the No drama of Japan. In order to get away from the Elizabethan or later European drama—too obvious and commonplace a theme—she had gone to the Orient. It was not quite at random that she had chosen her subject, slight as must have been her claims to have been considered an authority upon it.

Finally, and most important of all, the one literary production of hers that merits attention for its own sake is the series of conferences she wrote as a novice. They are remarkable for several reasons, as will appear when they come to be considered later; one of these reasons is the sense of "theatre" she showed in them. It is accordingly not fanciful to find in her salutatorian speech in the Bayonne High School the first intimation of a talent that she never dreamed of exploiting and in all likelihood never imagined she possessed.

CHAPTER FIVE

Interlude

AT the time of Teresa's graduation from high school, she was not yet sixteen, though her dignified aspect and erect carriage made her look rather older. In the ordinary course of events she would have entered college that fall, though she had at the back of her mind very different plans for herself, about which she said nothing. But eventually it was decided—not so much by Teresa as by the rest of the family, though Teresa completely concurred—that she had better stay at home and look after her mother, whose health was giving cause for anxiety. Johanna was only in her middle fifties, but she had worked herself to the bone and had never been very robust.

All this was looked upon by the family (and by Teresa herself, for reasons somewhat different to theirs) as a marking of time. Mary in particular, who had obtained a very good position in the public-school system at a time when the qualifications demanded from teachers were not very great, felt that Teresa, with the better qualifications she might acquire, and with her varied gifts, might be able to go even further. While the family might not have thought of Teresa as a saint—though they did not exclude the possibility from their minds that she might be—they all agreed that she was talented and versatile and would make an excellent teacher.

Mary's own case stood before them all as a kind of beacon. As Miss Herbert's secretary, she had proved herself so efficient that she had virtually established herself as an unofficial supervisor of schools. Her conscientiousness was such that, even when she had nothing to do in the office, she would not read a magazine to kill time or write a personal letter—a conscientiousness which seems to me a bit excessive and which should be remembered later in considering Teresa, for she was, in this, much akin to Mary. The older sister's conscientiousness was, in fact, even rather perplexing at times to Miss Herbert. She had obtained her appointment largely because of the prestige she had acquired as one of John Dewey's students at Columbia, where his relativism and pragmatism do not seem to have hurt her religious faith. Occasionally she would have liked Mary to utilize slack periods during the school day by typing letters on various more or less political affairs. This the scrupulous Mary refused to do, on the ground that such things could not be considered strictly school work. For this Anna Herbert respected her, and now, many years later, she realizes that Mary was a paragon, never failing in any task to which she was assigned, or making any error when acting on her own initiative; indeed, Mary was an alter ego who needed no instructions.

In view of her own success, it was only natural that Mary, who acknowledged that her sister was more gifted than herself, should want Teresa to go to college and prepare to become a teacher in her turn. College was now indispensable because of the raising of educational standards. The only drawback in all this was that the mere thought of teaching made Teresa's blood run cold. She believed (and upon the whole rightly, though some qualifications will have to be made at the proper place) that she was lacking in the natural aptitude for the teacher's life; instead she was thinking more and more (but still secretly) of becoming a nun in a contemplative order, in which the label of a college degree would not be needed. But while seeing what was being planned for her, and being grateful to those whose generosity might bring it about, she hoped to avoid college, whose four years she hoped to spend in the cloister. It was because she saw that the issue of making a definite choice between college or cloister would not immediately arise that she said nothing about what was at the back of her mind. Her duty at the moment was clear. It was that of looking after her mother.

Her sister Anne also had a private ambition: it was that of becoming a nurse, which in fact she eventually did become. To this she must have had a clear vocation, because she was the office manager of a local company, earning a high salary for a young woman in those days, a good deal more than she could hope to obtain as a nurse. If she deferred this change, it was to be able to contribute to Teresa's college education, about the advantages of which she thoroughly agreed with Mary.

John Demjanovich shortly after this time was drafted into the army upon the entrance of the United States into the First World War. Though his regiment, the 317th, went overseas, John did not, having been transferred to an artillery unit at Fort Niagara about five hours before the regiment sailed from New York. He had held positions with a paper-box company in Jersey City and with a ship's chandler. His being in the army made it impossible for him to contribute towards Teresa's college fees. Therefore the whole scheme, though it was by no means abandoned, was now looked upon as not much more than an eventual possibility—much to Teresa's relief. That she was needed at home was a perfect excuse for her not committing herself to the four years of college. Looking back upon it all, it is possible to see how beautifully the providential pattern was worked out.

It must not be thought that Teresa was called upon to be

her mother's nurse, except during the last two weeks of her life. Johanna was not bedridden, but continued to perform her household duties. Teresa merely did what she had done for years past, only now doing a good deal more, so as to lighten her mother's burdens. Though nobody knew how close Johanna was to death, it was obvious that she needed some help.

Teresa was glad of this respite, dull though it must have been according to ordinary standards. Her work was not so heavy as not to leave her plenty of time for thought and prayer. In the first place she was happy that she was able to be of some service to her mother. In the second place, it put off her attendance at the college where she was to do so brilliantly and whose social life she enjoyed. But in the third place she felt that she needed further time to consider what religious order she should enter.

If her mind ran mainly on the Carmelites, this was probably because she had read a life of St. Teresa of Ávila given her by her brother Charles about the time he left for Seton Hall. Whether she had read the autobiography of the Little Flower as yet is uncertain, though it is likely that she had, as the book was being much talked about, and we know that during her college years a copy of it was always on her desk. The book has no doubt implanted in the minds of many girls an attraction towards Carmel, though it must have shown a good many others that Carmel was not for them. Teresa of Ávila and Thérèse of Lisieux confirmed our Teresa that her vocation was for the contemplative life. Yet the Carmelites are only one of the contemplative orders for women, and apparently Teresa knew nothing about the Poor Clares or the Dominican Second Order, for she never once, so far as we are aware, so much as gave a thought to them. The particular order here is of little consequence; what does matter is that Teresa wanted to be a contemplative.

It would appear from the statements she made to Father

Benedict—at all events from the statements regarding her case that he was at liberty to publish—that she did not consult any of the priests at St. Vincent's. When she went to confession, one must infer that she did what she had been accustomed to do when she had been actively connected with the Eastern Rite; that is, mention her sins, such as they were, but not to seek any spiritual direction. Five or six years afterwards, while she was still in college and her brother was a seminarian, she did talk to Father (now Monsignor) Dolan, and he tried to put her in touch with the Carmelites, but at this time she seems to have been as close-lipped with him as with her family on the point. She wished to think things out for herself and to be quite sure as to her vocation before making any move.

The period of waiting lasted longer than anybody had expected—over one and a half years—ending only with Johanna Demjanovich's death on November 27, 1918. Such a delay would have given most girls—even those who were not pressing on to an unachieved ambition—a sense of frustration; to others it would have been merely boring. Even Teresa, though she did not regret this interlude of time, must occasionally have thought that it was a little too long drawn out. Yet she was always cheerful and uncomplaining, however dull and dreary were many of her days. Her sister Mary says that when others snapped at her, as, being human, they sometimes did, after a hard day's work in the office (of course they thought of Teresa's position at home as "soft"), she never attempted any defence. "But," adds Mary, "this was so characteristic of her that we took it for granted and did not consider it unusual." It would be no wonder if Mary's nerves were a bit on edge because of Teresa's lack of enthusiasm about the fine plans that were so generously projected for her. It was not that Teresa was at all ungrateful but that her own plans were of a totally different sort.

Whether or not Teresa knew it at the time, Johanna had

extracted a promise from Mary to send Teresa to college. The idea of doing so had seemingly originated with Mary, but of course there is considerable difference between getting an idea and seeing it through. Johanna therefore tied Mary down, knowing that no Demjanovich goes back on his word. This pledge in a way bound Teresa herself: a promise given to the dying woman could be honored only with her acquiescence. Though she knew that she was not under any positive obligation in the matter, in the end she acted as though such an obligation had been created.

The one and a half years slipped by in helping her mother run the house on East 44th Street, in reading and in music. So much we can say of Teresa's external life, but only later do we find that it was also filled with spiritual experiences of an unusual sort. One would suppose that she read voraciously were it not that the evidence points to her never having been a great reader. But she read enough to give her, when at last she entered college, a larger fund of general information than a freshman usually has. Though she definitely did not read with college requirements in mind—for she still had the hope that she would avoid college altogether—her reading, and still more the power for concentrated thought that she was developing, laid the foundation of a brilliant college career. Of spiritual books she read practically none, for the Public Library at Bayonne carried very few, and at home there were only the Bible and the basic liturgical works, which she already knew almost by heart. But this lack of reading mattered little in her case; it was more than made up for by the infused knowledge of divine things she was receiving.

Whatever reluctance she might have to anyone hearing her play the piano, she did not mind her mother hearing her. It was during this period that she acquired most of the skill she possessed. And had she been a real poet, she would have thought of the quiet of her days as priceless, yet even under these fortunate circumstances, only now and then did Teresa feel impelled to produce a set of verses. What is clear about these is that they were not written to relieve her tedium— even if they did do that—but as a relief to her emotions. Mediocre as her poems may be, never do we come across one of which one can suspect that it was turned out because Teresa had said to herself, "Let's see, what shall I write about now?" That is why they have so much autobiographical significance, little as Teresa thought of this during their composition.

Every day she was at early Mass at St. Vincent's, always receiving Holy Communion, and at intervals during the day, when she was able to slip away, she made visits to the Blessed Sacrament. While all this was a departure from the customs of the Eastern Rite, it must still be affirmed that she most unmistakably bore the marks of her early religious experience upon her. But all this time she was trying to find the "pattern" for her life, experiencing extraordinary manifestations of grace, and content, for the rest, that she was undistracted. Though she never, so far as I know, said anything about this (and may never have realised it) I am sure that she discovered during this time, when she was busy with housework, that contemplation was not in the least incompatible with it. That was the very core of the meaning of her life. Would it be far-fetched to suppose that God did not allow her to enter any convent until she had learned this lesson?

When her mother was on the point of death, Teresa and her father walked from 44th Street to fetch a priest. The hour was late—eleven o'clock—but Catholic priests consider themselves bound to answer such a summons at any time. But, possibly because he made his own long-range diagnosis from what he had been told, he promised to go at seven the following morning. Faithful to his undertaking, he arrived on the stroke of the clock—but Johanna had been dead for half an hour. In an extremity of this sort she would have been fully justified in asking for a priest from St. Vincent's, but she wished to receive the last sacraments according to her own rite—perhaps thinking that the recommendation of the Holy See in the matter was a positive command—and so did not receive the last sacraments at all. But few people can have prepared for death by a more holy life.

Teresa has left an account of her feelings at this time. Writing to Father Benedict on July 21, 1926, she tells him that on one occasion when her father was sick, she also became sick, so much was she affected. About her mother she says, "Only twelve months later did tears come to relieve the oppression, and then I wept for hours, with such torrents of tears as I have never experienced—not hysterical ones either."* In 1919 she wrote the first of the two poems of hers about her mother. About one of these, her brother Charles, who edited her poems, asks of the concluding lines, "Did Sister have a premonition of death?" These are the lines:

> The goal
> For which all strive I too shall see
> Ere long. Death will not frighten me.

But it seems to me that all such fancies should be dismissed: even in 1919 she still had six and a half years to live. But she had a melancholy streak in her, and many people of that sort "die daily," though perhaps not in the Pauline sense. I myself have had such premonitions for more than twenty years, and I have twice been anointed, and once afterwards given a year to live. Yet here am I writing this book. Even if Teresa was

*We hear of her crying a good deal in her last months in the novitiate, and some of those who were novices with her have explained this on the ground that she was at that time sick and weak, for they knew her as rather reserved, perhaps almost stoical. She did conceal her emotions, but under the façade she presented to the world she was always very sensitive. However, it is somewhat strange that she did not give way to weeping, when her mother died, until a year later—or would be except on the supposition that she tried to keep her emotions in check, until they broke the dam she had erected.

a saint, as I think she probably was, sanctity is not ordinarily accompanied with the gift of prophecy.

Johanna Demjanovich was buried from the church on East 25th Street, the remodelled Lutheran church that was taken over by those who remained faithful in the schism of 1916. It is called the Ukrainian Catholic Church to distinguish it from the much larger and finer building that was erected soon afterwards and is known as St. John the Baptist's Greek Catholic Church, from which Johanna's widower was to be buried in 1925. The other little church must present some difficulties for the conducting of funerals, as one encounters steep steps at the entrance; up these it cannot be easy to carry a coffin.

Johanna's death occurred on November 27th, too late in the year for Teresa to be able to execute the project of college that her family had been pressing upon her. Therefore she went on for the time being in the same way as before, but now in greater loneliness than ever, because until the working day had ended for the other members of the family she was completely alone in an empty house. Though her mother's death had set her free—except for the reluctance she felt to leave a father who, as she well knew, would be deeply grieved to lose her, though she also knew that he would not actively oppose her purpose to enter a convent— she submitted to the decision of the family council and agreed to register as a student at St. Elizabeth's College. She knew, however, that this could not be carried into effect until September of the following year, and she may have continued to hope that something would turn up before then. But she had been more or less committed to the college project, and she was not the kind of young woman to disappoint those who had made, and were willing to make, sacrifices for her.

CHAPTER SIX

❧

At St. Elizabeth's

Towards the end of September Teresa Demjanovich enrolled at St. Elizabeth College near Morristown, New Jersey. Because it had a railway station and because of its post office, it used to be called Convent Station, but is now simply Convent. The station is right at the convent gates, and one goes up a landscaped walk towards a long row of impressive if not very beautiful buildings, beginning at the left with the chapel, by far the best of them all, and from there to where the administration offices are housed, with accommodations for the Sisters and some of the students above, and ending in Xavier Hall, in which is the academy and the auditorium. Behind the chapel is "Nazareth," the novitiate, and further back upon a slight rise are other buildings that are newer and more handsome: O'Connor Hall, Santa Rita Hall, and the classrooms and library of Santa María Hall. Best of all— in fact, architecturally a little gem—is the home for rest or retirement where about a hundred Sisters have their residence. But that did not exist in Teresa's day; instead there was the old "Villa" used for the same purpose, and elsewhere are the original buildings of what is one of the oldest Catholic colleges for women in the United States.

Teresa's first room was in the main building, on the fourth

75

floor of what may be described as the convent wing, though of course completely separated from the Sisters' quarters. The corridor off which the freshman rooms opened was officially that of the Sacred Heart, but familiarly known to the girls as the "alley." At the other end of the building was "Broadway" —not the broad way that leadeth to destruction. Half a dozen freshmen were accommodated in Santa Rita Hall, to which all students were transferred in their sophomore year.

Teresa roomed by herself, having acquired a taste for solitude, but soon found she had much in common with the girl in the room opposite, Agatha Spinella, with whom she formed a close friendship that was to be life-long. Teresa became known to the other girls as "Treat," and Agatha "Spin."

Early in her freshman year Treat confided to Spin that she planned to enter religion—a measure of her confiding friendship, as she had hitherto been most reticent on the subject. One day the following year she showed her a letter she had received from the superior of a Carmelite convent which, in answer to a letter of enquiry from Teresa, explained their regulations. This was the first open move that Teresa had made in the direction of her vocation, and even this was not a formal application for admission, as first she was more or less under an obligation to her family to obtain her degree. Spin asked, "Did you ever think of becoming a Sister of Charity?" and received the emphatic reply, "Such a thought never entered my head." When two years later Spin put the same question again, Teresa only smiled. This may have meant that she was now considering the Sisters of Charity, but her inclinations were still for the Carmelites. It might be noticed that not even with her most intimate friend was she prepared to discuss the matter in any detail.

Among their friends were two girls who eventually entered convents, as did five others of this class at St. Elizabeth, but who were not quite on the same footing with Teresa as Spin, possibly because they were not members of Teresa's class.

These were Agnes Keenan and Mary McGarry, one of whom is now Sister St. Anthony of Maryknoll and the other, Mother McGarry of the Cenacle in New Brunswick. About other of Teresa's college friends we shall hear in a moment.

The headquarters of the group was Spin's room, partly, of course, because she was popular but partly also because, as she came of a rather well-to-do family, she had special furniture and always seemed to have available various goodies for the entertainment of her visitors, and even a drawer full of first-aid equipment. Treat was content—or had to be content—with what the college provided; her room was monastic even to the extent of being uncurtained, shutters serving instead. But Spin turned her comfortable room almost into a kind of club, having brought from home some wicker armchairs, a rug, a bookcase, pretty blue velour draperies and Madeira linen for her bureau. Those who gathered there included Agnes Murphy, Margaret Bennett (now Mrs. Stickley), who was class president during all her four years of college, Alice O'Toole, Gertrude Girourard, and Isabel (or "Izzy") Meisenzahl, all of whom became teachers.

Margaret Conklin, who became one of Teresa's biographers, during freshman year was not so much her friend as Spin's, though Treat's later letters to Margaret prove the eventual warmth of their affection. Margaret Bennett was the kind of girl whom all girls admire—tall, good-looking, smartly dressed, athletic, and always chosen to head committees. I would gather from my conversation with her that there was not much in common between her and Teresa in their early college days, for though she may be described as good all-round, she herself insists that she had no special intellectual or spiritual aspirations beyond those of the average college girl of her day.

It is evident from the information which I have gathered from many sources, including Teresa's own letters, that Teresa was not very popular at first, though this should not be

taken to mean that she was disliked. She was not of the type
that makes friends easily, and she was looked upon as something of an oddity. A few of the girls were devoted to her, and
all came to admire and respect her, but the majority, for reasons not always to be accounted for, did not take to her. One
suspects that there may possibly have been an element of
snobbishness in this; for though the girls at St. Elizabeth's
have always had a reputation for fine democratic spirit, it may
be that a few of the girls there tended to look down on one
who came from a working-class family and who also struck
them as being more than a little "foreign." The young are
usually somewhat conventional and are made ill at ease by
anything even a little out of the ordinary. As Teresa said a
little later in one of her letters to Father Benedict, she knew
she was always "different" from other people, though one
may attribute this to her being *made* to feel different, especially at this time. "That Greek" was a favorite way of dis-
missing her. She confided to one of her fellow novices some
years later: "When I came here to college I found it very
difficult to mix with the girls. They thought I was queer, and
of course I felt it keenly. As I advanced in college, though, I
learned more and more to act with a crowd." That her classmates did eventually value her accomplishments and friendship is proved by the fact that in her senior year Treat was
elected vice president. Those who knew her only slightly may
have considered her too serious and too studious; those who
won her confidence discovered that she had a keen, lively
sense of humour and that she could be very amusing.

Some of the girls had a sense of humour of a less pleasant
kind. They may not have intended to inflict pain (though
they did) but merely to have a little fun when they asked
Treat to sing for them, knowing that she was much too good-
natured to refuse, even though she well understood that she
was being made game of. Her voice, as has already been remarked, was rather high-pitched, especially when she was

excited. The girls would ask her to sing, and they would even suggest the song, which was usually "Kiss Me Again," a ditty with very high notes. The combination of that fact and the sentiment and her thick-lensed glasses made the occasion delightful to those who, without perhaps meaning to torment her, did so very effectually. It was characteristic of Teresa that she always responded to these requests, though she well understood the motive behind them; her humility accepted them as a mortification, but I think also that her sense of humour operated: Why not give the girls a little amusement, if this was the kind of amusement they wanted?

Teresa, as described in the brief biography Margaret Conklin wrote, was rather stocky, her complexion and hair were light, and her eyes grey-green. Her carriage was so erect that it seemed to some almost military. She wore her hair in the "pompadour" style, and this, though very common in America at the time, was set down as "too European," though Europe had long since abandoned it. My wife tells me, however, that Teresa's "hairdo" was not exactly a pompadour, but was puffed out in "buns" over her ears. She adds that when she was a little girl at school at Elmhurst some of "the big girls" affected this manner; they called the combing part of it "ratting" the hair. It is hard for me to believe that Treat would have bothered about her personal appearance to that extent.

Mrs. Stickley tells me that there was nothing freakish about the way she dressed, though St. Elizabeth's did have some who were freaks in this respect. Teresa did not have many dresses, and many of these were made by herself, but ordinarily she went about in a plain skirt and a red jumper of her own making, very similar to the clothes of most of the other girls.

Whatever antipathy there was towards Teresa was by degrees worn down, for the girls discovered that nobody was more willing to give them help than Treat, whether it was in an essay they had to write or in the drawing of a poster for some class project. Furthermore she often joined in the daring little suppers they had—of pickles and similar delicacies—just before midnight. Then if they happened to be caught at the forbidden feast and sent to report to the prefect, Sister Mercedita, Teresa would be asked to be their spokesman, for she could usually get the Sister laughing so that the escapade was passed off harmlessly. In one of Teresa's "Junior Jingles" she refers to this sort of thing, which at least shows that she was "one of the girls":

One night we felt that life was dull, we formed into parade,
The hour was late, the hall was dim, but we were not afraid.
We marched, we ran, we slid, we hid,
   You know we did,
   You know we hid,
And Sister knew we hid, she did,
   Oh! we'll say she did.
   They made new rules,
   We broke them not,
   We kept them not,
We looked abused, for innocent were we.

Lines like these show that Teresa might have developed into a good "light-verse" poet. It is not often recognised that Cardinal Newman was often at his happiest in this vein. Apart from his verse, his lecture in *The Present Position of Catholics in England* on the Russian count who denounced the enormities of the British Constitution (quoting chapter and verse) is one of the unrecognised masterpieces of satire. Yet Newman is generally supposed not to have had much humour, and probably the same thing may be said of Teresa.*

---

*I have mentioned her hearty laugh, in which sometimes she bent forward towards the ground. On the other hand, some very humorous people (Edwin Arlington Robinson, for instance) never permit themselves more than a somewhat wry smile. Chesterton, by way of contrast, used to chuckle at his witticisms in advance, when he was giving a lecture—much to the mystification of his audience.

Teresa was reasonably good at games. I find from the year-book of her graduating class that she was on the track team for three years. But though she played basketball, she was not rated good enough to be on the college team, not even on a team which, as she records in her "Jingles," won during her four years only one game! Teresa did not even manage to secure a place on her class team, and most of the sports at St. Elizabeth's at that time were of the intramural sort. Her eyesight was a handicap here, and of course made tennis out of the question for her. Indeed, her college work made her eyesight definitely worse. Though I, of course, am not competent to give a medical diagnosis, I cannot avoid the layman's impression that eventually she would have gone stone blind. What I can report is that sometimes—especially if she had been doing some close work the day before—the pain in her eyes was so great that she was unable to get up for early Mass, greatly though she wished to do so.

It would not appear that her brilliance in the classroom was resented. Such resentment would be extremely ungenerous, and the young are rarely that. They are, however, quick to perceive parade and pretence, but Teresa had not the slightest trace of either about her, and kept as far as she could in the background, only speaking in answer to a direct question from one of her instructors. Yet the head of the English department, Sister Mary Vincent, when I asked her what kind of student Teresa was, said, "I would not call her brilliant, but she wrote well, and prepared her work thoroughly." On the other hand, Margaret Bennett, speaking from the student's point of view, said: "Well, I disagree there with Sister Mary Vincent, though she herself is very brilliant. Why, one could see Treat's intelligence positively shining from her eyes." While I would not attach too much importance to Teresa's college grades (and I have her excellent record before me), as I know that it is possible for the dull and industrious to surpass the gifted, it seems to me that only a remarkable mind could have produced the conferences she wrote as a novice.

Margaret Bennett was equally forthright about Teresa's piety, saying, "I never suspected that all through those four years I had been living with a saint." I gathered that she was almost shocked when she heard that Teresa's cause for beatification had been introduced, not because she had any fault to find with her but because, as she put it to me, "In those days *all* of the girls were holy."

The explanation may be that, though all the girls at St. Elizabeth's were pious after their fashion, not all of them went to undue trouble about it. There was no obligation (such as prevails, or used to prevail at some Catholic colleges) to attend Mass every day; but many went of their own accord. Some who asked to be called early for chapel, however, were hard to wake, but Sister Esther Maria, the freshman prefect, says that when she went to summon Teresa she used to find her at five thirty kneeling in prayer by her bed, as though she had been there a long time. This sort of thing escaped the notice of girls who took religion in a more easygoing fashion, though it did command the quiet respect of Sister Esther Maria, who eventually became Teresa's sponsor in religion.

Teresa and Agnes Keenan used to go to chapel every evening, meeting in what were called the "Catacombs," where one or the other would bring college caps for both. They chose seven forty-five for this, as the chapel was then empty, and then they usually made the Stations of the Cross, Teresa kneeling at the Twelfth Station with arms outspread in the form of a cross. In this she was probably imitating the Sisters. Some who by accident saw her there whispered that she was in "ecstasy," but that I think we may disregard. But Mother Alexandrine, the superior-general of the Sisters, saw her there one evening and asked, "Who is that girl?" They were to have much to do with each other a few years later.

Margaret Conklin says that Teresa always crossed her hands over her breast after Holy Communion (and this certainly was an Eastern Rite mode), and adds that at these times heat radiated from Teresa's body. It was a phenomenon that we hear of in connection with St. Philip Neri, but Sister Zita, when I questioned her about it, said this was something she had never noticed. This may be because Sister Zita, coming into the novitiate after Teresa had entered, did not have a place in chapel near her. All these places were, as in every religious house, assigned strictly according to seniority. But it may be presumed that, if this radiation of heat occurred, it did so only now and then. In any event it must be said most emphatically that the Church never canonizes anybody for manifestations that may be merely "psychic," but only for heroic virtue. While I record these things, I do so only as one passing on what I have been told; even if I could personally vouch for them I would not know (nor would anybody else) the precise significance they have.

I leave until later a fuller consideration of Teresa's spiritual life at this time and remark only that her conscientiousness, while theoretically admirable, was not a quality that would ingratiate her with everyone. It rarely goes with spontaneity, which is considered far more charming. Thus in her sophomore year, when she had the privilege of "hazing" the freshmen, she looked upon this as a duty and was almost grim in its performance. In men's colleges hazing used to be so rough as now and then to result in death, but recently it has moderated; girls' colleges are a pallid and refined counterpart of the masculine example. The whole thing is silly and should be forbidden. But let us see how the sophomore Teresa treated the freshmen.

She took hazing quite seriously. If this was the rule (or custom), it should be observed. Therefore when a freshman passed a sophomore she was rigorous in demanding kneeling as a mark of respect. During this period, when Teresa was waiting for a class to assemble, some freshmen crossed the room and, noticing that she was reading, did not make the required genuflection. Teresa called them back and demanded the obeisance. The former Agnes Keenan was one of her victims and felt that she had to undergo three days of torture. Now, nearly thirty years later, she says laughingly, "How I hated that woman!" Poor Agnes was made to wear, instead of shoes, rubbers, each on the wrong foot, and to walk backwards along the corridors, though her foot was sore. But one night, when she was ordered to draw baths for all the girls in Santa Rita Hall, she felt this was a little too much, and hid, for several hours, until her absence really made the college authorities fear that she had run away. "If they liked Teresa, they liked her; if they didn't they didn't," was her terse summing up. At the party at the end of the hazing period Teresa went out of her way to be attentive to Agnes, by way of making amends, and they became friends.

Let me say that I set down these things, and what is to follow, with some distaste, though I suppose they show that Teresa was a normal American college girl or that at least she wished to be looked upon as such. But along with that must go the admission that her sportive moods were not quite in the vein of the high-spirited girls with whom she now found herself but were, no doubt because of her racial origin and her upbringing, rather dour. Most people would prefer something less deliberately planned than the elaborate practical joke that may be recounted to illustrate this side of her. I confess that I find what I am about to relate not very funny, but I do not think that any "cruelty," such as some people have suggested, was intended; it was merely overdone.

It seems that one of the girls was going to take a late sleep on April Fool's Day. Therefore Teresa undertook to bring her her breakfast in bed. But she was deputized by her tablemates to put on the tray a banana, from which the fruit had been extracted and the skin filled with soap. That would have sufficed for most jokesters, but not for Teresa. When the girl decided to keep her room for the rest of the day, lest she be "caught" again, the bell was rung for her and, when she did not answer, Teresa knocked on the door and said that the prefect wanted her. Then the girl hurried breathlessly to the prefect, who had been made a party to the joke and who pretended to be displeased at her tardiness. At last she said, "Well, here is a note for you," and it was found to be in the writing of the girl's favourite Sister, asking that she come to see her at seven that evening. She decided that another hoax was planned and so went to bed immediately after supper. At eight the telephone rang and she was summoned to the office. There she was told by the telephone operator, who was also an accomplice, that the Sister had waited for her for half an hour and wanted to know how much longer she was to be kept waiting. Of course when she reached the designated place at last there was nobody there. Before the day was out Teresa asked her victim if she had not received a package from home. "Yes," was the reply, "but I haven't opened it yet." She must have been an easy mark, because in spite of all that had happened she was persuaded to open it then—and found a collection of old shoes and hats that she had gathered to give to the poor.*

Like Queen Victoria, I am not amused. But all this shows Teresa's thoroughness. It was at least very clever of her to pack up hats and shoes in such a way—presumably using the wrapping and address that were on an earlier package—as to hoodwink, late at night, a girl who had been befooled by her so many times the same day. My explanation of this affair is that Teresa, precisely because she knew that some of the girls considered her a little "queer," was trying desperately to prove that she was not.

*I have always understood that the rule about April Fool's hoaxes was that they were not to be perpetrated after midday. In any case they are extremely foolish.

If Teresa was prepared to go to a good deal of trouble over trifles, over serious matters the pains she took were boundless. She explained her own temperament when writing some years later to Father Benedict Bradley: "My nature is such that no matter how much I have to do (the kind of work is immaterial) I ordinarily can't come down from being keyed up to Z until it's all finished. I'm like a fiddle-string, taut. If I stop in the middle of my work (although physically I may be ready to drop) and relax, I'm good for nothing, like the fiddle-string that suddenly loosens. . . . In college in order to finish a colored poster I've gone without supper—otherwise it would never have been completed, because once the brush is down, and the string loosens, the hands tremble so, that I couldn't even hold a brush or pencil with any degree of firmness." This tenseness of hers made even those who admired her conscientiousness a bit uncomfortable, but it helps us to understand the complete exhaustion that overtook her in the end when the overstretched fiddle-string suddenly snapped.

Most people of this sort are inclined to be self-centered and may be, without intending it, rather unkind. This was not at all the case with Teresa. If she saw that one of the girls at college was unhappy over something or depressed, she would go to her room and do what she could to comfort or encourage her. Miss Spinella tells of one particular occasion when Teresa noticed that one of those at a gathering in Spin's room was nearly in tears after the teasing that had been inflicted on her. That could not be allowed, so after the party had broken up, Teresa made it her business to seek the girl out and make up for the others. Over and over again Teresa carried her solicitude to those who needed it; nor did she content herself with a bluff, "Oh, pay no attention to them! They don't mean it," but tactfully making no reference to what had happened perhaps a couple of hours before, she would show a real interest in all the poor girl's concerns. A conscientiousness that was

perhaps excessive was one side of her; the other was her un-
failing kindness.

About midway in Teresa's college career there appeared
at St. Elizabeth's a figure who gave a good deal of color to the
place, though perhaps at times some embarrassment as well.
This was no less a personage than Archbishop Seton, the
grandson of Mother Seton, the foundress of the Sisters of
Charity in the United States. He had been named an archbishop in 1903—Archbishop of Heliopolis in Phrygia, that
is, *in partibus infidelium,* but never exercised the functions
of an ordinary. Made a monsignor a year after ordination—
the first American to receive that title—he had served at the
cathedral in Newark under his cousin Bishop Bayley. Many
years before this time, because he was thought to be threat-
ened with tuberculosis, he had been appointed chaplain at
St. Elizabeth's, where from the start he revealed himself to be
a "character." In knee breeches and buckled shoes he used to
run up and down in front of the academy, which was hardly
conducive to a cure for the disease he was supposed to have.
Nevertheless his constitution was so rugged that after nine
years of this he served for another twenty-seven as pastor of
St. Joseph's Church in Jersey City.

He was inordinately proud of his ancestry, and boasted of
being descended from one of the "Four Maries" who accompanied Mary Queen of Scots when she went to France to
marry the Dauphin. This was, of course, Mary Seton, the
others being Mary Beaton, Mary Livingston, and Mary
Fleming, though the famous old ballad, which is supposed to
have been spoken by a Mary Hamilton, lists them as having
been "Mary Beaton and Mary Seton and Mary Carmichael
and me." How he could have made this claim is not easily to
be explained—unless on the ridiculous supposition that there
was a bar sinister somewhere! Although one could relate
many amusing stories of the elderly gentleman, they have

been told and retold by students and friends of the school until they have become legendary.

In advanced age he somewhat resembled Cardinal Newman in features, though in nothing else, just as he was quite unlike Mother Seton in almost every possible way. It might have been said of him, as he said of the Duke of Grafton, that he was "antique and aristocratic, projecting a superb Roman nose before his face." Blue blood was his foible, but he had the justification of being a Roosevelt, a second cousin of the two Presidents of that name. At the Vatican Council he had been present in some capacity or other, and the current quip was, "There was Satan in the midst of them," such being the old Scotch pronunciation of his name.

Now back at St. Elizabeth's in extreme old age, his dignity was as impressive as ever, and so was his vehement speech. I often saw him, but I confess that I always fled his approach and so never actually met him. The nearest I came to this was that, whenever I gave a lecture in the auditorium, he would arrive, invariably late, so that I had to stop until he had been escorted to an armchair in the very middle of the centre aisle. Then we would bow gravely to each other, after which I went on with what I had been saying. His escorts were always two college girls, and if he was not satisfied with the looks or dress of those provided he was quite capable of sending them away with instructions to ask the dean for others. When they took him back afterwards to his apartments, he would reward them with a handful of cookies, a rare old book, a pair of cuff links, or a baked apple. On one occasion it was an unset amethyst.

For some reason he took a great fancy to Agatha Spinella from the moment he set eyes on her. She tried to escape (as everybody did), but it was no use; when she pretended not to hear, he raised his voice: "Hey! You there in the blue dress; come here." Well might Teresa commiserate, "Spin, you're doomed." He was always wanting her for something or other, and Treat also was dragged into the wake of so powerful a comet.

There were, however, compensations of a kind. The old archbishop would go to Morristown in a taxi and return with $20 worth of chocolates, most of which he gave away. When Sister Josepha, the novice appointed to wait on his table (she also waited on mine, when I had dinner at St. Elizabeth's), pleased him he would give her a half-pound box of these candies, but no more, for he wanted her to eat these herself and knew that a larger amount would have to be handed around in the novitiate. She earned all that she got from him; on one occasion he was complaining about the food with which he was served. So Sister Josepha, pretending that she was going to the kitchen to get something else, went to the next room and rearranged what was on the plate so that it looked different. Archbishop Seton was not only satisfied but roared, "Now *you* know how to look after me!"

Teresa of course saw the amusing side of such a character, but the only reference I can find to him is the reminiscence of one of her fellow novices that one day they saw him in the main corridor just when the dinner bell rang. Immediately the archbishop clapped his hands in joy, whereupon the novices with Teresa tittered, until she reminded them that he was a man to whom great respect was due. Quite so; nevertheless he *was* funny.

Teresa's own sense of humour comes out in the series of drawings she made for the 1923 issue of the college yearbook, the *Elizabethan*. It was shown when, on a page that contained three rather clever and amusing caricatures of her classmates, she wrote in the fourth corner: THAT WHICH MIGHT HAVE BEEN—Thirty Others." Some of the girls were supposed to help her by offering suggestions as to the familiar foibles of their classmates, so that this one could be depicted eating a chocolate bar, that one holding a letter postmarked "Yale," and so forth. But they let her down and she was (very justifiably) annoyed. She had not intended, however, that the inscription in the fourth corner should be printed; it was the editor who decided to allow it to go through, because it was so "cute." She had never had any drawing lessons, and her drawings show it, but they also show natural talent. Teresa was certainly a most versatile young woman. Not only did she act as art editor; she did a quite disproportionate amount of the letterpress of the *Elizabethan* both in prose and in verse. It was here that were printed her "Junior Jingles" of the year before, celebrating what went on when the lights went off at nine, with only a single gas jet in each corridor. Then those who wished to continue to read had to do so by flashlight (no wonder Teresa became almost blind), though sometimes with the welcome illumination of Spin's electric battery lamp a group of girls gathered in her room for unauthorized little parties the *pièce de résistance* of which was usually a jar of pickles. It was the day of the "lost generation," but even then there were innocent souls to whom this sort of thing seemed very "dashing."

Teresa was the inevitable choice for class poet. She had won a kind of fame among those at the college by having a poem accepted by the *Messenger of the Sacred Heart* and others by a college anthology entitled *Poets of the Future*. Moreover once—only once—she was cajoled into reading some of her verses to a group of her friends. And for the class of 1922 she had written a song and some more ambitious lines. Her class poem, though owing something to the influence of Lowell and Oliver Wendell Holmes, selected as its symbol, instead of the dandelion or the chambered nautilus, the industrious spider:

> A friendly spider who, with uncertain care
> And restless ease,
> Now spun, again withdrew his shimmering snare
> Of filmy leaves,

Until the sunlight found the silken chain
That fastened him to ceiling-home again.
　　And seeming with delight
　　To wonder at the sight,
He ceased a pause, then speedily upclomb
The ladder home.

Sister Mary Vincent thought that Teresa ought not to read her poem to an audience for she (and others too) feared that Teresa's high-pitched voice might grate upon the ears of an audience largely made up of strangers. She therefore suggested as tactfully as possible that somebody else read the poem. Teresa herself decided, however, to get some coaching from the teacher of elocution and dramatics. It was represented to Teresa—more tact being brought into play—that of course she would want what was good to seem better; so she consented to rehearsals in the auditorium that gave special attention to modulation and pitch. The result was that Teresa's delivery was considerably improved, and she made a good showing in the graduation exercises of June 14, 1923.

She and Helen O'Leary—now Mrs. Coyle of Hastings-on-Hudson—were the only members of the class to graduate *summa cum laude,* Teresa getting the degree of B.Litt., not of A.B. As a former college professor I attach no very superstitious value to grades, but I cannot fail to be impressed with the steady and consistent showing she made. She had entered St. Elizabeth's with only two units of high-school Latin instead of the required four. This was because she had never intended to go to college at all. As a consequence she was obliged to take a "make-up" course in this subject from Sister Marie Victoire, and it must be said that she came to display a greater familiarity with Latin than those who have made it one of their college subjects. It is perhaps hardly surprising that in Organic Chemistry she received the lowest mark of her whole four years—a "C," but one wonders why, after having four units of high-school German, she obtained only a "B" in the freshman course in Selected Works of Lessing, Goethe, and Schiller—especially since German was one of the languages her parents had brought with them from the Carpathians. But of course Slovak was what they usually spoke, and it may be that Teresa's scanty knowledge of colloquial German handicapped her when she came to the literary German, which is so different. For the rest of that year she obtained nothing but A's, her subjects being English prose style, the sources of Church history, higher algebra, trigonometry and solid geometry, physics, and Religion.

In her sophomore year Teresa's record shows straight A's, her main subjects being English, history and Spanish. Her teacher in this last was Sister Marie Dolores, a Central American who became a close friend and, in later years, a disciple of Teresa's in the spiritual life. It was under her direction that Teresa took the leading part in a Spanish play, performing so well that Sister Marie Dolores declares that even those who did not understand the language were able to follow the plot, and even the dialogue.

The junior year was again one of straight A's, with English still Teresa's major, but with history reduced to an hour a week on the Church in Modern Times. French now replaced Spanish, and there were courses in logic and the Old Testament. But as she was suffering from eye-strain, she asked the Dean if she could lighten her course during her senior year. This, Sister Marie José told me, was the only conversation she ever had with Teresa, and the matter was soon arranged to the extent of permission being given for courses in the history of painting and the appreciation of music. Such courses can be very stiff, but as ordinarily given in American colleges (and only in America would they be considered as proper to college studies) they are designed to give the necessary credits with the minimum of effort. The curious fact is that, for the first time in three years, Teresa dropped to a "B"—in the music course. But taking her work as a whole, her scholastic record is one of very remarkable proficiency.

One further comment seems to be called for. As Teresa had not wanted to go to college and had done so only in deference to her family, she might have contented herself with mechanically, or even sullenly, "going through the motions." Instead she did her very best by way of repaying those who were making sacrifices for her. Moreover, she had too much intellectual curiosity to neglect the opportunities that had come her way. The page of the 1923 *Elizabethan* which sums up each member of that year's graduating class in a single word has for Teresa "versatile."

One should not, of course, take such productions seriously, but it is worth noting that the "Class Prophecy," while often going wide of the mark, calls Teresa "our only religious—but we ask you why do you not let the world enjoy all the beautiful thoughts and pictures your talents produced in college?" Though she was not the only member of the class to enter religion, and though only by doing so did her talents become known, it is evident from this that the class president's opinion was not shared by the very shrewd girl who wrote this "Prophecy." This was Anita Greco of Waterbury, Connecticut, now Mrs. D. S. Pisani of Peekskill, New York, who would certainly have been startled had she known then that Teresa would one day be proposed for beatification.

My last comment upon her scholastic record is that though many of the students—perhaps the majority—at St. Elizabeth's intended to become teachers and prepared for this by taking courses in pedagogy, Teresa avoided doing so. Though she did join the Sisters of Charity, a teaching order (but not exclusively so), they were not at this time in her range of vision. It is therefore clear that, while she would do her very best at college, if only by way of repaying those who had sent her there, her heart was set upon being a nun in a contemplative order.

Teresa had gone to St. Elizabeth's on a partial scholarship

that required her to spend two hours a day helping the present superior-general, Mother Benita, who was at that time librarian. This was a congenial task, and Mother Benita tells me that Teresa was a perfectionist and that she trusted her judgment to such an extent that she let her decide whether a particular book might wisely be put on the shelves for the girls or a particular article in a magazine in the reading rack. But that she had a job which cut so much into her time—in addition to which she undertook so many extra-curricular activities—makes her college record all the more noteworthy. And all this was done in spite of the handicap of her weak eyes, which in fact were probably damaged by the amount of close work she undertook.

With regard to her eyesight, she offered to God what remained of it as a sacrifice that another should return to the Faith. It was something that was injudicious and that any priest who had been consulted would have told her not to do. Father Charles tells me—saying that he has never told anybody else this*—that the person for whom the offering was made was their brother John. It was not exactly that he had lost religious belief but rather that he had ceased for a while to practice religion. God did not accept the sacrifice, and the terrible headaches that Teresa endured for some months were probably only due to eye-strain. But John did come back to the religious duties he had neglected for a while.

After this it may seem something of an anticlimax to say that Teresa always managed to find something left over for her friends. If so, I can only remark that in the life of a really spiritual person the natural and the supernatural are closely twined. Teresa did not live much beyond the time when she was a college girl, and she may be taken by all such girls as their patron, if she should be beatified, and even now may be prayed to privately. As a college girl she was always friendly, at any rate after one had got beyond the carapace of her some-

*He gives me permission to mention his brother's name.

what aloof bearing. Sister Mary Gertrude has said: "She was always ready to go to New York for a day with the other girls, and enjoyed going to the theatre or attending a concert as the case might be. A day's shopping might be planned or a visit to the museum and Teresa would enter into the spirit of the occasion just like anybody else." Though this must not be overstressed, for the simple reason that Teresa did not have much money to spend, her classmate Florine Yocham told me about a day when she and Agnes Murphy and Teresa went together to see Bernard Shaw's play *Saint Joan*. This, however, was after Teresa's graduation and at a time when she had, for a brief period, a job. It seems that Miss Yocham had come to town to buy some clothes just before entering the novitiate. And she places the date as April 24, 1924, in Easter Week.* The three girls were all interested, but were naturally amused by Shaw's presentation of Joan of Arc as a Protestant before her time.

Teresa did no doubt go occasionally at other times to the theatre, and we hear of pre-matinee lunches at Enrico's Italian restaurant, but I still cannot believe that she was often a member of the party. The only definite record that I find of any excursion in a big way was when, in her senior year, being vice president of her class, Teresa felt it incumbent on her to go to the "prom" at the Waldorf-Astoria. Most of the girls had many "boy-friends," but as this was not true of Teresa one of her classmates had to supply the escorts—two Fordham students. Miss Conklin remembers her dress as a Nile-green crepe with silver beads embroidered in a Greek key pattern around the neck. Agnes Keenan had to make it suitable by removing the long sleeves at the last moment. This would seem to indicate a last-minute decision to go; but Teresa said that she thoroughly enjoyed the evening—no doubt a very mild dissipation.

*The play was sponsored by the Theatre Guild, with Winifred Lenihan in the title role. It opened on Dec. 28, 1923, and ran for 211 performances.

Miss Conklin recalls another happening of a somewhat similar sort during the same year. The juniors had all gone to their tea dance in New York, and Teresa was somewhere on the campus—probably the library—engaged in one of her many chores. One of her friends remembered that the day, March 26th, was Teresa's birthday, and so while she was out of her room her friend arranged a party there. Teresa arrived, laden with what she had brought back to work upon, to be greeted with the Happy Birthday song. For the rest of the afternoon she was hostess to those who had assembled.

Pleasant though Teresa found such occasions, her greatest joy was in going to see her brother Charles. Now that he had completed college at South Orange and was in its seminary, he could not leave the campus and visitors were allowed to go there only once a month. On one of these Sundays Margaret Conklin noticed such a look of happiness on Teresa's face that she asked the reason and was told, "I'm going to see Charlie." To Father Benedict Miss Conklin wrote after Teresa's death that she had never seen anybody so radiant as Teresa was on these South Orange days.

Not even with Spin did Teresa discuss very often the question of her vocation, though she let her friend know what was in her mind. But we have seen how the "Class Prophet" said of her, and of her alone, that she would become a religious. There were other girls of whom this might have been said, and there were several among them who entered the novitiate at St. Elizabeth's. But Teresa, though her college years were happy, was quite definite that the vocation of the Sisters of Charity was not hers. As she wrote to Father Benedict a few years later: "While I was at college I could not help but realize what was the general attitude toward contemplative orders and the value of contemplation. But I was sure it was all wrong; and that it was the very thing that was needed to give soul to the place. . . . Up to two weeks before I petitioned, my dominant thought was that this would be the last place I'd ever enter."

Teresa's spiritual life during her college years was, except in matters in which all shared, something that she went to considerable trouble to keep hidden. If she paid frequent visits to the Blessed Sacrament, so did many other girls, and therefore this excited no special comment. But now and then somebody would by accident stumble upon her secret or at least have reason to suspect that she was set apart. Thus one girl who entered her room found her so absorbed in prayer that she had to speak to her several times before any answer was given. Then, "What is the matter, Treat?" she asked, somewhat frightened by the face lifted up a little and wearing a look of radiant intensity. And we gather from a letter she wrote to Father Benedict, that she often prayed late into the night, for she tells him of "falling asleep at my bedside . . . in the cold nights and getting up without feeling a bit cramped or shivering, with a zest for work which could have cleaned up the world if needed." It was probably this that she paid for during the last year of her life, when she often confessed to an unutterable weariness, an exhaustion which undoubtedly hastened her death.

Perhaps the most remarkable instance of her being "found out" is what Agatha Spinella has to relate. But first it must be said that many, if not most, apparitions, like locutions, may be within the soul and not heard or seen with the physical eyes and ears. Teresa a little later was quite sure that she had heard God speaking to her, but she did not claim, when telling Father Benedict about this, that the Voice was audible except within. In the case of Joan of Arc it was otherwise: under most searching cross-examination at her trial she steadily maintained that her visions and voices were exterior. So with what now has to be recorded.

It happened during her sophomore year. Then one night, about ten, after the electric lights lit from the college's dynamo had been off for an hour, Spin went into Teresa's room and found her kneeling on the window seat. Spin asked her why she was there, and after a long silence (of the kind that Spin was used to from her friend) Teresa told her: "You remember how beautiful the sky was last night? Well, I was kneeling here saying my Rosary and then prayed a long time. It must have been about midnight that the heavens seemed to get brighter and brighter. Finally, when the light was almost unbearable, I saw our Blessed Mother in the midst of the light. After a few moments she disappeared and the light gradually faded. After that I could not go to bed but stayed kneeling here until it was time for Mass. Oh, do you think I could have imagined it all?"

Agatha gave the question some thought before answering: "No, I don't think it was your imagination. If one of the other girls had told me this, I think I might doubt. But I have no doubt in your case." After that, at Teresa's insistence, she gave her promise to tell nobody about what had happened.

Another incident seems equally startling. Florine Yocham (known to everybody as "Float") tells me that one day, as Treat had not gone to her classes, she went to see if she was ill. She was in bed, but there was nothing worse with her other than that she had broken her glasses. But when her friend made a movement as though she were going to sit on the chair by the bed, Teresa exclaimed in alarm, "Oh, Float, don't sit there!" This was rather surprising, as there seemed no reason for the remark, but when a few minutes later there came, "It's all right now," the inference was inescapable. But who Teresa's visitor was, her classmate never discovered.

CHAPTER SEVEN

First Teaching

As was the custom, Teresa stayed on at St. Elizabeth's for a few days after commencement, savoring, so it was supposed, with the others the grandeur of their new condition. Actually, the fact that she had finished college made Teresa a little apprehensive, for she knew that, in spite of the fact that her family knew she would like to be a nun, they would expect her to carry out her part of the implied bargain and become a teacher, or at least join a teaching order. Yet she had had four pleasant years at St. Elizabeth's, and even the girls who had started by having fun at her expense had all developed respect for her, and in some instances warm affection. As a group they might never meet again. Now that they were about to part, they found how strong were the ties that had been formed; so the moment of parting was deferred.

A further joy was that her brother Charles had been ordained only a few weeks before—on May 26, 1923, to be exact—and he, "Father Charles" at last, came over with the brother of another member of the graduating class to say Mass for them during this time.* Teresa acted as her brother's "altar

*The rest of the data about Father Charles might be supplied at this point. Immediately after ordination he was appointed procurator of the seminary at Seton Hall, a very responsible position. The seminary was trans-

boy" in the sense of kneeling in the first pew and making the responses. For his birthday the previous year she had written him a sonnet. Now for his ordination she wrote another:

> The silence of the ages veils your soul,
> One trembling, awful moment. Tier on tier
> Of wond'ring angels glorify your fear,
> Your love exalt, while slow descends the whole
> Celestial sphere, and burning sighs control
> The Trinity, Majestic now appear
> The Three. They speak, "For even as the seer
> Melchisedech art thou a priest." Far roll
> The echoes down th' eternal years, unite
> With every beat of life-inspiring heart,
> And striking all the hours, re-vow the tryst
> He made with you, within the angel's sight
> When you were marked a man of God, apart
> From other men, and sealed another Christ.

That Father Charles was now a priest meant that he was able to give Teresa active help to obtain admission to the Carmelites of whom she had long been thinking. But this had to be done tactfully, for those who had made real sacrifices to see Teresa through college, though they did not object, were not at all enthusiastic about the idea of her entering a convent. Mary could not understand why Teresa found the idea of teaching so repugnant, and her father, who retired in that year, while he was not actually opposed to her going into a convent certainly showed that he would prefer to have her at home. He was not very old, and his health was not bad, ex-

---

ferred to Darlington, N.J., in 1926, and Father Charles moved there on Oct. 4th of that year to prepare for the seminarians who did not go there until the third week of April, 1927. The Rector of the seminary, Monsignor McLaughlin, whose brother married Anne Demjanovich, was made bishop of Paterson. Archbishop Walsh appointed Father Demjanovich pastor of St. Mary's Church, Rutherford, N.J., on Jan. 11, 1951. Until then Father Charles had been procurator at Darlington.

cept for his asthma; but he could not do much more than put-
ter around the tiny back yard of 15 East 44th Street. But
Teresa did not wish to distress him, and such inquiries as she
made about convents were conducted with some secrecy. But
they were made; not for a moment did she abandon her plans,
though she was still uncertain as to details.

Teaching was something that Teresa had tried to remove
from the range of possibilities by taking no courses in pedagogy. (One cannot but suspect that Mary knew nothing about
that; otherwise she would have been annoyed, and rightly so,
though naturally such courses could have been taken later.)
Yet from what her friend Aileen Flynn writes to me, it would
seem that when Teresa came home she did some job hunting,
though without any success.

It was during the summer of 1923 that Teresa at last consented to do what she had hitherto treated very lightly; under
pressure from Mary (Anne by now was carrying out her own
ambition and was training to be a nurse) Teresa took some
music lessons. Her teacher spoke as though she had considerable talent, which may be so but which may merely indicate
that he was speaking to please; I am inclined to discount all
this, though in view of what we have heard recently about
self-taught doctors (always regarded as "impostors," however
brilliant their surgical operations) perhaps one may be self-
taught in music. What is certain is that, during her four years
at St. Elizabeth's, Teresa never once, so far as one hears, so
much as touched the piano, being very shy about the talent
with which her family credited her. What may, however, be
believed is that her teacher was astonished at the proficiency
that this "beginner" showed.

As Teresa had no job, most of the summer of the year she
graduated was spent in running the house. Just before she
went to college she had been all alone there, whereas now her
father was always somewhere about, but needing very little
attention from her, so that one does not quite see why nearly

all of the twenty-four hours of the day should not have been almost completely free. Yet that it was not quite so must be gathered from a letter she wrote to Spin during the previous summer vacation: "I am doing the housekeeping stunt all over again. That accounts for my negligence in writing." She added: "I don't mean that I haven't had time, but you see I'm rarely in the mood to do anything lately. I rather dislike inflicting my melancholic and conflicting emotions upon my friends; and when I'm tired and irritable into the bargain, I'm not responsible for what I put on paper. Hence I prefer to refrain from committing myself." If Teresa was on edge, it is probably safe to attribute this not so much to work as to anxiety as to her future. It was probably worse now than it had been a year before.

It may seem a little strange that, though Spin lived at Paterson and Treat at Bayonne, they never visited each other. The explanation that in the early twenties few people had cars hardly suffices, for trains and buses would have served, especially for distances that were not very great. I cannot help thinking that Teresa's sensitiveness had suffered a good deal during college and that she was not very anxious that college friends, who might be considered as belonging to a higher social milieu than her own, should go to her house, as they would naturally expect to do, if she went to theirs. But whatever the reason for it, none of these friends went to stay with her in Bayonne, just as she never went to stay with them.

As the "convent idea" hung fire, Teresa did what she had always told herself she would never do; she took a teaching position. She looked upon it as being merely temporary, as indeed it was, for had she meant to make teaching her life's work she would have gone to a normal school or done graduate work. She obtained a teaching position at St. Aloysius Academy, an institution conducted by the Sisters of Charity in Jersey City. At that time they were housed at 555 Bergen Avenue, to which they had moved from Grand Street, before finally establishing themselves in 1928 in a much finer building on the Boulevard.

Miss Anna Herbert, the assistant supervisor of schools in Bayonne, under whom Mary Demjanovich served as secretary, would probably have been willing to stretch a point in Teresa's case, and may have advised her as to how best to equip herself for the position her scholastic record indicated was within her reach. But if so, a further obligation would have been created, and with obligations Teresa had already had enough. The St. Aloysius job suited her as being no more than a marking of time. Her face was turned towards the Carmelites, and it may be that Teresa accepted a teaching position as a way of proving to her family that she was no good as a teacher. She could then say to Mary: "Well, you see! As you wanted me to be a teacher I took this job, but look what happened."

Her subjects were English and Latin and drawing. In English she was undoubtedly very competent, for though she could hardly have had profound scholarship she had that inner grasp of her subject which few teachers possess. With regard to Latin, one must say that she was not, on the face of it, too well qualified. She had gone to St. Elizabeth's with only two units of high-school Latin, so that she had privately to take a "make-up" course. But either she was an extremely intelligent student or Sister Marie Victoire a brilliant teacher (or perhaps both), for Teresa showed in her subsequent writings that she was better grounded than many students, who after six years of Latin, know very little about it. The Sisters at St. Aloysius were therefore glad to secure her services.

Teresa was the abject failure she knew she would be. From Sister Aurora, a teacher at St. Aloysius at the time, but who is now in retirement, I hear that Teresa was the only secular teacher employed, that she had charge of the first-year students, and that she could not exert much discipline. Her high squeaky voice, which had been the subject of unkind jests at St. Elizabeth's when she first went there, again brought derision upon her. Teresa was deeply hurt by the rudeness that some of these youngsters showed her—which they would never have dared to show to a Sister—and especially by the nickname "Demi" that they fastened upon her. Her weak and flickering eyes also gave these young rascals an opportunity to make fun of her. Little boys can make life miserable for a teacher, and, I suppose that, in a different way, little girls can be equally devilish. At any rate teaching at St. Aloysius was, for Teresa, anything but a pleasant experience.

She sometimes had to be "coached" for her classes, to the extent of being advised how best to handle her charges. One day Sister Aurora asked her, "Teresa, why don't you enter?" To this Teresa returned, "Why do you say that?" but then dropped the subject. Even the clocks seemed to be unruly, or showed some difference in time, and the ringing of the bell was one of Teresa's duties. When one of the Sisters said that she had rung the bell a little too early (and sometimes it was too late) the poor girl exclaimed, "How can I help the tantrums of the clocks?"

She was not interested in the "make-up" commonly used by young women, though she was always neatly dressed. Perhaps the fact that she was not glamorous went against her in the eyes of her students. These teen-agers probably intended no harm, and were merely hoping to get a little fun, but one of their tricks in the drawing class was to pass around their drawing portfolios behind her back so that "Demi" would get confused when she came to inspect the work.

Usually she travelled by bus between Bayonne and Jersey City, but Aileen Flynn says that on fine days she sometimes walked for the sake of the exercise. We do not hear of her walking with anyone. By now she knew no men except her father and brothers; with the boys—now grown up—who used to play baseball with her on the sandlot she exchanged no more than a casual "Hello" when she encountered them on the street. Hers was a completely withdrawn life. She did her work at St. Aloysius—and waited.

The work at the academy would have been hard even had Teresa's students been less intractable. Her main difficulty seems to have been that, as Miss Conklin (herself a teacher) says, she treated these children as though they were Ph.D.'s and habitually talked over their heads. Teresa was too kind and gentle to be able to control her classes. I suppose that it is possible to be so brilliantly fascinating as to hold children spellbound, but while this method may work with those of more mature age (and with *them* Teresa may well have been more of a success) it must be admitted that it did not work with the teen-agers of Jersey City. Only in retrospect did one of them say, "Along with her lesson in Latin she was a lesson in patience." Alas, such lessons are often learned too late. Even so, it is consoling that at least some of Teresa's students appreciated her.

One surmises that when the year of teaching came to an end, the Sisters made no attempt to engage Teresa for another year. Yet it would be putting it much too strongly to say that she was "dropped"; the truth undoubtedly is that on both sides it was recognised that the experiment had been somewhat unfortunate. Teresa was certainly glad to be relieved of work which she had always heartily detested and which she knew before she undertook it she would detest. The wonder is that after her view of life in a teaching order was so completely confirmed, she should nevertheless in the end have chosen that life. Or this would be a wonder were it not that the final decision was taken out of her hands, so that she felt that she was acting only according to the will of God.

CHAPTER EIGHT

❧

The Problem of Vocation

TERESA's priest-brother tells me that soon after her twenty-first birthday she announced to the family that she intended to become a nun. "I'm twenty-one now, and I'm going to be a nun," she said very definitely. Though Teresa had never been given to talking about her plans, her family had known for some time in a general way what was in her mind, though they may not have taken it very seriously and they may have hoped that, once she had obtained her degree, she would settle down to put it to use in teaching. As she still had more than a year of college ahead of her, nothing could be quite certain until then.

We have seen how for a long time she had been thinking of the Carmelites, but except for a single letter of enquiry she had sent out—and that did not amount to an actual application—the matter had not gone any further. During the summer of 1920, she would at last have been free to do a little more "convent hunting" with her brother. They went, for instance, to the Carmelite Convent on Gunhill Road in the Bronx. There Charles waited in the back office while Teresa talked to the superior at the grille. One would surmise that the heavy veil usually kept across it was removed at this time, for the superior would naturally want to look at the young woman who was applying. This would seem to be borne out by the fact that it was noticed that Teresa's eyes were weak and flickering; because of this she got nothing better than conditional acceptance; she might come back in two years if her eyes improved.

Teresa must have understood that this was virtually a refusal, as there was no reason to hope that her eyes would ever get any better, short of a miracle. Yet she was not entirely cast down, for Father Dolan gave her and her brother Charles the address of another convent which might be more willing to take her than was the one in Gunhill Road. It was an address in Philadelphia, but they could not find any Carmelite convent there. Only after they had returned to Bayonne did they discover that it was not Philadelphia but St. Louis, Missouri, to which they should have gone! Father Dolan had made a mistake, giving them the right street address but the wrong city. St. Louis was certainly too far away, and by now one may suppose that they were rather discouraged. And then in 1923 the job at St. Aloysius Academy was offered and apparently Teresa decided to put the whole matter in abeyance for a year. It may also be that she had at first intended to hold the Academy job for a couple of years—the period of waiting that the Carmelites had stipulated—but that she could endure no more than a single year.

One may hazard the guess that it was at this time that she wore a hair shirt, something far less painful to her than her teaching. As a matter of fact she did not find it painful at all, but gave it up because the irritating hair seemed as soft to her skin as delicate silk underwear. One realizes, of course, that it was only from the Carmelites that Teresa could have obtained such an article, for excessive austerities are not encouraged by American religious congregations. Aline Kilmer wrote an entertaining article on the subject. It was not that she wanted a hair shirt for herself; she was simply curious: she did not believe that in a department store one could ask to be directed to the section where they were sold, or, as a friend suggested, buy an old horse-hair sofa and cut it down, or, like the old lady in the fairy tale, weave her own hair into cloth. The old lady's hair had always grown again by morning, and Mrs. Kilmer was afraid that hers would not! As the hair shirt that Teresa obtained did not work with her, she concluded that physical austerities of the kind were not suited to her. In a conversation on this matter with her brother Charles, he told her that he deduced from this episode that Our Lord did not want her in Carmel.

As events turned out, after Teresa had given up teaching at St. Aloysius she remained at home for almost another year. The reason was probably that, since she had been told to wait two years, she meant to do just that, though she could have had little hope that her eyes would show any improvement. And though in the end she chose the Sisters of Charity —clean contrary to all her previous resolves—while the unmistakable prompting from on high was the main factor, the natural motive for the choice was not without some weight. At St. Elizabeth's, where her gifts were recognised, she knew that she would be accepted if she applied, whereas she was coming to feel that neither the Carmelites nor any other community where she was unknown would admit anybody with her poor eyes.

Meanwhile she resumed her familiar occupation of housekeeping. Quite literally this "Mary" was also a "Martha" concerned about many things. Among them was her father's health, and though he was only going on sixty-three, and in no sense an invalid, it was because he was not the man that he used to be that he had retired. Here Teresa made the immemorial complaint of solicitous women about their menfolk, that her father was "so careless about himself," meaning that he did not always do what he was told. There was nothing very obviously the matter with him except that he was troubled with asthma, though that can be very hard to bear.

Even so it was supposed that he should have ten easy years ahead of him. While he did not need her as her mother had, Teresa was glad that she could look after him, while dreading the day when she had to leave him, knowing how much of a blow this would be.

As before, Teresa's diversions were reading, music, and occasional visiting. These visits were, so far as we know, all a mere dropping into the houses of the young women whose acquaintance she had made in St. Vincent's parish. Gradually she had established a kind of ascendency there, for even before this date she had been serving in effect as a secretary to Father Dolan at the time he was building a new church, doing so at least during her vacations, while the seminarian Charles Demjanovich occupied himself with more manual tasks. Father Dolan had come to rely on Teresa a good deal and, in spite of her youth, often consulted her. The money for the fine edifice came in rather slowly, as the parishioners were not very well-to-do, and Aileen Flynn, who was also one of his helpers, remembers him saying to her, "Teresa, do you think I have tempted Divine Providence too far in trying to build such a big church?" She answered at once: "No, Father; God's resources are infinite." But that the church did go up was accounted for by some on the grounds that the angels must have helped to build it.

Teresa had by now become a leading spirit in the Sodality, a group rewarded by Father Dolan with a boat excursion to Rye Beach. He had not provided any lunch for the party, however, so each of them had to bring her own sandwiches, his contribution consisting only of a large box of candies. Alas, this, when passed around, proved to be mildewed, and when Teresa was appealed to as their "Emily Post" as to what to do, she very sensibly decided that, even at the risk of hurting Father Dolan's feelings, the candy had better be left uneaten. On another occasion, when the Sodality made a pilgrimage to Maryknoll, Miss Flynn describes Teresa as being the life of the party, but without supplying any of the details one would like to have.

Aileen's sister Kathleen was another member, and so was Alice Pratt, who later entered the Benedictine Order, where she is known as Sister Marie de Lourdes and about whom we shall hear a little more later. Aileen Flynn says that at a party held at Alice's home, she (Aileen) read the tea leaves and among other things told Teresa, "You are going on a long journey and there will be no return." She wonders rather naïvely at the accuracy of her own "prophecy," forgetting that when fortunes are told in this way, or with cards, it is hardly possible not to be right sometimes. The pleasures of these girls were evidently of an extremely simple sort.

From notes made by Sister Marie de Lourdes we learn that her friendship with Teresa began in 1922, that is, while she was still at college. It could only have been during vacations that Teresa could have taken any very active part in the Sodality, yet she found it possible to accept the position of secretary to St. Vincent's branch of the National Conference of Catholic Women, another indication of her capacity for leadership. This, however, was not developed at once. Teresa was only about sixteen when the family moved to 15 East 44th Street. In the Eastern Rite parish in which she had been brought up until this time, the people are content to play a passive role, except in liturgical matters, and to leave whatever organizing work is necessary to their priest. Even when she went to St. Elizabeth's (by which time she was eighteen and a half), she was at first rather retiring and shy, so that it was not until her last couple of years that the students succeeded in drawing her out. But once she had accepted the more bustling American temperament, one might almost say that she accepted it with a vengeance. St. Elizabeth's and St. Vincent's did a great deal for the Americanization of one who, until then, had lived in what was in those days more or less a foreign enclave. When she did at last respond to the calls that were made upon her, she threw herself with the utmost energy and decisiveness into whatever she was asked to do.

These external activities, however, or her occupations at home, were never allowed to interfere with her interior life. Regarding this year her sister Mary has given a vivid account: "From July, 1924, to February, 1925, she was at home again, doing the housework and planning her future. It was during this period that I found her several times in deep meditation, when apparently doing something else. She might be sitting with a book in her hands, but her eyes were not on the pages, and her mind was evidently miles away. Once I happened to pass through the dining room where she was cleaning. She was standing in the middle of the room lost in thought. As I approached, she remarked that there she was doing nothing when she should be working. Then, as formerly, she would never admit that she was tired, but kept at the work nearly all day. If we happened to be doing something together she always insisted on doing the hard part, because she was stronger, she said. One day, after washing some clothes, I noticed that her fingers were almost bleeding. I remarked that she should rub the clothes and not her fingers. Because it was noticed, she never hurt herself in that way again.

"She asked Father Charles and me where we thought she belonged. We agreed that she should join the Sisters of Charity, and make use of the talents that God had given her in teaching others. Her own choice was the secluded quiet of the contemplative life, but never having had her own way, she submitted all to the will of God, who showed in a remarkable way that He wanted her at St. Elizabeth's." That of course was written after Teresa's death and in the light of Mary's later knowledge—how else *could* it be written? Father Charles thought that she should use her talents in teaching, though Father Charles, as he understood Teresa better than anybody else did, did not want her to become a teacher unless it were clearly God's will.

Normally a choice of this sort comes about by force of circumstances, associations, the offering of opportunities, advice that is given, and so forth. And these were not quite absent in Teresa's case. But Father Charles was obliged to admit the force of Mary's arguments that Teresa had talents to give, and though he knew of Teresa's violent distaste for teaching he may have thought that this would be overcome in time. If there is such a thing as a teaching technique that can be acquired, Teresa, with her indomitable doggedness, could have been counted upon to have acquired it. Moreover, Teresa was, scholastically speaking, excellently equipped; and he and Mary probably reasoned that one with her brilliant record would in all likelihood be sent out to obtain a Master's degree and then a doctorate, after which she would have been given a college professorship. In this—especially if she were wearing a Sister's habit—she would undoubtedly have done much better than she did in her early and almost catastrophic venture. It was perfectly reasonable for him and Mary to believe that Teresa was making too much of her qualms.

Teaching, as it turned out, was what Teresa did eventually choose—to the extent of entering a congregation in which she knew that it was almost certain that she would have to teach for the rest of her life. Moreover, she did not quite escape it even during her last year at home, for during part of December, 1924, and a part of the following January, she substituted in a Jersey City high school for a former pupil of St. Elizabeth's who was ill, showing her versatility by this time teaching Spanish. One may surmise that she did this at the solicitation of the Sisters of Charity, who wanted to help one of their alumnae, and that the kindhearted Teresa did not feel that she could refuse. (It seems that the principal was so pleased with the teaching of the young lady who was ill, that he did everything in his power to get another St. Elizabeth College graduate.) About what happened at Jersey City we have no information, but no doubt though the work was still distasteful it could be endured, since it was going to be for only a brief period.

But note how sudden and even startling was her decision: we know that it was reached on or about December 8th, even before she accepted the temporary position, and that as soon as Teresa had made up her mind, she wanted to enter St. Elizabeth's novitiate by Christmas, and that it was only in deference to the wishes of the superior there that she put this off until early February, the Feast of the Purification of the Blessed Virgin being settled upon as an appropriate date.

December 8th, it will be remembered, is the Feast of the Immaculate Conception, and Teresa had gone to St. Elizabeth's that day to see Sister Angela Marie, who had been in college with her. She had not intended to spend the night there but was persuaded to do so. And on that day all doubts were ended. Sister Esther Maria, the prefect for freshmen at the college, who was one of her best friends, had been writing advising her not to put off her decision too long and suggesting that she make a novena in honor of the Blessed Virgin, in which her friends there would join, asking for God's guidance as to her vocation.

Here we should give Teresa's own words as written to Father Benedict: "Up until two weeks before I petitioned [for admission] my dominant thought was that this would be the last place I would ever enter. And the first serious thought I gave Convent was one night just about a fortnight before I applied, when I had come to visit Sister Angela Marie, a classmate, and was prevailed upon in spite of great disinclination, to remain until the following day, I then began to think that perhaps I had been battling against Providence all along. I saw that circumstances were still pointing in this direction; that my great hatred for teaching was precisely the principal source of assurance that it was God's will, since Carmel was to me naturally more attractive." This is all simple and natural; what is a bit breath-taking is that she adds: "The important thing is that then was the first inkling I had of the real reason God wanted me to be here: to teach them that Martha draws all her strength from Mary. And honestly, Father, I had no idea I knew even the a b c of the matter. And with the peace came absolute conviction. And once I was certain of God's will, I didn't delay a moment in carrying it out." Let us be unequivocally plain: Teresa joined the Sisters of Charity because she believed God had directly commanded her to do so; and this Father Benedict believed. He also believed that Teresa had received a definite commission from God to bring a greater degree of the contemplative spirit into her community.*

If Teresa was referring to the date of her decision about her vocation and the date of her application, actually five days intervened. But she was so certain on December 8th that later she told Father Benedict that from that date, though the earth tremble and the stars from heaven fall around her, nothing could disturb her calm. But she did not make her application to be admitted to the novitiate until December 13th, and it was only because she was told that she had better wait until February 2nd that she accepted a temporary position in the Jersey City high school. (It was probably represented to her by Mother Alexandrine, then the superior-general, that the delay would be a short one and that the alumna of St. Elizabeth's needed somebody to take her place.)

Sister Esther Marie was startled to find Teresa at St. Elizabeth's again on the 13th and even more so when she heard that she had come there to ask to be accepted as a postulant.

*This matter will be discussed more fully later, but as it cannot but constantly recur in any life of Teresa it must be said that many members of her community greatly resent such a suggestion. Well, I am not going to thrust it on them (if I could), but I ask them merely to be tolerant: all I need say at this point is that I can see the force of their objections; but I can also see all that the "other side" may urge.

Not even to this Sister (close friend though she was) did she confide all that had happened. That was reserved for Father Benedict, when he had become her spiritual director: to him she made it clear that she had seen no vision nor heard any Voice, in the ordinary sense, but that she had been directed by God to do what she had done. Once she had received this assurance, she acted upon it with the utmost promptitude.

Even so we do not find her dashing out with the news. But to Margaret Conklin she wrote, on January 15th, to tell her that she was going back to Convent "for good," adding: "To make matters more interesting, I haven't a thing ready, except some hankies that Charlie gave me for Christmas, anticipating my need. Everything came about very suddenly. The trouble was that I wasn't sure whether it would be Convent or not.* With half of the world making a novena for me (they all took it upon themselves) to the Immaculate Conception, Our Blessed Mother finally helped me to decide. . . . Did you ever see me when I wasn't rushed to death? I suppose I'll die that way, too—rushed to the undertaker."

Teresa had her suitcase all packed—having by now supplied herself with more than "hankies"—when her father came down with pneumonia, and with asthma on top of this he had little chance. A few days carried him off: on January 30th, two and a half days after he was taken ill, he died. Teresa was with him night and day, but there was little she could do for him.

Dying when he did spared Alexander Demjanovich a good deal. He had never been able to bear the thought of Teresa's leaving him, and it was partly because of this that she had put off her decision for so long. He was buried from the fine new brick church of St. John the Baptist on the very day that had been appointed as the one on which Teresa should enter St. Elizabeth's. But two of the nuns who attended the funeral—

*From which one derives further inference that St. Elizabeth's had come to seem more and more of a possibility before a final decision was reached.

one of them was Sister Benita, now Mother Benita—brought word from Mother Alexandrine that Teresa had better wait until February 11th. (Otherwise she would have gone straight from her father's grave to St. Elizabeth's.) As usual, Teresa did not make any contrary contention.

Teresa had been asked to write a poem for the centenary that year of the foundress of the Sisters of Charity of New Jersey, Mother Mary Xavier Mehegan. I have heard somebody say that some of the Sisters complained that this assignment was given to a college girl instead of to one of the members of the community. If so, it merely serves to show that people will complain about anything; actually Teresa was asked to write the poem when she had been accepted as a postulant by St. Elizabeth's. The whole objection was beside the point: Teresa did not start her poem until January 27th, and the last lines were written within three hours after her father's death. The entire piece (possibly her best) was composed by her father's deathbed. She had to write under pressure, for she believed that she was leaving for St. Elizabeth's on February 2nd, and the centenary celebration had been fixed for the 19th.

❧

CHAPTER NINE

The Sisters of Charity

IN view of the fact that Teresa acted in complete variance with her declared intention when she joined the Sisters of Charity, it should be explained just what is the nature of their life. Yet to get any real idea of the New Jersey branch—there are four other distinct branches in the United States—a brief sketch of their history must be attempted. Nor would it be sufficient to begin with Elizabeth Seton, the American foundress; we must indicate what was in the mind of St. Vincent de Paul when, with the help of his coadjutor St. Louise de Marillac, he brought the original group into being.

Vincent's was a departure so radical in religious life that it would have seemed startling, or even in some eyes scandalous, had it not been disguised. Shortly before he successfully tackled the problem, his friend St. Francis de Sales had approached it (or something like it) from an angle from which it was shown to be unattainable. Francis in founding the Visitation order wished to provide women who were not sufficiently robust to endure the rigors of Carmel with a contemplative life under less austere conditions, but he envisaged them doing a certain amount of outside charitable work. Only when he encountered the opposition of Cardinal de Rougemont, the archbishop of Lyons, who held the opinion that was almost universal in his time that all religious women should be cloistered, did Francis give up part of his plan. Vincent de Paul, however, in gathering his first Daughters, did not intend them to be nuns at all; they were merely a band of sturdy country girls who would help his aristocratic Ladies of Charity in whatever work was too much for their dainty little hands. These Daughters of his wore no habit, but a uniform—if the ordinary dress of peasant girls is to be called that—though it is from this that the habit of the "cornette" Sisters (and even this is not, strictly speaking, a habit) has gradually evolved. Nor were they to take any vows, though in Vincent's last years annual vows were permitted them. As for a cloister, they were to have none, though they lived in community. Actually, of course, what Vincent had intended to found was merely a pious society; no objection regarding their lack of a cloister could be brought against his Daughters. So far from that, they came to be everywhere enthusiastically accepted and have provided the model upon which many subsequent congregations of women were formed.

This point must be stressed at the outset, for if Teresa (who was one of St. Vincent's Daughters) seemed to depart from his ideas, it was to draw closer to those of Vincent's comrade-in-arms, St. Francis de Sales. Moreover, had the plans of Francis not been obstructed, Vincent would have established, not a copy of the Visitation, of course, but a group of women who would have been given from the start a habit and allowed to take vows, though their main purpose was active works of charity. His peasant sagacity had devised a scheme for by-passing the criticism he knew he would have received had he attempted more. But under changed conditions it is hardly reasonable to demand that what was merely a very clever device in the seventeenth century must be regarded as sacrosanct in the twentieth. In other words there is now no reason why a Martha should not have a strong infusion of her sister Mary, as for that matter was true of the original Martha whose name has been given to the active life. Because of what he first planned, Francis de Sales made Martha the patron of the Visitation.

The first convents established in the United States were of course established after the Revolution, for until then Catholics everywhere, except to some extent in Maryland and Pennsylvania, lived under penal laws. Of these early convents there were just three, but because of the crying needs even those of the Carmelites and Poor Clares conducted schools for a short while, until they saw that this work was incompatible with their rule. Only the Visitation school, founded at Georgetown, still survives.

The same year (1805) that the Poor Clares packed up to return to Europe, Elizabeth Seton, a widow just under thirty with five children, came into the Church shortly after the death of her husband. Her Episcopalian relatives—both on the Seton and Bayley side—gave her little if any help, though they were well able to do so, and when she opened a school in New York to support those dependent upon her they put so many difficulties in her way that in 1808 she migrated to Baltimore, where again she set up a private school, being assigned for the purpose a small house on the grounds of the Sulpician seminary on Paca Street.

She had been brought into the Church largely through correspondence with that most charming man, Bishop Cheverus of Boston, who died as a cardinal archbishop in France but who while he was in Boston chopped his own firewood. Elizabeth did not meet him until some years later, when, as he was in Baltimore on ecclesiastical business, he drove over to Emmitsburg, Maryland, where she was then living and announced himself, when she went down to the parlor to meet him, "I am Cheverus."

She had moved to Emmitsburg because a former sea captain

named Samuel Cooper, who was studying for the priesthood, had bought a farm for her there, and because a group of ex-Sulpicians had opened Mount St. Mary's college only a mile or so away. They conducted an institution which included a school for small boys (she wanted some such place for her own sons), a college department, and also a seminary. Elizabeth and those with her, a very small group of women (including two of her dead husband's sisters), came over the hills of Western Maryland in prairie schooners, and, after they were established at Emmitsburg, those who intended to live a religious life adopted, not even the uniform of the Sisters of Charity, but the kind of widow's weeds that Elizabeth (and for that matter Louise de Marillac) adopted. Canonically they had no standing, and their funds were often so low that they almost starved to death, but somehow they kept going.

At her convent Mrs. Seton received some young girls as pupils, and for the children of Emmitsburg she also established what can claim to be the first of American Catholic parochial schools, one that is still in operation. It was in this fashion that the Sisters of Charity began in America, as a most strongly flavored American enterprise.

Elizabeth Seton did not live to be old, but in her comparatively short life she set an indelible mark upon all who knew her, and soon the rapidly expanding Church in the Republic was sending out appeals to the congregation of which she was the foundress. New York received as its bishop Jean Dubois, who had been president of Mount St. Mary's College; Cincinnati received another Mount St. Mary's man as its ordinary, and each wanted Sisters of Charity, but under diocesan direction. Emmitsburg itself eventually became affiliated with the world-wide organization of the Sisters, under the direction of the superior-general of the Vincentian Fathers in Paris, thereby no doubt gaining a good deal, but also losing some part of their distinctive American character.

The New Jersey Sisters, an offshoot from those of New

York, were brought into the state by the bishop of Newark, Elizabeth Seton's nephew, James Roosevelt Bayley, who rose to be archbishop of Baltimore. He is buried beside his aunt's body at Emmitsburg, though his tomb does not bear the disarming inscription he had requested—"Here lies the poor old Archbishop." He was born in 1814 and educated at Amherst and Trinity College, Hartford, when, after being called to the Episcopalian ministry, he was received into the Catholic Church in Rome in 1842. A year later, after only a year's study at St. Sulpice in Paris, he was ordained a priest and immediately appointed president of Fordham, not as yet under the charge of the Jesuits. Eight years later he was made bishop of Newark, when he lost little time in seeking the services of the Sisters of Charity, who were led by Catherine Josephine Mehegan (known in religion as Mother Xavier). She was a young woman who was born in Ireland in 1825, and she lived until 1915, establishing a great work which has followed to this day the lines of development she initiated. One might perhaps have expected that her niece might have helped in her enterprises, for she was married to the railroad tycoon James J. Hill; actually, however, she made no material contribution, though she remained on friendly terms with her aunt. Presumably her husband considered that he had done enough in building the seminary at St. Paul, Minnesota, using steel railroad rails so freely in its construction that it would probably be proof against an atom bomb.

It was Bishop Bayley who founded Seton Hall (named for Mother Seton), at first in a very small way at Madison before he transferred it to South Orange, when he made over the Madison property to the Sisters for an academy. The transferred college naturally retained the name of Seton, but it was Elizabeth's Christian name which was used by the new academy, to which a college was eventually added. There was a second transfer before the present fine campus was secured, and even then the start was made in some woefully small

wooden buildings. In the name Mother Xavier had in mind
the saint of Visitation memories, whereas Bishop Bayley was
thinking of his aunt. His comment upon the diplomatic
achievement was "Cork, Blarney, Ireland"—for, after all,
Elizabeth Seton has not yet been proclaimed a saint.

Though the community has members of all nationalities,
yet it is decidedly more American-Irish; for, being near large
cities, it was natural that it should draw largely, if not quite
exclusively, upon those of Irish descent, who formed the
main part of their Catholic population. What is more important is that its spirit was distinctively American, as was
that of Mother Seton, whereas Emmitsburg adopted some
French ways of thought with the French habit. The American
branches, though they decidedly differ from one another in
habit, have, in their American practicality, discarded the
cornette (which, by the way, did not exist in St. Vincent's
day but was hardly more than a white bonnet), as cornettes
are not too well suited for the kind of work that the Sisters
have to do. And their rule has been modified with American
conditions in mind.*

Most of the American branches have laid their main em-
phasis on educational work, which was Mother Seton's idea,
but without limiting themselves to this. The Sisters of Charity
of Emmitsburg, on the other hand, have done more in the
way of conducting hospitals of various types than have the
other branches, though most of these (if not all of them) have
also established hospitals, the Sisters of New York and New
Jersey notably so. By definition the Sisters of Charity are
committed to any form of charitable activity, and what is
the chief work done here or done there depends upon local
needs. What has to be borne in mind is that this was the life

---

*My mother-in-law tells me that she was much amused in Paris to see
Sisters of Charity calmly riding bicycles, with large pieces of cellophane protecting their cornettes from the winter rains!

that Saint Vincent de Paul—so excellent an example of the Saint of the active life—envisaged for his Daughters.

This, however, does not mean that Teresa Demjanovich was an undutiful Daughter of his because she laid so much stress on the contemplative mode. Nor should it be said (though it often is) that she was out of place among them, for she did them the highest possible service in making it her mission to remind them that an active life, when devoid of sufficient spiritual nourishment, can become rather sterile. On the other hand, those who point out that a good many Sisters have attained to great sanctity while engaged in a multiplicity of activities merely prove what nobody has ever denied: Teresa found that it could be so in her own experience, and explicitly said as much in her Conferences. To put what seem contradictory propositions in a nutshell: one must not allow one's self to become clogged by "business"; at the same time it must be remembered that it is possible to be deeply engrossed in all sorts of affairs and yet to keep the heart hid with Christ in God.

The distinction often drawn between the active and the contemplative life indicates, except in a few instances, not so much a real difference in purpose (for the purpose of both is the attainment of perfection) as a difference in stress. While the most active should give some time to prayer, human beings, as they are only human, can hardly be contemplatives and nothing else. Though the Church maintains that in itself the contemplative life is higher than the active, St. Thomas Aquinas has expressed the conviction that the most perfect life is a combination of both—*tradere contemplata.*

Quite recently the Pope has indicated that all contemplative orders of women (the Carmelites excepted) should engage in some external activity, thus ending the putting of everything connected with the religious life in hermetically sealed water-tight compartments. Yet it need hardly be said that he was not abandoning the traditional Catholic view;

he was saying no more than that charitable works need not interfere with the spirit of contemplation, just as the active life is made more fruitful by prayer.

The various American branches have sought to differentiate themselves from one another by modifications in their habit. Mother Seton wore merely widow's weeds, and so did St. Louise de Marillac, who, though co-foundress of the Sisters with St. Vincent, never was one of his Daughters but remained a Lady of Charity, while acting as his Daughter's superior. She was never addressed as "Sister" or "Mother," but always as "Mademoiselle le Gras."* In New York the Sisters of Charity modified her headdress in what I hope I shall be pardoned for saying was not a very becoming style, wearing until fairly recently a bonnet of black oilcloth. This is now discarded for a bonnet of black silk, and I have heard rumours that this was designed for them by Hattie Carnegie! In New Jersey the New York habit was adopted, but eventually an elaborate fluted white cap was introduced. We hear in the excellent three-volume history of their community that, when it was introduced, the older Sisters (who showed by this that they must have been set free from all the vanities of the world) bemoaned the change and kept their old beloved headpieces in a closet in the hope that they would eventually be restored.

Only during the past few years has this branch of the Sisters of Charity taken perpetual vows, and though the same thing may be true of the other American branches, I understand that the Sisters of Charity of Emmitsburg, as they follow the Vincentian Rule under a superior-general abroad, still have only annual vows. The formula of petition used in Teresa's time reads: "We, the undersigned, do most humbly petition the Council of the Motherhouse, to be allowed to re-

---

*Marillac was her maiden name. According to the usage of the time, only ladies of very exalted rank rated the Madame, and Louise, though of good and indeed illustrious family, could only be "Mademoiselle."

new our consecration to God, by the HOLY VOWS OF POVERTY, CHASTITY, AND OBEDIENCE, in the sense and manner in which they are made at the Motherhouse of the Sisters of Charity of Saint Vincent de Paul, in the Diocese of Newark, New Jersey." But these vows were taken only for a twelve-month period, and "the sense and manner" in which they were "renewed" allowed only another twelve months.

The Sisters' Rules are based on the Conference that St. Vincent de Paul gave to his first Daughters. One of the most important passages is that defining the purpose of the Sisters: "Although they do not constitute an enclosed Order, that state not being compatible with the objects of their Institution,—nevertheless, as they are more exposed than nuns, in most circumstances, their only monastery being a hospital, the houses of the sick or an asylum; their chapel the parish church; their cloister the public streets; having no enclosure but obedience, no grate but the fear of God, no veil but holy modesty;—they should lead as virtuous lives as if they were professed in an enclosed Order, and comport themselves in all their intercourse with the world, with as much recollection, purity of heart and body, and detachment from creatures, as nuns in the retirement of their monastery." Regarding their devotions, a paragraph reads: "They shall not on week days spend their time in saying any prayers but those prescribed by the Rule, without a special permission from the Mother, who is not to grant it if those devotions would interfere with their exterior duties; nor should they hear more than one Mass, unless obliged to do so, by some extraordinary circumstance." In their devotions the Little Office of Our Lady is not included—not even the Little Office in English; instead there are a number of prescribed prayers to be said, when feasible, at stated times during the day, as well as half an hour's daily adoration of the Blessed Sacrament. To any Sister who suggested additional prayers or pious practices, Mother Xavier made an invariable rejoinder: "Keep your Rule, and it will keep you."

These were the ideas—clear and precise, if somewhat limited—that prevailed when Teresa Demjanovich laid aside her longing for Carmel to enter the novitiate at St. Elizabeth's. Under the circumstances the act was heroic, for she not only renounced all her own natural inclination but went forward into a future which she knew would be full of misunderstandings and difficulties. Teresa's life is not to be understood unless we are able to see what were the obstacles she had to overcome.

CHAPTER TEN

Taking the Habit

FEBRUARY 11th, the Feast of Our Lady of Lourdes, was the day set for Teresa to enter "Nazareth," the novitiate at St. Elizabeth's. The night before she left there was a reception, and Alice Pratt and two of the other girls in the Sodality were deputized to bring her to the meeting and take her home afterwards. The next morning, saying goodbye to her brother John, and accompanied by her other brother, Charles the priest, and her sisters Mary and Anne, she went to Convent Station. She described it in a letter to Margaret Conklin as the day "when I really began to live."

The start, however, was not very auspicious, so far as the weather went. The walk from the railway station cannot be more than a quarter of a mile; even so, as there was a downpour of rain, Mother Alexandrine had sent a carriage to meet the train. It was an example of the kindness and sympathy she was to show Teresa during the two years that followed, a time when she was often badly in need of some sympathy.

As soon as the carriage drew up under the porte-cochere at the entrance, Teresa jumped out and ran eagerly up the steps, as though unwilling to lose a moment's time in putting on her postulant's dress, a long black skirt with a cape and starched collar and a black net cap. It was this that she was to wear until she was given the novice's habit (which is slightly different from that worn by the professed Sisters) and her name in religion. Ordinarily that was then three months from the day of arrival; now it is six.

Eight days later, in the auditorium in Xavier Hall, the academy building, the celebration of Mother Xavier's centenary was held. I have before me the program as printed in Sister Mary Agnes Sharkey's *The New Jersey Sisters of Charity*.* The celebrated Dr. James J. Walsh, appearing as the representative of scholarship, delivered an erudite address on Modern Monasticism. An alumna, Mrs. Josephine McMullen, of the class of 1905, delivered a very brilliant speech on "Our Founder's Message." She was a few years later to be delegate at large from her state of Ohio to the Democratic Convention, where she was one of those who spoke seconding the nomination of Governor Smith as presidential candidate. The third item was supposed to be offered on behalf of the religious. The author is set down as "Teresa Miriam Demjanovich, Litt.B. '23," though the "Miriam" does not appear either on her baptismal certificate or on the Community Record, so it is evidently a mistake. As for the name "Sister Miriam Teresa, 1926," which follows in brackets, this was not then on the program but was added afterwards by Sister Mary Agnes. It was stretching a point quite a long way to allow Teresa to appear as the representative of the Sisters, as she was only a postulant; but she did not deliver her poem herself for it was assigned to one of the Sisters. It was a great honor that she had been commissioned to write it.

The Mother-General at this time—that is, the head not only of St. Elizabeth's but of all the New Jersey Sisters of Charity, was Mother Mary Alexandrine Jackson. She, like those who had gone before her in this office—and those who

*II, 270.

succeeded her—had so very "Irish" a face that one would almost think they were members of the same family. And most of the names one finds mentioned in Sister Mary Agnes's three-volume *History* are also of Irish descent, which perhaps had some bearing upon Teresa's case in the novitiate, as in college, where she was considered a bit "foreign." Mother Alexandrine was obviously a very kind woman, though she may have lacked some of the largeness and decisiveness of mind of the Foundress; she had been elected in 1921, after having been stationed at the mission of St. Michael in West Hoboken (now Union City), and had taught at the academy at St. Elizabeth's, held the position of prefect of discipline at the college, and was assistant mother in the Community Council from 1915 to 1918. She had therefore had considerable administrative experience.

Sister Mary Ellen, the novice-mistress, who will figure even more prominently in these pages, was a personage of force and pungency. She had entered in religion in 1868, and had been a sister close on to sixty years and in fact celebrated her diamond jubilee before her death in 1932. During most of that period she had been novice-mistress, serving two long terms, interspersing this extremely important work (upon which depended the formation of the younger Sisters) by periods of superiorship at Jersey City, Newark, and Hoboken, during one of which she had had Mother Alexandrine as a subject. As was only to be expected, she was definitely of the old school in her outlook, and as most of the younger Sisters had passed under her hands (including many who could no longer be called "young") she was able to exercise considerable influence.

She and Teresa were a real trial to each other, a trial each of them tried to support with Christian patience. While it is true that Sister Mary Ellen told Father Benedict, soon after the new postulant had arrived, that there was now a "little mystic" among them, it became evident as time went on that

Teresa was a good deal more of a mystic than had been bargained for. Excellent woman though she was, Sister Mary Ellen's view was that mystics were no doubt all right in their place but that their place was not in that community. She did not have much elasticity in her makeup, for she was old and her spiritual habits had long since set.

Sister Mary Ellen probably had scant regard for Father Benedict. Or rather, while she sometimes drew out his praise after a conference, she suspected him (not without cause) of encouraging a contemplative spirit which she thought should not be stressed among the Sisters of Charity. She was rather strict and had little sympathy with the sick. Unlike most of the great founders, all of whom showed solicitude for those who were unwell, Sister Mary Ellen could never quite believe that any of the ailments the novices had were really genuine, because she had such good health herself, in spite of her years. Even those who returned from hospital after an operation were not allowed to take things easy for a week or two afterwards. Her attitude seems to have been that of St. Teresa of Ávila, who said that there were nuns who asked to be excused from their duties because they had a headache, and would ask to be excused the next day because they had had a headache, and for a third day in case the headache returned. If the novice was not well, so Sister Mary Ellen held, she should go home; illness showed that she was not fitted for the religious life. She therefore not only came to object to our Teresa's mysticism but to the semi-invalidism from which she suffered during the last year of her life. On both counts a good deal of pain was inflicted. It is unfair to hold anybody responsible for her temperament, but had Sister Mary Ellen recognised that Teresa was a very sick woman, a very valuable life might have been saved.

On the other hand, she had a tart kind of humour, and this alone made her liked; and everybody admired her single-minded devotion to her duty as she understood it. I have been told what were her comments when some postulants were being given their religious names the evening before they received the habit. Sister Zita, who had asked for that name, was very much pleased when told she was to have it. Why she wanted it I do not know, for she tells me that the reason did not have its source in Reginald Balfour's charming couplet:

Z is for Zita, the good kitchen maid;
She prayed and she prayed and she prayed and she prayed.

Another postulant was given "Carmela," and Sister Mary Ellen added kindly, "Our Lady's Child"; but when Carmela asked how her name was spelled she was told sharply, "One 'L' is enough for you!" "Ursulina?" another novice stammered in surprise and got, "Yes, Little Bear!" And when the fourth girl, to be known as "Josepha," asked timidly, "What language is that?" she was told: "It's God's language. Now run along to bed all of you." I confess to finding the old lady rather amusing, though her charges were a bit afraid of her. As my only fear is that she may appear in a somewhat unfortunate light, it must always be remembered that to a great extent she was placed in this situation in spite of herself. There was always much to be said for her side of the case.

Father Benedict Bradley, a monk of St. Mary's Abbey, Newark, was a person of a very different type, and he had to play a more important part than anybody else in Teresa's spiritual development. He had been appointed spiritual director of the novices, giving also a weekly conference to the professed Sisters. About the end of September, 1924, he succeeded Father Gilbert Nolan, also of St. Mary's, and served for three years. He was tall, handsome, urbane, and by this time approaching his mid-sixties. He had been born in the Mississippi Valley and had been educated by the Benedictines of Atchison, Kansas, passing through their college before making his novitiate at St. Vincent's Archabbey in Pennsylvania, from which he returned to Atchison to complete his studies for the priesthood. He taught in the college there for a time, then was pastor of a large parish in Kansas City until appointed a professor at St. Anselm's College, Manchester, New Hampshire. During these years he gave much of his time as spiritual director of convents, a work which was crowned by what he did at St. Elizabeth's.

In his guidance of Teresa I daresay that some people doubt whether he always showed good judgment, but so far as I can make out from the documents that lie before me his was rather a case of exceptionally keen insight. Few priests would have ventured to act as he did—that may be admitted—but it is not often that a spiritual director encounters a Teresa Demjanovich. As the proof of the pudding is in the eating, it must be said that Father Benedict, using most unusual methods, succeeded in directing to very great heights the "little mystic" put in his keeping. Without prophesying what would have happened had she met a confessor of different type—for sanctity might have overcome all obstacles—it may be that by another spiritual director she would have been so discouraged as to have found it safest to subside into mediocrity. Discouragement (theoretically) may have been even better for her aspirations, but this may be doubted, for human nature needs encouragement. One may tremble at the risks Father Benedict accepted, for by urging her on as he did she might have been spoiled and made insufferable. But tentatively, to give my opinion for what it is worth—for the readers of Teresa's life will have to judge for themselves—it seems to me that, while even in retrospect one sometimes trembles, Father Benedict's way of directing Teresa justified itself. What cannot be questioned is the objective honesty with which Father Benedict recorded the relationship between them. Had it not been for his preservation of her letters and his own ample statements about what happened, we should know very little about her. At most she could have been only a fragrant memory, shyly cherished by those who had been with her in the novitiate.

For Teresa the postulancy was stretched a few days beyond the three months then required; this was because on May 17th the Little Flower was to be canonized, and that was considered a very suitable occasion for Teresa's clothing. Her devotion to the Saint of Lisieux had not escaped notice while she was at college, and this was perhaps the reason why she was allowed the unusual privilege of retaining her baptismal name in religion, with the addition of the "Miriam," for in some form or other nearly all the Sisters (and even some monks, particularly the Trappists), take the name of Mary, though it is not always used except in formal designations.

Mother Benita—still at that time Sister Benita and the college librarian—met Teresa after she had received the habit and, naturally, her religious name. "So it's Miriam Teresa, is it? The Miriam is for Our Lady, of course, but which Teresa —the Little Flower?"

"No, the Old Lady," was Teresa's quick reply.

But she was delighted that her reception of the habit fell on the day the "Young Lady," who died about the age Miriam Teresa was then, was being declared a saint. Her happiness was increased by the fact that her brother Charles said the community Mass that day, and that she was permitted to serve it, kneeling in the front pew and making the responses.

The Little Flower was regarded by her as her secondary patron. But it seems to me that Miss Conklin suggests too much when trying to show that Teresa Demjanovich and Thérèse Martin were very much alike. There were of course some points of resemblance: both were young, both came of exceptionally pious families, and both laid great stress in their religious life upon observing the Rule down to its smallest details. But all religious should do the last, and most of them are the children of very devout parents; some even die while young. For the rest I cannot see that these two have much resemblance to each other. Their families were of a different social milieu, the Martins being well-to-do French bourgeois and the Demjanoviches of the working class. More important still, there was no trace in our Teresa of Thérèse's somewhat prattling literary style, which at moments came distressingly close to being baby talk about "little Jesus" and the "little Virgin Mary" and her own "little soul." Moreover, we hear nothing whatever of the Little Flower's ever having experienced the concomitants of mysticism, whereas Teresa several times (and as Father Benedict hints, many times) had known these. As for Thérèse's "Little Way"—which is far from being an easy way or a short cut to heaven—though we know that Teresa had studied *The History of a Soul* she gives no indication of following its method. Instead she reaffirmed the classical system of asceticism, though somewhat softened, as it had been after St. Francis de Sales and those of his school had done their work. The Little Flower was by no means so cozy and coy as she may appear to be on the surface, displaying qualities which have charmed most people but also setting many teeth on edge, whereas our Teresa showed an astonishing maturity in the case of one so young, and her occasional—very occasional—exhibitions of cuteness are so sedate as seriously to trouble no one. There is, however, this much that the two have in common: in what they wrote they drew very slightly upon what they had read—the truth is that neither was either deeply or widely read—but primarily upon their own experience. Even here there is a difference: broadly, one might say that Thérèse was a psychologist, whereas Teresa was a philosopher and theologian, even though her amateur status is sometimes apparent.

At the time that Teresa applied for admission to the Sisters of Charity, many of the community were surprised at the suddenness of her decision, though some of them had been praying for her to do so for years. But nobody took this as a whim, for all who knew her also knew how solid was her character. Therefore, without the long examination that such applications sometimes get, she was accepted at once, Mother Alexandrine waiting only to obtain the approval of her council and the bishop, which was promptly given.

Even before actually entering, Teresa believed herself to have received from God Himself the mission of making the community realize the value of the contemplative spirit. Yet at that time she did not really understand what this meant, for she was to write to Father Benedict: "I am only speaking from my own experience, Father, for even while thinking of entering Carmel, I never supposed that I knew what contemplation was, but I thought I might strive to learn. All I knew was that I had a natural attraction for quiet, and a supernatural attraction for penance and seeking God." Then most astonishingly she goes on: "When I entered I came to know all. It was only after your first conference and a rapid perusal of Vaubert that I began to realize that I had been living an interior life. In fact it was the first time I had ever heard the term mentioned in connection with the life of the soul."

To Vaubert I shall come in a moment, but one wonders how she could have spent four years in a Catholic college and not have heard at least the gist of what was in the little book to which she refers. It is clear that she could not have done much reading in spiritual works prior to this time—possibly because she was much too busy while at college and also because when she was in Bayonne she could find nothing of the kind in the public library. But she did have at least one vision of Our Lady, and Father Benedict makes it plain that such things were frequent with her, for in a statement prepared by him at the request of Archbishop Walsh he says: "Though Sister Miriam Teresa enjoyed from childhood the extraordinary privileges of the great mystics, such as ecstasies, raptures, visions, locutions, she carefully concealed from all the Secrets of the King. It was not until she entered the novitiate that she revealed to her spiritual director the hidden privileges of her spiritual life. To him alone she confided all her secrets, and that under obedience. Until her death she was obliged to disclose to me all the extraordinary manifestations of grace in her soul. This was the weekly ordeal that she went through with the greatest aversion." To this we may add that Teresa was a mystic without having the least suspicion that this was so.

As to the spiritual benefit of what are, after all, only the concomitants of mysticism and not mysticism itself, she wrote in one of the conferences she prepared for Father Benedict to deliver: "Look at the voices heard by Jeanne d'Arc and the visions seen by Teresa [of Ávila], who wouldn't be holy with all these extraordinary helps? We can't measure up against them. No, we haven't heard the voice that Jeanne d'Arc heard, and the better we haven't. Our ordinary way is much safer for us. And we have even more than Jeanne had. We have the absolutely safe and audible voice of our superiors and our rule. No possible mistake here to know the will of God. And Jeanne could easily have slipped. Do we ever stop to think, though, that it was not the voices that made Jeanne a saint, nor the command to do God's will, but her doing it?"

In another conference she reverts to the same idea, saying: "A word of warning. Don't confuse visions and revelations and ecstasies and the gift of tears with the essential part of perfection." Then out of her personal experience she adds, "And here's another thing; it is possible for a soul to have attained this end and not be conscious of it." To go back to Father Benedict again, he says: "The first grace of her life seems to have come in childhood. She did not specify the exact year. Speaking of this, she told me that as a child Our Lord had given her the grace to understand the meaning of life. Rather curious, I asked her what it was. In reply she said it was to do His will." But Father Benedict does not suggest that this came to her in vision or locution, and indeed, it is no more than a logical inference to be drawn from the relationship that should exist between the Creator and His creatures, few as are the people who, while perceiving this, act upon it.

In another of several statements made by Father Benedict, he writes: "It was about three weeks after Sister's entrance that I came to recognize in the confessional that I probably had an extraordinary soul to deal with. . . . Up to this time, Our Lord, and He alone, was her spiritual director in all things extraordinary, and He continued to direct her until the end of her life."

Now we come to the book that Teresa said opened her eyes. It is *How to Walk Before God, or the Holy Exercise of the Presence of God,* by the Jesuit T. F. Vaubert. In the 1925 edition that I have, it is a volume of only 149 pages bound in dark blue with its titles stamped in black, and this presumably is the edition the novices used. All of them were expected to read it, though whether all of them did I cannot say; if they found it a bit on the dry side, so do I. Its gist is in this passage towards the end: "To become interior we have only to change the objects on which the powers of our soul act—that is, to substitute God for the creature, to accustom ourselves to recollect in Him our minds, which are incessantly dissipated on creatures, and to keep our hearts closely united to Him by affection and love; to enter into ourselves, and to keep ourselves retired in the solitude of the heart as much as we can, and there to speak to, look at, and listen to God." That contains none of the exalted considerations that are found in St. John of the Cross or in St. Teresa, but attempts merely to point out what may eventually lead to the heights of contemplation. As such, it was thought by Father Benedict a suitable little manual for beginners in the spiritual life, for such as might have been daunted by more technical studies in mysticism, especially since these would probably have been quite beyond their comprehension. The Practice of the Presence of God is one that many Christians follow, including lay people, and has been explained in many works, perhaps never more charmingly than by the French seventeenth century Carmelite, lay brother Lawrence.

Another book assigned for study—actually a pamphlet of only 43 pages—was *The Little Secret* by the German Capuchin Cassian Karg. The "secret" itself was merely the taking of some ejaculatory prayer, such as "All for the love of Jesus!" and making it the axiom of one's life. On page 35 Father Cassian writes: "We should all be guided in our choice by the inner promptings of the Holy Ghost. Only he who does not enjoy the liberty of the Holy Ghost imagines he must adopt every religious practice and despises those who do not. This gives rise to pharisaical and abnormal devotees. This is by no means the purpose of the little secret. It produces true, earnest and interior Christians, whose prayer continually grows simpler until it reaches that stage where the soul only says: 'Jesus, Jesus' (the great secret)." It is to this that the author tells us that the "little secret" is intended to lead. He concludes, "He who has really grasped the idea of the little secret, has laid the foundation for an interior life rich in spiritual benefits, for the progress of the soul, for a practical and at the same time ideal Christianity." But again it is evident that Father Benedict was proceeding on the principle of giving babes milk before going on to more difficultly digested food.

Teresa reveals some indebtedness to both of these books, for though she does not quote from them directly, or in so many words recommend the practice of the "little secret," she does in one of her conferences allude to the modern multiplication of "devotions" but shows on almost every page that she wrote that her own spiritual life was nourished on the Liturgy and the Bible. In all this it might seem odd that she gives no sign of having read the life of St. Teresa her brother had given her years earlier. But at Father Benedict's suggestion she did read *The Interior Castle* and something of St. John of the Cross. When she did so, she found in them a confirmation of what she had already discovered for herself.

Teresa's great devotion then, and throughout life, was for the Blessed Trinity. Concerning this, Father Benedict writes: "Among the most remarkable of the passive unions which some of God's saints have experienced is the Vision of the Trinity. According to her own admission, Sister Miriam Teresa had enjoyed this privilege. The purpose and fruit of this grace are a marvellous strengthening of the faith. The intellect is illuminated and the will is so strengthened by the light received in this vision of the greatest of all mysteries that the soul is firmly established in God." He goes on to quote a passage from the Seventh Mansion of *The Interior Castle,* in which St. Teresa describes this vision, saying that the soul now, "so to speak [that is, by analogy] understands by sight, though it beholds the Blessed Trinity neither by the eyes of the body nor of the soul, this being no imaginary vision"; meaning, of course, not a fantasy, but that which appertains to the faculty of the imagination. St. Teresa continues: "All the Three Persons here communicate themselves to the soul, and speak to it and make it understand the words of Our Lord in the Gospel; that He and the Father and the Holy Ghost will come and make Their abode with the soul which loves Him and keeps His commandments." This does not mean—and cannot mean—a "vision" in either of the forms as ordinarily understood, for of course "No man hath seen God at any time" (I John 4: 12), and furthermore the Blessed Trinity indwells millions of hearts. But, as St. Teresa makes clear in the next section, there may be a consciousness of the presence of the Blessed Trinity in the soul's depths, "though," she adds, "for want of learning it cannot describe how." If the copious and exact utterance of the great Spanish mystic fails Teresa Demjanovich, the most that ordinary people can say is that this experience of the most real of realities is given to very few; but our Teresa seems to have been among them.

Some further explanation seems to be called for. *Deum, tamquam ignotum cognoscimus*, as St. Thomas Aquinas says, is the pithiest and truest statement of the matter. God is at once unknown, but also knowable experimentally. As Thomas Merton, a modern monk professed to contemplation, says: "When the mind admits that God is too great for our knowledge, Love replies: 'I know Him!' "* Teresa may not have known the term to use, but she knew the truth that the terms sometimes inadequately convey.

In her very fragmentary autobiography Teresa notes, among other things, that she was "not a beauty"—which may convey more than is true, for she was certainly not ill-favored —but adds that her powers of observation were never more acute, despite her weak eyes. (This means that she observed people more easily than she observed, let us say, buildings.) She goes on: "Neither am I insensible to heat and cold; kindness and contempt; weariness and comfort. But now all these natural cravings are in bondage, for the will has absolute control over them." As that does not tell us all that we would like to know, we may find some of the specific details in what Sister Dolorine, a fellow novice, supplied at Father Benedict's request. But Sister Dolorine did not even discover the color of Teresa's eyes for two months. Otherwise she was observant, for she reports: "I have never seen her doing nothing. She talks only when necessary, and of course, at recreation. The sunshine of her charity falls equally on all. She is 'apart.' Associated only with Jesus. I have never seen her take a restful position, except at recreation. When sitting, she does not lean back. Kneeling, she used to keep away from the bench in front. Now she rests her hands on it, because that is the way our Mistress wishes us all to kneel. . . . She appears to walk very slowly. It is a mistake. Her gait is quick. Her bearing is very erect, holding her head as if listening to somebody, i.e. slightly raised to the left. . . . She is positively noiseless."

*Ascent to Truth, p. 296 (New York, Harcourt Brace and Co., 1951).

Towards the end of her time at St. Elizabeth's, Teresa, at Father Benedict's request, began an autobiography, but did not proceed very far in it because of the illness that soon overtook her. A passage or two from it has already been drawn upon, and more will be said later. It was completely on her own initiative, however, that she began a diary on the day she entered, and she kept it until the end of the retreat in July. This must be one of the most laconic documents of the sort ever to be produced, and from it a few samples may be cited. For February 11, 1925, the day she became a postulant, she has: "I am all His; He is all mine. How powerful I am!" Six days later appears a more extended passage: "Beloved, I live only to be united with Thee. Every step that I shall take shall be made in union with Thy weary journeyings in search of souls; every physical labor, in union with the work of Thy hands during Thy hidden life at Nazareth; every mouthful of food, an act of gratitude and praise for Thy solicitude for my temporal welfare; every breath, a sigh of desire for Thee; every beat of my heart, a throb of love, magnified infinitely by Thy Divinity present within me; every look, a glance of love towards Thee; every word, a prayer; every thought—all Thine own—reconsecrated to the Holy Spirit."

Three days later, in another relatively extended passage, she says: "With sorrows, and sufferings, and reproaches, and humiliations, will I assuage Thy thirst, O my Beloved, by so aiding Thee in the redemption of souls." In other words, she not only entered the Novitiate already completely yielded to God, but expecting, even then, that she would have much to undergo (in which she was not mistaken) and—most surprising of all, perhaps—that it is all to aid Christ in the redemption of souls, so positive was she from the outset that hers was an apostolic mission and that she had been called to the Sisters of Charity to fulfill a special purpose.

By the end of March her daily entries became reduced to a

mere exclamation for the entire day: on one it is "Deo Gratias!" on another, "God!" and on the following day, "Amen." She records for each day her guiding principle, the patron she has taken, and the reading she is doing—all confined to the Bible and *The Imitation of Christ,* with the precise passages read set down, and the subject of her self-examination. It is all as cut and dried as a ship's log, and does, in fact, indicate the point of the ocean where she found herself in the journey on which she had embarked.

She concludes this time of retreat, and the diary itself by recording the resolutions she had made. These are so characteristic of her that they are worth reproducing:

"1. Never to let slip an opportunity of performing an act of charity.

"2. To keep a weather-eye open for all occasions that offer humiliations and make use of them.

"3. To be the servant of all.

"4. In time of desolation to keep strict watch over every movement of soul that purity of intention may be preserved and heightened.

"5. At recreation, to overcome my natural desire for quietness and give myself up completely to helping my sisters really recreate.

"6. Daily to say at least 100 Glorias and 100 Deo Gratias in honor of each of the three Divine Persons.

"7. Always to make the Sign of the Cross fervently.

"8. Never to be idle a moment."

The whole of her brief diary would be worth quoting, but for this there is not sufficient space. It will be enough if we observe that from the moment Teresa crosses the threshold of Nazareth she is a dedicated soul, and that she concludes this bit of writing with practical resolutions. Yet it does not quite come to an end with the eight resolutions that have been listed, but with a ninth, "Prepare to begin now for your retreat"—and the next retreat was a year ahead.

CHAPTER ELEVEN

The Private Vows

IT must be borne in mind that the Sisters of Charity of New Jersey until quite recently took only temporal vows, such as bound them for a year but were renewable annually if the individual Sisters and the council of the Motherhouse mutually agreed upon it. Nevertheless, in 1926, only nine months after she had received the habit, and when she still had more than a year of her novitiate ahead of her, Teresa took a series of private vows that were perpetually binding, and that under pain of mortal sin.

It should perhaps be explained that, while there is nothing to prevent anybody's making a private vow, these are not supposed to be made without the confessor's consent. This consent a confessor is ordinarily very reluctant to give, and when he does so, will allow a vow to be taken only for a short period. For while the Church holds that the making of a vow is good, it is better not to make a vow at all than to make one and then fail to keep it. Yet Teresa received permission from Father Benedict to make a whole series of vows—a most unusual procedure known at the time only to Teresa and to her spiritual director himself.

Teresa appears to have derived the idea of taking these vows from her reading of the life of Benigna Consolata, a young Italian Visitandine who had recently died.* Two pas-

*This book seems to be the one translated by the Visitation nun of Georgetown who wrote under the name of M. S. Pine. I knew her in the early thirties when she was a very old lady. She also wrote a life of Father Tabb and a volume or two of verse. Though this verse was rather wooden, she

sages should be specially noted: The Visitandine believed that Christ had appeared to her, "and urged her to do always what she believed to be most perfect in order to become more agreeable to Him." Though on page 33 there is no explicit mention of any vows, on page 135 we read that on June 30, 1916, in the presence of the bishop and the superior of her convent, she took a series of five vows. If one of these "vows" —that of the Sacrifice of her Life—was not strictly that in July, but merely an "offering," it was given the full force of a vow in the following September. It was after reading this book that Teresa wrote to Father Benedict: "I wonder if you would permit me to make those similar to hers which I have not yet taken: the vow to do all from a motive of pure love; the vow of perfect abandonment (that would be a good answer to the devil!); and the vow of humility (I've read the chapter on it in Marmion). I think I can truthfully say that I've been trying to practice all that these vows imply for many years, and I feel that God would thereby be more glorified." Though this letter, headed only "Monday," would seem to have been written in August, and we know that Teresa had taken the first of her vows in March, one more than suspects that the idea of taking any of her private vows was inspired by this book.

She began with what is called the vow of Greater Perfection, which is clearly indicated as an ideal (though not as a vow) in the first of the two passages quoted from the life of Sister Benigna Consolata. The term is a strange one, and few people have so much as heard of it. Grammatically one might object that, as perfection is an absolute, it does not admit of a comparative degree. It is rather like that "banner with the strange device"—a very strange device in view of its Latinity —which the young man in Longfellow's poem bore "through

---

inspired the devotion of Harriet Monroe, her pupil at the Georgetown Visitation Convent. The last time I saw Harriet was when I took her there about 1933 to see her old teacher.

snow and ice"—*Excelsior*. However we may let such things pass, there are some matters for which ordinary language seems to be not quite adequate. To make sure that Teresa understood what she proposed doing, Father Benedict made her read an explanation of "Greater Perfection" given by the Abbé Saudreau, the director of the Motherhouse of the Good Shepherd at Angers, in the second volume of *Degrees of the Spiritual Life*.

Two passages from this book—one on pages 165–166, and the other on page 168—now follow. The Abbé writes: "First to make it clear what this vow is. A vow that is vague and obscure in its manner of operation would assuredly result in difficulties and scruples, and would be most harmful to the soul. Every vow must bear upon deliberate acts. A vow to abstain from the faults of human frailty would be void, say the theologians, because it is impossible of performance. We may, however, make a vow not to commit some venial fault of deliberate purpose. This vow is valid and binds in conscience, because it is feasible. Acts of a semi-deliberate nature are therefore excluded from the vow of greater perfection. Acts the perfection of which remains doubtful are also excluded. . . . Finally we must add that this vow does not aim at absolute perfection or any act considered entirely on its own merits without any regard to circumstances, but at the most perfect relatively. In itself it is more perfect to fast than not to fast, but for the great majority of Christians frequent fasts would be an imperfection, because they would be rendering themselves less capable of performing the duties of their state, and also because it would constitute a culpable singularity. To bind oneself by vow to a greater perfection is, therefore, to vow that whenever there shall be time to reflect upon the relative advantages of two possible courses of action, we will always choose the one which, after a due consideration of circumstances, is obviously the more pleasing to God."

That is a moderate statement of the case, and is amplified

by the passage on page 168: "God will do the rest; His purifying action will continue to operate by means of ordeals
which the soul must accept in all submission and trust. At the
same time the Divine workings will never be discontinued,
in prayer and out of prayer, will not cease from purifying it
and sanctifying it yet further, always provided that it is careful not to impede the action of grace."

Father Benedict says that when Teresa first asked him for
permission to make this vow, he refused. When she raised the
question again, he gave her Saudreau to read; and when she
returned the book and he felt assured that she understood it
he told her she might make it for one week—at the end of
which she was to account to him of her experience. When she
said that she had undergone no disturbance of soul in keeping the vow, and that the only time she had hesitated was
when she had stopped to consider which was the most perfect
thing to do, he extended his permission for a month. While
he was hesitating to allow her to make the vow perpetual,
she told him one day, "From childhood I have always tried to
do the most perfect thing." On May 1st, accordingly, she was
permitted to give the vow perpetual force.

A third volume should be mentioned, that by the Jesuit
Peter Cotel entitled *A Catechism of the Vows for the Use of
Persons Consecrated to God in the Religious State*. The copy
before me belonged to her, and a series of resolutions has
been written in it, which I have been told was posted on the
bulletin board in the novitiate as a help to the novices. Apparently they were drawn from a biography of Father Wil-
liam Doyle, yet they are so much in Teresa's spirit that I
shall quote them here: they are headed "What must I do to
become a Saint?":

"1. Excite in yourself an ardent desire and *determination*
to become one, cost what it may.

"2. Beg and pray without ceasing for this grace and the desire of holiness.

"3. Take each occasion and duty as if it were the last and the only one of your life, and perform it with extraordinary fervour.

"4. Have a fixed duty for each moment and not depart from it; never waste a moment.

"5. The spirit of constant prayer.

"6. Relentless war against my will and inclination; *agere contra* at every moment to all things.

"7. The fearless practice of little mortifications."

Now we can come to some of the things said by Père Cotel, which may be offered without further comment, except that Teresa had evidently studied what he had to say, and may have been directed to do this when she was planning her series of vows. This is the little catena I offer: "Separate the obligations imposed by the vow from the practice of the *virtue* required"; "In order to be a vow [*sic*], we must have the intention of obliging ourselves under the pain of sin"; "Since it is an obligation voluntarily imposed on one's self, the vow obliges only so much as we wish to oblige ourselves"; "The spiritual power possesses, in regard to the vows, the same right that the civil power has with regard to contracts"; "The acts that can form the matter of a vow may be reduced to three classes: 1st, Acts already obligatory; 2nd, Acts which are only of counsel; 3rd, Acts indifferent in themselves. . . . Thus when one who has made a vow to observe the sixth commandment of God, resists the temptation to violate it, he adds to the merit of observing the precept the merit of the virtue of religion, and his act thus becomes better"; "Merit before God and men consist much less in making vows than in keeping them"; "The vow is therefore as the *means,* the virtue as the end."

At this point it would be as well to give a complete list of all the private vows taken by Teresa in 1926; it is truly astonishing. In some instances—those referring to such a matter as promptness or the performance of something already inculcated by the Rule—one would hardly suppose a vow was necessary. But as both Saudreau and Cotel say, even obligations that already rest upon us become all the more meritorious when enforced by a vow. Yet it is doubtful whether she was ever actuated by the idea of obtaining merit; rather it was her burning desire to give glory to God. Love forces some holy souls to do unusual things—things that are often more admirable than imitable.

1.	Of greater perfection (temporary)	March 20 or 14
	Of greater perfection (perpetual)	May 1
2.	Of chastity (absolute)	June 5
3.	Of obedience to Director	June 5
4.	Of poverty	July 9
5.	Of abandonment	August 18
6.	Of humility	August 18
7.	Of doing all through love	September 3
8.	Of sacrificing life	September 18
9.	Of simplicity	October 2
10.	Of meekness	October 2
11.	Of patience	October 2
12.	Of obedience to superiors	October 9
13.	Of obedience to neighbors in matters of indifference	October 9
14.	Of charity	October 9
15.	Of obedience to rule	October 16
16.	Of obedience to custom	October 16
17.	Of mortification	October 16
18.	Of obedience to Holy Ghost	October 23
19.	Of promptness	October 23
20.	Of heroic charity (temporary)	November 6
21.	Of servitude to Mary (temporary)	November 6
	Of servitude to Mary (perpetual)	November 19
	Of heroic charity (perpetual)	November 19
22.	Of silence, according to rule and custom	November 19*

*Teresa herself drew up this list, at Father Benedict's request.

From this list it is clear that the vows up to September 18th were more or less directly inspired by Benigna Consolata; after that date, while Teresa may still owe an indirect inspiration to the same source, she proceeds along her own path, often taking three or more vows on the same day, and hardly allowing a week to go by without binding herself with some new obligation. As not even her closest friends, inside the convent or out, knew what was happening, her conduct sometimes puzzled them. Thus Agatha Spinella, her closest friend in college, when on a visit to Teresa at St. Elizabeth's was waiting for Teresa in the corridor when she was passed without a word or so much as a sign of recognition until Teresa had rung the bell—her duty at the moment. Spin would have wondered less had she been aware of vows 16, 19, and 22. But of course when the duty had been performed, Teresa, on her return journey down the corridor, stopped and spoke to her old friend.

Father Benedict has left an account of this matter of the vows. He must have been aware that his part in what was done would have subjected him to considerable criticism, so had he been concerned with protecting himself it would have been easy to have kept silence and to have allowed everything to sink into oblivion after Teresa's death. But he felt, much to his credit, that he should tell the whole truth, for only this would reveal what kind of soul it was he had the privilege of directing. He showed reluctance to the taking of the first vow —that of greater perfection—but eventually permitted it. Similarly, he was reluctant to allow Teresa to take a vow of perpetual obedience to himself. He pointed out that he was old, that before long she would probably be sent to one of the other houses and that, even did she remain at St. Elizabeth's, his term of office as spiritual director would come to an end soon afterwards. He may have argued that should all this happen, the vow would be cancelled because it was impossible of being carried out. What he wrote about it was: "I permitted her to take the vow nevertheless, for I thought that Our Lord wanted it."

He had some reason for thinking so, as he had discovered that Our Lord, "for her humiliation . . . obliged her to submit to the confessor she happened to find in the novitiate, and her obedience was heroic, so heroic that she made a vow of perpetual obedience to him." He continues, though, "It was definitely stipulated that the vow should bind only in cases in which there was no conflict with the rule under which she was living." The second point he makes goes without saying, but concerning the first, Father Benedict means that Christ's command about an absolute obedience to her spiritual director was given about the time she received a divine intimation as to her special mission, for at that time, of course, she had never met Father Benedict and probably had not so much as heard his name. So it must be understood that all this was without any reference to personal devotion to him as a man or a priest, though such a devotion was developed in the course of their acquaintance.

As for Teresa's vow of poverty, Father Benedict, before allowing her to take it, made her read the tenth chapter of Abbot Marmion's *Christ, the Ideal of the Monk,* so that she should clearly know in what sense poverty was to be understood. This was necessary lest Teresa give too rigorous an interpretation to the matter. The Benedictines have a somewhat milder view than had, let us say, St. Francis of Assisi; yet both views are thoroughly in accordance with the mind of the Church.

For her vow of humility, Teresa was obliged to read Marmion's eleventh chapter. In it the abbot, though basing himself on the Benedictine Rule, does not follow exactly the classical exposition of the twelve degrees of the virtue found there, but regroups more compactly, just as St. Bernard (who also followed the Benedictine Rule) had another slightly different version of the matter. All this was done to safeguard

Teresa from binding herself too drastically, or from taking the vows according to a private standard which makes them very difficult to carry out, and so burden her soul with scruples. In other words, Father Benedict was careful to make sure that Teresa fully understood what she was undertaking.

The spiritual director records his conviction that Teresa had never in her whole life committed a single deliberate venial sin, and so adds, "In her case I judged that perpetual vows would be not only permissible but also pleasing to God." In a letter that Teresa wrote to him on July 26, 1926, shortly after she had taken the fourth vow of the long series, she says: "Father, I'm beginning to appreciate the fact that the devil hates me cordially, and do you know what I think is eating him especially? The vows. Particularly that they are perpetual. What wonderful mercy and favor God has shown me in letting me make them! And I have willed to renew them at every beat of my heart and at every breath I draw. Truly they impart a stability never known before." Father Benedict comments: "Before making them, she had experienced severe temptations, particularly against her vocation to religious life, which was not the case after she had made them. Once she had sealed her own fate by perpetual vows, the devil found it useless to tempt her much, and this is why she thought he showed such anger."

Though her spiritual director mentions as his motives only his belief that she might safely be allowed to make these vows and that they would be pleasing to God, he may well have had in mind also the thought that in this way she would secure the peace of heart that he knew had been often disturbed. He shared her conviction that she would not take the ordinary vows of the Sisters of Charity when the rest of the novices took theirs. As he interpreted this as meaning that she had had an intimation from heaven that she would die early, he wished to give her the joy of binding herself in this special way in the event that she would not be able to bind herself as would the others. Events justified his belief, though neither of them knew that on her deathbed he himself would receive the vows as taken by her community.

A final word about these private vows, as made in another statement by Father Benedict: "After making the perpetual vows of Poverty, Chastity and Obedience, she told me that Our Lord had expressed to her His great pleasure and had called her His spouse. She also refers to the indignation of the devil. . . . Before this he had tempted her to abandon the novitiate, picturing to her the bright future the world had in store for her. After making the three perpetual vows, it was no longer possible for him to tempt her in this way. . . . Burdened as she was with so many vows, all of which were perpetual, she experienced no disturbance of spirit. The perfect life, however, which she had vowed to live demanded constant watchfulness, and to this heavy cross she refers in one of her letters. She never once expressed a regret for having taken the vows. These were the cause of her joy."

Probably very few spiritual directors would have adopted Father Benedict's course of action, and it is made abundantly clear that he decided to follow it only after deep thought upon the situation and because of his observation as to the effect of the first vows he had permitted Teresa to make. As to these effects we not only have his testimony but may also be presumed that his knowledge of the case was even fuller than he allows to appear, for as to what was under the seal of the confessional Father Benedict of course had to preserve silence.

Chapter Twelve

Fledgling Instructress

Strictly speaking, Teresa was hardly a "fledgling" by now, for she had had two periods of teaching before entering the novitiate—one of a year and one of about a month. Each of them she had detested; and though she could be morally certain that, by becoming a Sister of Charity, she would eventually be called upon to teach in one of the schools of the community, she did not expect that she would be summoned to do so as soon as she was. But if any word had reached St. Elizabeth as to Teresa's lack of success at St. Aloysius Academy, this would have been discounted; dressed in a habit she would be able to exercise the discipline not possible before. There could be no question as to the scholastic qualifications of the star graduate of the class of 1923. As the academy at St. Elizabeth's found itself in need of teachers, three novices were assigned to this task—Sister Zita, her future biographer; Sister Canice, and Teresa herself.

Teaching was, to her, the severest of mortifications. She had thought of it with such horror that it was, at first, the greatest of deterrents to her joining the Sisters of Charity, apart from the attraction she felt for the life of contemplation. While she admired and respected the Sisters and had affection for the St. Elizabeth's where she had spent four happy years of college, she had always said, "Any place rather than that!" But, as we have seen, the matter had been taken out of her hands. On the natural plane her road to Carmel had been barred by a virtual refusal—that is, an acceptance conditional upon the improvement of her eyesight, and this she knew to be most unlikely; on the supernatural plane she had received what she looked upon as a divine command to enter at St. Elizabeth's, after which there was never a moment's hesitation.

Yet she may well have felt consternation that she was not given even so much as a couple of years' respite. At the same time, as she had made her choice with her eyes wide open, she found that her positive dislike for teaching made it penitential, and therefore a reason for becoming a teacher.

We know that she did not have to endure this for long, for death did not delay. God called her to submit her neck to the galling yoke for a time, but He did not intend that it should be for a greater period than would suffice for her further sanctification. She was called to a teaching order, not to teach in the ordinary sense, but to instil a new spirit into the community she joined, and also to show many other active orders—and many Christian souls in the world—that the doing of the world's work is not incompatible with the contemplative religious mode. While this cannot be said to have been an original discovery on Teresa's part—for it had been said over and over again by some of the most notable exponents of mysticism—a new exemplification was needed. This she saw from the outset was to be her distinctive mission.

Teresa's abhorrence of the classroom may seem very strange to the hundreds of thousands of people who like teaching. It is true that a good many people are not enamoured of this work but take it up only because of force of circumstances. To these, teaching is merely a job that has rather more security than most jobs, reasonable pay upon the whole, and brings long vacations that provide them with the leisure for doing other things that are more to their taste. Such people never become very good teachers, but at least they are usually adequate, and they are able to solace themselves with the reflection that almost any occupation has a certain amount of inescapable drudgery. Therefore they have no actual dislike of their lot in life; if they do, they can usually get out of it easily enough, as they are well educated and, as a rule, have some degree of talent.

Had Teresa lived, it is probable that sooner or later she would have been appointed a professor at St. Elizabeth's College, and that would have been a kinder fate. For one of her troubles was that she did not find it easy to gauge the minds of high-school students, and she habitually talked over their heads—"treating us all as though we were Ph.D.'s" was how one of them put it. We may be sure she would have done brilliantly in the graduate studies that would have been necessary to prepare her for a college position, and in such a position, when dealing with more or less mature minds— more or less!—she might have done well. Assuredly she would have done much better than she was able to do when trying to handle gawky adolescents.

This teaching of hers was, at any rate during the first year of the novitiate, at variance with Canon Law. A novitiate is supposed to be devoted wholly to spiritual training, a contemplative training for the active work ahead. Strictly enforced, the rule permits no regular courses of secular study, let alone the instruction of others. But among the Sisters of Charity of New Jersey Canon Law was not observed in all its details at that time. There was no such thing as a canonical year of novitiate for those who were asked to teach, and the second year of novitiate was commonly spent on one of the many missions of the community. Teresa's teaching was therefore not at all anomalous.

To ensure respect for the novices who taught in the academy, they were obliged to wear, instead of the novices' habit, that of the professed Sisters. The novices had a rather heavier veil, a slightly different headdress, and wore no rosary at the waist but kept a smaller one in the pocket. Teresa was given an old large rosary which had belonged to one of the deceased Sisters. Only during vacations did these three novice teachers put on the novice cap again.

Teresa took her meals with the students in the main building, presiding at one of the tables, and she slept in the students' dormitory. It seemed to be the custom to have the youngest religious sleep in one of the alcoves at the end of the dormitory. Thus Teresa kept in close contact with the girls. By them she was liked very much, though some considered her a little queer, if only because of her flickering eyes and her high voice, described to me by person after person who knew her, as "squeaky." And it is to be feared that even her most endearing quality, her kindness, was taken advantage of by the lazy, mischievous, and ill-disposed. But if she was somewhat lacking as a disciplinarian, it should be remembered that there are teachers who are disciplinarians and nothing else. They may be feared but do not impart much knowledge, as Teresa could do.

That she spent most of her time with the academy students does not mean that she was never in Nazareth, the novitiate. She went there to attend the half-hour's instruction that the Rule prescribes be given daily, as well as other required spiritual exercises. She would have much preferred it could she have been at Nazareth all the time. In fact, after being given the habit, she had been assigned to help in the normal school conducted in the novitiate, until some change of plan, or unexpected need, brought about the decision that she should be sent instead to Xavier Hall to conduct classes in English, history, and Religion.

By some of the novices she was criticised on the ground that she did none of the housework that the others performed, and which she would gladly have done had she not been otherwise employed. And later, when, as we shall see, she was given some work to do—nobody had any idea what it was—it was interpreted by some as an artful device on her part for getting out of the usual novitiate chores. But those who considered her as unfairly privileged did not realize that these so-called privileges were to her a torment.

As formerly at St. Aloysius Academy in Jersey City, so now at St. Elizabeth's—though now to a lesser degree, for the habit itself imposed some respect—there were those who behaved pretty much as they liked because they had discovered Teresa's constitutional inability to be severe. The fact that she was inclined to talk above the heads of some of these adolescents was supposed to absolve the rest from paying attention. It did not help matters that the English classroom of the academy, which was on the third floor, gave a good view of the tennis courts, the athletic field, and the miniature golf course. Moreover, in the spring and fall the gymnasium classes disported themselves on the green, or a soft-ball baseball game was played there. While making some pretence to listen to their teacher (not a very great pretence, as they knew she was nearsighted), many of the girls were peeping out of the windows. All this need not be exaggerated, but anybody who has ever taught knows what a temptation this sort of thing can be when spring stirs the young blood.

We are told also—and here I cannot help believing that there must be much exaggeration—that Teresa spent a good deal of her time with her back turned to the class and writing on the blackboard. My surmise is that when this happened it was because Teresa hoped that what was written down had more chance of being learned than what was merely spoken. This circumstance, however, has given circulation to the story that she sometimes taught while in an ecstasy and that she turned her back on the class so that this would pass unnoticed. This seems to be supported by a note, dated March 6, 1926, made by Father Benedict. "For many weeks it was a continuation of raptures, ecstasies and visions during prayer and out of it, even while teaching in the class-room." What seems to have gone unnoticed is that he added that these were "unattended by sensible devotion" and that "her chief mystical phenomena were of the intellectual kind."

We have to add to this what was reported by Sister Gertrude, who was the community supervisor when Teresa taught at St. Aloysius Academy, and as such had the duty to visit the classes. Sister Zita assures me that Sister Gertrude had told her that she now and then sensed that Teresa was in a kind of ecstasy. But that she habitually taught with her back to her class is simply not to be believed; at any rate I cannot believe anything of the sort. Sister Zita, who it must be remembered was teaching with her at St. Elizabeth's, says that if Teresa turned her back to the class it was to write something on the blackboard and that she is sure that Teresa did not keep her back to the class long. Of course no teacher can afford to do so. Just what little girls can concoct in the way of deviltry I do not know, but little boys are very likely to throw a spitball or a piece of chalk, and then be found sitting with a face of angelic innocence when the teacher swings round with an indignation which is to their inexpressible pleasure.

What Father Benedict said about this has been quoted. This is what Teresa said in a letter to him: "It happened occasionally that even while teaching I am conscious of the operations of the soul in the superior part, while the inferior was actively employed." But does this mean ecstasy? It does not seem to me that the words need be forced to bear such a meaning but that they merely convey—though this was sufficiently wonderful—that she was conscious of her union with God even while conducting her classes. The fancies and surmises of other people need not be accepted.

Teresa's lack of success as a teacher is not to be attributed to this reason but to the simple fact that she never mastered the knack of teaching. Yet she was called upon to teach—as we shall soon see—in a much more striking way. Her true vocation was to give her fellow novices, most of whom were destined for the classroom, something vastly more important than they would extract from their courses in pedagogy. That was why God had called her to a teaching order.

As to Teresa's own teaching in the academy, we have a statement by herself. "I seem to like those best in the class who ask the most questions, even those who are pert. Then I become so enthusiastic that my voice rises and I speak louder. I like the fighting type now. When I was a pupil myself, however, I was not like that. I seldom spoke unless called upon." One wonders, though, whether there were not occasions when the students did not deliberately lure her into a discussion, as they had discovered that this would get her excited and that then her voice would become shrill. That they considered amusing. Besides, a discussion—especially if it could be adroitly carried far afield—would give the class a respite from the work in hand. But while a skilled teacher is able to detect that object, he also knows that discussions, even when quite unconnected with the subject being studied, may be of greater intellectual value than a close keeping to the textbook.

Some of the stories that have been remembered about Teresa show that she had an appreciation of the juvenile sense of humour and that she utilized this to effect. Thus, when she told her lazy little girls that Bassanio pressed Antonio's suit, they thought it exquisitely funny. So also when one day she wrote on the blackboard the sentence, "A five-dollar bill blew around the corner," and asked how they would punctuate it. Of course no punctuation was possible except what Teresa supplied when the whole class gave up—"I would make a dash after it." She was less fortunate when her students were studying Hawthorne's short story "The Great Stone Face," and she asked one of them, "Do you not think a brook majestic?" When most of them were of the opinion that it was not, Teresa asked, "But is it not when you think of its Creator?" The fallacy should have been (and probably was) obvious. A mountain is lower in the order of creation—because it is inanimate—than an oyster, but it is vastly more majestic because it reminds us more than such a thing as an oyster can do of the glory of God. Still, I suppose the comment was useful as provoking thought.

Moreover, she was versatile, and had almost everything of the good teacher about her except the ability to get the range of the minds of the children before her and the art of keeping them under control. In the college yearbook at the time of her graduation—a compilation in which all the graduates were described in a single word besides the usual fulsome paragraph which makes each of them out to be a saint or a genius (or both)—the word considered most fitting for Teresa was "versatile." She deprecated this and said to a friend, "People seem to think I can do anything." In the same way she now deprecated attribution to her of a wide range of information, saying, "I've always been given much more credit for knowledge than I really deserve." Yet as such things go —both among students and teachers—Teresa did know a good deal, though hers was not so much a richly stored mind as one that was exceptionally quick and acute.

Then there was her kindness. It would not be quite accurate to say that she was *too* kind, for that can never be true; but the form of her kindness led her to be imposed upon. Firm though she was with herself, she was not firm enough with other people, and firmness is often an essential part of kindness. To Father Benedict she wrote, "I have suffered and still would suffer untold tortures myself rather than hurt another, no matter whom, even by a pin prick, even unconsciously." Quite so, but this meant that she had to suffer tortures at the hands of those whom she was teaching; it would have been better for them had she been prepared to administer, metaphorically speaking, the lash now and then. Outside the classroom, however, her solicitude was noticed and appreciated, touching even those who had been most troublesome, and sometimes winning them over. For instance, if she thought that one of her charges, over whose dormitory she presided, needed it, she would give the child one of her blankets or her own pillow.

Though she cannot be called a success as a teacher, neither must she be set down as a failure. She found some admirers, or some who expressed their admiration years later. One of these said of her, "She really taught, and not from a book." The accounts she sometimes gave the girls of the Eastern Rite in which she had been brought up (and to which she still canonically belonged) they found extremely interesting, though one suspects that the very fact that her youth had been passed in the care of a succession of married priests confirmed her pupils in the idea that she was in some way "odd." But as to her personal religious fervour none of them doubted. And one of her third-year students wrote after her death a poem in which Teresa was compared to

> A perfect Ostensorium
> A monstrance for her mighty King.

Another declared, "She was the nearest to perfection that we have ever seen. She was the ideal woman, a model for this generation and for future generations to come. She was a light from the Great Light to guide us poor mortals nearer to Him." Still another, whom she had taught as Peggy Burke, writing as Mrs. Angevine and the mother of three children in the *Sister Miriam Teresa Bulletin,* says in retrospect: "When I was a sophomore at the Academy of St. Elizabeth at Convent, I had a desperate 'crush' on a young novice who was teaching our English class. To me, she was ideal. As far as I was concerned, she walked in a splendor of light that was truly celestial. . . . I haunted her, and waylaid her, and tried to ply her with gifts, as all other girls were doing to their respective heroines. . . . After 'lights out' Sister used to walk down a long, long corridor from some mysterious region where she had gone to prepare for bed, to her curtained alcove, where she slept with her charges. A single gas light burned in the hall. I shall always see her walking in the light. She never failed to be sweet and kind to me who often lay awake to be able to whisper the last 'Good-night, Sister' as she passed close to my bed on the way to hers."*

Teresa tried to teach Peggy Burke to write poetry, but with what success does not appear. And she did her best to arouse an interest in poetry among her students by reading it to them, once or twice bits of her own. But from what one hears of her high and "thin" voice, she could not have been a very good reader. In any event a girlish "crush" and some admirers were not quite enough to make her a satisfactory teacher, though there is no need to make her out as incompetent.

The main point to seize is that though she certainly did better at St. Elizabeth's than she had at St. Aloysius, she still disliked teaching and looked upon it as a much greater mortification than the hair shirt she had once worn. As such it served the purpose of developing her holiness, and as such she welcomed it. Yet it was not without profit to some of her students; and the profit of others, especially their spiritual profit, was now her main concern, or second only to (if separable from) her personal spiritual life. Even on the merely academic plane she did much for those girls who had intellectual gifts and who were willing to learn. But she always knew that her real mission lay in another kind of teaching— about which we shall soon hear.

*Vol. III, No. 4, p. 4.

Chapter Thirteen

≈

Influence—Conscious and Unconscious

JUST as during Teresa's first years at college the girls were not attracted by her, so some of the sixty or so novices at Nazareth were not naturally drawn to her. Indeed, in many ways things were now worse than they ever had been, for whereas Teresa had suffered no active dislike at college, now she did. The trouble seems to have been that at college, while there were some who set her down as an oddity, if only because her seriousness and studiousness prevented her from taking part in some of the things in which the others were interested, in the novitiate her zeal was a standing rebuke to those inclined to be slack. Many, perhaps the majority, accepted this rebuke and were inspired by her example to seek a higher degree of perfection; but a few definitely resented it.

Women are upon the whole more conscientious than men, and they can be, in extreme cases, rather painfully so. Moreover, young women who enter convents are likely to be among the most conscientious of their sex. Because of this they were often willing to accept Teresa's careful exactness as a standard for themselves and would consult her upon small points concerning which the Rule was silent. It was to that extent college all over again, where in doubt or difficulty so many said, "Let us ask Treat."

One point, however, must be made clear: Teresa was not scrupulous in the sense in which this is understood by those who have the direction of souls; about that Father Benedict was very explicit. Scrupulosity is a kind of spiritual neurasthenia that is constantly imagining the commission of faults, or even sins, where none exist. As such it can be a disease that hinders spiritual progress simply because it is the counterfeit of true spirituality.

Punctilious she was; that cannot be denied. We may see this in the illumination she was making for a "spiritual bouquet" to be presented to Mother Alexandrine, but left unfinished because she was overtaken by illness. In it she stopped while making an "O," for the community bell rang at that moment. Here she was like the Little Flower, who often stopped short in her letters at such times, even in the middle of a word; but Teresa did not know this and so was not imitating her, because at that time St. Thérèse's letters had not been published. That much nobody minded, even if they did think she overdid things, but naturally enough it was held against her that she corrected others. A novice from Central America, Sister Rose Anita, records: "I once heard two remarks by schoolmates of Sister's. One said that Teresa was so exact that she could not help loving her; the other said that Teresa was so exact that one could not help hating her. These remarks put the situation regarding her companions in a nutshell. While they could not deny Teresa's goodness, some said that they disliked 'her type of holiness.' Other criticisms were heard occasionally, such as: 'She gets on my nerves'; 'She would be better off if she did more work'; 'She spends too much time in the confessional'; 'She walks as if she were a queen'; 'Her so-called sanctity is too obvious'; 'I cannot stand her' etc. But in spite of all this, the same people who passed such remarks would acknowledge on other occasions that she was a model religious."

Other comments are in some notes made by Sister Zita,

which to some extent she drew upon when writing her book, but from which I now quote directly: "A group of novices seemed to be enjoying a story told by one of their friends. It ran something like this: 'You should have seen her come out in the park. (I think it was the day Sister received the habit.) I had to paint one of the statues. She was all dressed up with her new clothes, but do you think she would help me to paint? She sat on a nearby bench and read a book!' " If so, she might be pardoned by not wanting to get any paint on her new habit.

Sister Zita continues: "Sister Miriam Teresa brought a good deal of censure upon herself because she corrected others. Often she would go to the reader after meals and tell her of mispronounced words. This seemed to annoy many novices. On one particular occasion a Sister was reading for the first time. She made several mistakes. Sister Miriam Teresa went to her after the meal and told her of the errors. Some of the novices, seeing Sister do that said, 'Wouldn't you think she'd give her a chance in the beginning anyway?' One novice suggested that perhaps Sister had been given that charge because of her superior knowledge. At this there was a general outburst of amusement." Yet she did have this superior knowledge, and later it was learned that she had been asked for such corrections by the reader herself.

She corrected her companions in other ways: to one—Sister Carrice—she said that she had too many friends, meaning to convey that in a novitiate special friendships are not encouraged on the ground that it is better to have everybody on a general friendly level than for couples to go off habitually by themselves. On that occasion the admonition was taken in good part. And one of the other novices has told me that she is sure that Teresa's corrections were offered, not in a censorious spirit, but to share what she had. Even so, there was probably a failure of tact now and then. Nobody particularly likes being corrected, and least of all by one who has no authority over them. That Teresa did this gently and with a smile did not help matters a great deal. It is not hard to imagine how even the smile could have been misinterpreted. Some, even while they had to admit that Teresa was justified, could not but mutter to their friends, "But what *right* has she got?" It is usually best to allow minor errors to pass unnoticed and to be content with the force of example. The "superior" person is disliked; there are times when it is advisable to hide one's light under a bushel. It was acknowledged that Teresa always practiced what she preached, that she was in fact perfect, but it is understandable that her perfection was an offence. As Disraeli said of Gladstone, "He does not have a single redeeming vice." And as Lord Byron said of his estranged wife, "She has no fault—the greatest fault of all." It was not, of course, as bad as all that in Teresa's case, but this gives the general idea.

As novitiate librarian Teresa was asked by Father Benedict to report to him about the novices' reading. This is what she wrote to him: "I have tried to get permission to allow them to keep a book out as long as they wish but have failed repeatedly. The opposing argument is this: They have the New Testament, the Following [the *Imitation*] and How to Walk Before God, and that's enough. Let them read what they are told to. Now, my argument is this: The Following is read at table every day at dinner, besides the life of a saint; unless a Sister is specially fond of the Imitation from long usage, she's not going to pick it up when she hears it read day after day and listens because she has to. As to the New Testament, I doubt if five of them ever handle it, and it's a pity. I intend to plan a course of class study of the Life of Our Lord using the New Testament as a textbook. It's one of the ways, I think, by which they will be made to realize the reality and humaneness [*sic*] of Our Lord. As regards Vaubert they should be made to read it every day, I agree. But the simple fact that it's a duty, and that it requires concentration and study, in itself predisposes them to attack it with the same spirit (the devil does his part)—well, it has to be read, so I'll get over it as quickly as possible. Now, they have not yet reached that degree of spirituality when they can pick up any book, simple, compound, or complex, and derive spiritual benefit therefrom. And I feel that if they are permitted to keep in their possession the book towards which the Holy Ghost attracts them, they will have an incentive to get as much as possible out of what they read and apply it. And this spirit is I think in them now to a good extent. Besides, having at least a little sense of freedom in this matter will incline them to enter on the required reading with a different attitude, and anxious to imitate what they see. They will be drawn to study the method of the interior life in Vaubert . . . Of course you have to find some method of introducing the subject."

In this passage it was not so much the novices themselves who were being criticized as Sister Mary Ellen the novice-mistress. She was, as Father Benedict knew, opposed to her charges reading any books that might give their minds a contemplative bent, for which she did not consider them suited. Accordingly they took their cue from her and tended to confine themselves to the required manuals. On Sunday afternoons, however, the novices who did not have company were allowed the privilege of reading, for about an hour, any book in the library. If it should appear that Teresa was being rather officious in this report, it must be remembered that she had made a vow of obedience to Father Benedict under pain of mortal sin; therefore she was obliged to follow his instructions.

One of the fullest statements comes from Sister Rose Anita, and is painful, if not even startling. She writes: "Of course I think it impossible to have 'enemies' in the convent. [But] there are always some persons whose tastes and inclinations differ so much from our own that from this difference can easily grow even among religious feelings of aversion if not carefully checked, [and this] makes of those who experience it what one would call 'enemies.' Keeping in mind this meaning of the word 'enemies' I think our Sister had at least a few of them. . . . It seemed to me that the dislike felt by many Sisters for Sister Miriam Teresa was only a repetition of the story of 'The Fox and the Grapes'; because they were fully aware of their not being as good as Sister, they contented themselves with thinking (and very often saying) that she was not the 'right type of saint.' But in my opinion (perhaps I am altogether wrong) the ones to blame for the remarks passed against our Sister were about six novices who disliked Sister so intensely that they did not lose any opportunity of showing it by cutting remarks and by ridiculing her as much as possible. The leader of this group, in her efforts to be 'funny,' often made Sister Miriam Teresa a source of ridicule. Sister Miriam Teresa must have known all this, because sometimes the novices saw her hands tremble or tears fall silently from her eyes, after they themselves had overheard one of those remarks. I have had the opportunity of talking recently to one of the novices (who was a member of this group) and she told me that although Sister Miriam Teresa was very holy, she 'hated her even at college.' She also expressed her disgust because one of the Sisters (a college teacher) was making a novena at Sister Miriam Teresa's grave. 'I gave her credit for more intelligence' was her comment."

One wonders that such treatment (even if meted out only by a small group) did not drive Teresa out of the novitiate. That she accepted it without complaint, and with nothing even faintly approaching a quarrel, is proof of her strength of character, if not of her sanctity. She knew that she was where God wanted her to be; she felt that she had a special mission (about which none of the novices had the slightest inkling), so she endured the spite shown her by some of the novices and misunderstandings on the part of the novice-mistress.

A temperamental, perhaps racial, factor also entered in; Teresa was very intense and, in the opinion of some, too careful about trifles. For example, she used to pick up any pin she found lying around, or any bit of silver paper, as this last was of some slight use in the support of the missions. One of the novices sarcastically asked her when she expected to be sent to China, and got the answer, "When I'm sent." Others noted Teresa's zeal in the very tone of her voice, so that a postulant (later Sister Electa) on the first morning she was at meditation heard the preparatory prayer read in such a way that it made her feel that whoever was reading it "was talking directly to Our Lord." Nobody could possibly regard Teresa as one of those innocuous and ineffectual people who glide through life, more or less liked by everybody but leaving no impression. Even those who said they "hated" her (of course using a feminine exaggeration) could not withhold a reluctant admiration. Teresa put a mark upon all those with whom she came into contact. Whether or not she was a saint, she was a remarkable personality.

Ordinary ridicule, even cruel ridicule, Teresa bore patiently, and though she was often hurt by it she made no rejoinder. What she could not bear was to be praised for her goodness. Mild though she was, her weak eyes could flash, as when one day a novice on the stairs behind her called up, "Hurry up, St. Teresa!" The remark was probably a harmless jest in intention, but at once Teresa swung round, saying, "*Never* say that again!"

Father Benedict must have caught some wind of the criticism that his protégée was receiving (though never, so far as there is any record, from her), because once or twice he went out of his way to suggest that some of the novices would not have liked the Little Flower had they lived with her. It probably is true that a real saint may sometimes be a disconcerting person to live with. It is easier to read about some of them than it would have been to be in close contact with them. So also sometimes with characters in books: Juliet's nurse, known in the flesh, would have seemed a great bore, and Mr. Micawber an ineffectual fool.

Apparently nobody caught the point of Father Benedict's remarks about the Little Flower. Certainly Sister Zita did not realise that he was obliquely referring to the "saint" they had among them. For one day when she and Teresa were walking back from the "Old Villa," where exposition of the Blessed Sacrament was being held, Sister Zita remarked, "I was thinking about what Father Benedict said in his last conference that probably we would not like the Little Flower if we had her in the novitiate because her exactness in keeping the rule would seem a silent reproach." To this Teresa smiled and said, "Don't you agree with Father?" Sister Zita returned, "No; I'm sure that if the Little Flower lived with us I would love her." This brought out Teresa's hearty laugh, and the characteristic bending of her body halfway down to the ground. She said: "Yes, you're right; I think I'd love her too. Father Benedict should not say such things." As she knew what he had been getting at, she begged him not to make that kind of remark again, for if he did it often enough, even the stupidest among the novices would become aware of what he meant. She wanted to be a saint; she did not wish to be thought a saint.

One of the Popes (I believe it was Clement VIII) once said, "Show me a religious who keeps his rule perfectly and I will canonize him." Well, Teresa kept her rule with as great perfection as seems possible. To many, indeed, it seemed an impossible perfection, and I must confess that the perfection was sometimes, in my opinion, unnecessary. One day when the group was assembled a few minutes before eight for communal spiritual reading, the senior among them remarked, "Sister Miriam Teresa said that we should not start before eight." (Teresa was evidently not present for some reason.) To which a novice retorted, "We're supposed to use our common sense and not wait for the clock to strike when there is so much to do." I cannot help sympathising with the novice—nevertheless, they sat sewing in silence until the clock struck eight.

Teresa herself, let us hope, would have agreed with the practical little novice, had she been there. In one of her conferences she referred to those Jews of Our Lord's time "who conformed to the *letter* of these individual laws, even to the last comma. That was their religion. For the spirit of the law they had no regard." And she went on to make the application: "Certain religious may choose for themselves certain points of rule to which they adhere because they feel so disposed; for example, the prayers of rule, or the appointed times before the tabernacle; and ignore other points, as silence or community recreation, because these do not coincide with their natural inclinations. What are they really doing? Like the Pharisees, they are setting up for themselves a code different from the prescribed law." However, earlier in the same conference she had written: "Keep the rule perfectly and that is all you need to do. This applies to every detail of the rule, not only such as appeal naturally."

It was much the same thing that St. Thérèse of Lisieux set herself to carry out, and unlike her as our Teresa was in many ways, she was like her in this: she was not merely a pedant but one who sought the inner spirit of the religious life. The Little Flower did more than the letter of the law demanded—avoiding even any special association with her blood sisters in the same convent, taking with a smile the splashing she received at the washtub, enduring the rattling of beads that one of the nuns inflicted on the others (and a trifle like this can drive one nearly crazy), and making a heroic effort to make friends with a crabbed and crusty old Sister, out of whose way everybody else kept when they could.

None of the details of the rule, taken singly, may be particularly hard, yet in accumulation they may be a heavy burden. Here we know that our Teresa had bound herself by a private vow, under such stringent terms as to make infractions—such as might have passed with us—a mortal sin in her case. It really was a well-nigh impossible perfection that she aimed at.

The complaint that we know to have been made about her dodging her share of the novitiate chores was most unjust. She helped whenever she could, doing things that she was not called upon to do. Thus during the retreat of 1926, when the novices on their way to the dormitory for the prescribed afternoon rest passed Sister Zita, who was on her knees scrubbing the tile floor outside the novitiate (for the following day was that on which the vows were to be taken, so everything had to be immaculate), Teresa alone on that hot day came up from the basement with a pail of water and scrubbing brush to help her.

We hear too of an occasion when the water in the dishpan was so hot that the dishes had to be fished out with a fork. Teresa put her hands into the scalding water and did the work with a smile. Here was a little mortification she would not miss. If it be wonderingly asked why on earth did it never occur to anybody to add a little cold water to the pan, the answer is that the dishes were washed at the tables at which the novices had been sitting, and the scullery was some distance away. Similarly she regularly carried out the garbage to the big can where it was deposited, so that a professed Sister who noticed this supposed that Teresa had been assigned to the unpleasant duty.

To those who were lonely or disconsolate she brought encouragement. In spite of the handful of novices who were, if not her enemies, at least rather antagonistic, she came to be revered by nearly everybody in the novitiate. One had to get to know Teresa well to appreciate her. If she had a fault—

and I think she did—it was the merely temperamental fault of her rigidity. It is a great pity that she did not live long enough to have some of her rough edges rubbed off, for many thought her censorious when she had a heart full of love. She came to be looked upon with awe, as a soul apart; but those who venerated her also loved her.

Among the reports left about her after her death by her fellow novices, one has to swing back and forth between extremes. A false impression could be conveyed by stressing too much the malice (for it was that) shown her by a few; on the other hand, an equally false impression would be given by discreetly omitting such unpleasant matters. So let us put black and white side by side. One of the novices recorded that "there was always a kind of universal respect for her. Upon her entering the room, the Sisters who were her contemporaries, or younger in religion, felt an impulse to stand up, and if they did so, as in fact oftentimes happened, she would laugh lightly or smile, and with a wave of the hand bid them be seated." Against this Sister Dolorine has written: "There was positive rudeness. Those who held contempt for Sister displayed it whenever possible although I know that in spite of their attitude they feared her. And thanks be to God, those *few* who *loved* her were never, on any occasion, ashamed of that fact, or of her." Sister Dolorine explains: "Some say there were two parties in the novitiate while Sister was there. I think there were three, not two. First, the majority against her; second, the few for her; and third, the more than few who did not know which party to join." If this differs from other accounts which say that Teresa's enemies were few— only a half-dozen out of sixty—the discrepancy may be resolved that the third party of the "neutrals" could be swayed against her, without too much trouble, when it was a matter of playing an unkind joke.

A favourite joke in the novitiate (as formerly in college) was to ask Teresa to sing at recreation, and then snicker. The song usually chosen for her at college was "Kiss Me Again," because of its high notes; but since that would have been inappropriate in the novitiate, "The Lost Chord" was now substituted, which was even better, for it began low down in the scale and rose to a delicious screech. Teresa knew she was being made fun of, but she never failed to oblige when asked to do something.

Apart from these malicious requests, many of the performances at recreation must have been rather foolish. Teresa recited poetry, occasionally her own, but others were simply ordered by Sister Mary Ellen to prepare something for the next day. Thus Sister Josepha, so she tells me, when given such an assignment, did her dusting with one hand while she held in the other a book from which she was learning a poem. Apparently Sister Mary Ellen looked upon this as an exercise in obedience rather than in art, for after Sister Josepha had recited a stanza or two, the novice-mistress said, "That'll do, Babe." "Babe" seems to have been the generic name for all her charges, and it certainly did not have the connotation that teen-agers would give it today.

Of Teresa, Sister Rose Anita writes, "As she was generally disliked, her performance met with little approval, and often her friends themselves (though perhaps they, too, preferred to recreate otherwise than listening to songs and poems) sympathised and were sorry for her because they well knew that while she recited or sang she was being made the object of ridicule. Personally, I liked to hear her recite (often her own poems) because of the life and feeling she gave each word. One could say after observing her closely that during recreation she practiced (at least) the virtues of charity, mortification, humility and obedience. But as I have just said, to notice this, one would have to observe her closely, because she was in no way singular and during recreation, at least, she was 'seemingly' like everybody else."

This Sister did not know of course that Teresa had made a

resolution "at recreation to overcome my natural desire for quietness and give myself up completely to helping my sisters recreate," or that this resolution was later enforced by some of her private vows. Even so, Sister Rose Anita sets down her personal opinion that Teresa was "a *perfect novice* (no one ever saw her breaking the rule), an extremely talented person (although most unconscious of it), a sympathetic and loving friend, and most forgiving to those who had in any way offended her." Yet she confesses that she thought her better qualified for a contemplative order. As for their personal relations, she says that Teresa was "too distant, too silent, and too unapproachable for my personal liking, and yet I longed to be her friend because I knew that her friendship was something to be treasured, and also because I knew she suffered much."

The pathetic thing is that Teresa was really trying to please everybody—even by her singing. Yet rarely, except when she played baseball in the novitiate park, did she escape being derided by some of her companions. At this game she was too good not to be admired. Probably even her playing of the piano would have been slighted, for no doubt there were some among the novices who were more accomplished. But as she had never played while at college, nobody knew that she could play at all; so she was never asked to perform. As Sister Zita says, while in the novitiate the only time she ever touched a piano was to dust it. We may feel glad that she was able to avoid exposing herself to possible ridicule on this account.

Her abstraction was so great that one of the novices records that in one of her classes at the academy she was asked to explain the stained-glass window over the high altar that represents the Blessed Trinity and the Holy Family. Teresa had to admit that she had never looked at the pictures in the glass but promised to do so the next time she went to chapel. This reminds us of St. Bernard who was obliged to say that he had never noticed whether the roof of his novitiate was flat or rounded. Teresa's eyesight was poor, but that was not the reason why she could not answer the question. The fact is that she habitually mortified her eyes, usually walking with them cast down, so that nothing should disturb the gaze she kept upon divine things.

There were other mortifications she practiced. For instance, she slept with one foot over the other, the position of Christ's feet on the cross; and she would have lain cruciform had not the narrow width of her bed made this impossible. In chapel she used to kneel erect, not so much as touching the pew in front, until Sister Mary Ellen, noticing it, gave precise instructions as to how the novices were to kneel, whereupon of course Teresa instantly obeyed. What went unobserved by the novice-mistress was that Teresa substituted for this a posture that kept her feet off the floor, something hard to maintain, and never without considerable physical discomfort. She had made a resolution "not to give in to fatigue and indulge in an easy posture during prayer," though St. Teresa of Ávila was of a different opinion, thinking that one could pray better when comfortable.

For further mortification she would never so much as wave away a mosquito when one alighted on her nose. Sister Zita (who is herself "the friend of novitiate days" she alludes to in her book) says that she used to do this for her lest her health be affected. About this Sister Zita was probably unnecessarily alarmed; but though mosquito stings are not particularly dangerous, they are annoying, and to endure them as Teresa did showed an iron self-control. About this she wrote to Father Benedict: "Sometimes in bed I have remarked that the members of my body occasionally jump around without my wishing to do so, especially when mosquitoes make their approach. Father, I'm an awful coward when it comes to mosquitoes. They're the very worst things I've ever had to endure. It's surprising how long they will hang on to you when

you let them. The ones this year are epicures, in my case anyway. Do you know what? They haven't missed a vein once in
their attacks. Maybe that's why every nerve in me responds.
And the park is thick with them, and we have our recreation
out there."

Sister Dolorine tells us that at table Teresa took whatever
was set before her, never indicating by word or sign whether
she liked or disliked it. About this we have a more extended
statement made by Teresa herself to Father Benedict: "With
regard to what you said concerning sweets, I have always
tried to act like others—and in fact, in all things possible. I
have been forbidden to mortify myself in the quantity of
food, so you need not have any apprehensions on that score.
And Father, I have always thought since that occurrence when
I was unable to eat (two spoonfuls of soup made me feel
stuffed) that Our Lord arranged matters thus in order that
my eating might be done through obedience." As Sister Mary
Ellen had ordered her to drink milk, thinking that she looked
a bit thin, Teresa did as she was instructed, telling Father
Benedict: "For ten consecutive months I drank milk at every
meal, and whenever I was told, but you'd never know it. And
I did it knowing that when I was at home milk and I did not
agree very well. But it not only had no ill effects, and the
same is true with regard to other foods that used to cause
trouble, but actually my digestive system has been in perfect
working order."

This has to be added: though Father Benedict approved
of Sister Mary Ellen's orders that Teresa was to eat well, he
raised no objection when she let him know that she was in
the habit of "eating dirt," that is, shaking a little sand over
her plate on the quiet. His only comment was that some of
the saints had done the same. Perhaps it was because of this
that Teresa lost all sense of taste until, shortly before her
death, it returned—no doubt because she could not give her
food in the hospital this "condiment."

Sister Dolorine records that Teresa "seemed to have absolutely no will whatever. If, at recreation, our Mistress asked, 'How many would like to go to bed early tonight?' some hands would be raised, some would not. Sister would laugh with us, await the outcome, and abide by it. It was the same always. If there was a lecture or musical recital in the auditorium and we had our choice whether to go or not (of course the majority rules) Sister would always wait, and then did what the rest did. If, however, opinions were asked, she would give it, simply and instantly."

Sister Mary Ellen was inclined to be unduly severe with Teresa, and one fears that this was because she remained fixed in her opinion that Teresa's place was with the Carmelites and not the Sisters of Charity. Yet nobody less needed correction than Teresa, except perhaps for her early posture when kneeling in chapel, which may have merited some reproof because of its singularity. Often and often Teresa left her interviews with the novice-mistress in tears. These interviews used to take place in an alcove off the community room at Nazareth, where nobody could be seen by the others, though the sound of their voices could be heard. Once, when Teresa came out crying, to kneel at the foot of the crucifix, little Sister Josepha made her way in to ask, "Why did you make Sister Miriam Teresa cry?" She could do this because she was one of the novice-mistress' favourites, and she was that probably in part because she showed no fear of Sister Mary Ellen, for she was one of the very few there who, never having been brought up by Sisters, stood in no awe of them. Nobody else in the novitiate would have ventured to use Sister Josepha's frankness and freedom with the redoubtable old lady. But these protests did little if any good; Sister Mary Ellen remained set in her opinion.

The novice-mistress was of course entitled to her views about the contemplative life being out of place at St. Elizabeth's. And she may have had some justification in considering Teresa secretive, for though actually she was perfectly candid in answering a point-blank question, she had never been accustomed, even among the members of her own family, to volunteering confidences. We have reason to believe that Sister Mary Ellen probed and pressed in such a way as to come close to flouting the regulation of Canon Law which, while it permits a subject to make disclosures as to the state of his soul to his superiors, forbids superiors to demand this.* For this reason the novice-mistress sometimes burst out against Teresa in a way that everybody could see to be unjust. Thus on one occasion in the novitiate, when Teresa was at the head of the table with some newly arrived postulants, and one of them clumsily knocked over the chair on which she was sitting, it was not the postulant who was ordered to stand up to be reprimanded but Teresa, who was quite blameless. Yet she accepted the rebuke without attempting to defend herself, and did not give the slightest indication of wounded feelings.

There were no tears that time, though sometimes Teresa did weep when things got too difficult. Sister Zita records: "Usually Sister was very happy, but several times I found her in tears. One evening, just before recreation, I found her alone in the basement weeping. I knew from past experience that it was useless to ask the cause of the tears, so I tried to cheer her up, and asked her if she would like to go out to the park with me. She dried her eyes, smiled, and said she would be very glad to go. It happened that no other novice joined us, so I was alone with her for an hour. . . . I had to do most of the talking that night, because as hard as Sister tried she could not repress her sobs, and more than once I saw her

*Canon 530 makes this ruling unmistakably clear, adding, however, that it is desirable that subjects approach their superiors with filial confidence, and, if the superiors be priests, expose to them their doubts and troubles of conscience also. But Sister Mary Ellen was not a priest, and one who was a priest, Father Benedict, had explicitly forbidden Teresa to say anything about such matters to the novice-mistress.

wipe the tears away. When we had returned to the novitiate, she said to me: 'I am sorry that I have been so unpleasant a companion tonight.' How I longed to be able to help her! Some time after Sister had died, her spiritual director asked me to tell him a few things about her. I related the above among other things and he said: 'No wonder she cried much that summer. She was going through hell.' "

Father Benedict acted according to the wise provision of his order that no monk must perform any special mortifications without the express permission of his abbot, and he held this position, in effect, towards Teresa. Therefore sometimes he had to restrain her, for he did not believe in too great a degree of physical asceticism. For example, when she asked his permission to sacrifice her eyes for the benefit of somebody who needed sight more than she did, he peremptorily told her to give up such an idea.

Another sacrifice about which she consulted him, he neither advised nor discouraged. This was what she called "the sacrifice of her honor," meaning by that the esteem in which she was held. In a letter she explained: "As a postulant, the first few days I was here I wondered whether the time would come when I would be forced to leave unwillingly. It seemed improbable then, but not impossible. . . . Only now it seems not only not impossible but not improbable. And you said, 'You are loved and honored by all; He was dishonored and hated.' And how that struck home. I've felt it often. And perhaps the resemblance to Him will be even outwardly achieved—maybe that's why all this is happening in my novitiate." In another letter to him she writes: "The one thought still haunts me: that He wants the sacrifice of my honor, too. I thought I had given Him everything, but I see that something still remains. . . . The blow, if it comes, will strike with sevenfold force in striking at those I love, and in dimming the lustre of a name that has always been above reproach. But after all, He will be only answering a prayer I made continually since childhood—that I might live despised of men, and known to Him alone, buried deep in His divine heart. . . . Only pray that I may not fail Him." All of which meant that Teresa was afraid that she would be asked to leave, but as this, had it happened, would have been coupled with the often repeated suggestion made by Sister Mary Ellen that she should join the Carmelites, it is not very easy to see why it need have been regarded as a disgrace. The point, however, is that Teresa would have regarded it as a terrible disgrace, and yet she was willing to accept it as one more sacrifice made to God.

Much that has been related would not seem to indicate an influence of any kind, except upon her small circle of devoted friends. Yet her influence was much greater than anybody suspected. Up to this time Teresa probably supposed that her influence could be of no very startling importance. But as she came to a keener and more clear realization of the doctrine of the Mystical Body—"if one member suffer, all the members suffer with it"—she saw that she was bound to have an effect, whether for good or for evil, upon those among whom she found herself, and determined to make it for good. First she would do this by example, and in the second place by word. Hardly conscious of her influence though she may have been at first, she afterwards came to be very conscious—some may even think too conscious—of her influence, and too deliberate in using it.

She did not act on her own initiative. There were long consultations in the confessional with Father Benedict about the spiritual life, and he soon came to the conviction that he had a saint on his hands. There were also occasional talks with her in the convent parlor—with Sister Mary Ellen's permission, of course, though this may have been somewhat reluctantly given. He laid Teresa under strict orders to tell him everything that had ever happened to her, and what it was she related comes out in her letters to him and in the various statements he made about her after her death. He was sure that she was a saint and that, moreover, she had a special mission. It was his function, as he conceived it, to direct her in the carrying out of this mission.

I gather that there are still a number of members of the community who strongly resent the suggestion that a novice should have had a mission at all, and consider her claims presumptuous. So, indeed, they would have to be considered at first glance; but one might remember the story of the child Samuel and reflect that it is not for us to say whom God is to choose as instruments, but rather to answer with Samuel, should the Voice come, "Speak, Lord, for Thy servant heareth." The presumption would lie in disobedience to such a summons. Actually, however, Teresa never made any claims at all, that anybody was allowed to hear of; she merely confided to Father Benedict that she believed God had called her to a very special work, and he thoroughly supported her in this belief.

Teresa had, as Father Benedict attests, a life of union with God since childhood, and though she was almost totally ignorant regarding formal knowledge of the mystical life, she had often experienced the phenomena that sometimes (but by no means always) go with it. Since entering the novitiate she had had her eyes opened by the rather dry little manuals which were the prescribed reading for the novices, and by Father Benedict's own conferences. Then when he asked her whether she had read St. Teresa's *Interior Castle*, she told him she had, and when he enquired what Mansion her soul was living in, she answered, quite simply, the Seventh. In other words, she was already far advanced in the spiritual life.

Concerning this mission of hers Teresa could not have been more explicit than in a letter she wrote to Father Benedict in August, 1926: "About the work God wishes me to do. First of all I wish to make it clear that my knowledge of it has not come to me in any extraordinary way. By that I mean that it has not been a case of interior locution. The only words Our Lord spoke to me in that manner were the two words I told you about, first, being called to sacrifice my life for the community, and second, His teachings through me were the culmination of those of Margaret Mary Alacoque."

That seems to be making a very large claim, so one must add that nobody is obliged to believe what is said in private revelation, except of course those things which are of course already part of the "deposit of faith." I for one simply refuse to believe that Our Lord used the language that St. Margaret Mary puts into His mouth. Yet I have a theory about this, which I have advanced elsewhere: it is that the divine message may be more or less refracted by the human medium through which it comes to us. To make such a proviso is not to reject the message but, so it seems to me, to make it more acceptable. I do not doubt that Margaret Mary did an immense amount for the spiritual life of Catholics—or rather, that Christ did it through her. But I believe her revelations only because of their consonance with the doctrines of the Church.

Teresa had nothing comparable to her colloquies to report. Her purpose is found expressed in her own words: "That is all I am living for—to comfort Him, to give Him delight. But what am I talking about? My comfort is to be without comfort, my consolation to be without consolation, my delight to be without delight. And after all it is He Who is suffering for me, and in me, and with me. And what a little little price has been the paying—purgatory, and a taste of perdition, and the boot of the world. But it's nothing, nothing, nothing, though it has been awful and it's getting worse. . . . Dear God, what must not Your thirst be! You've given me only a little bit of Yours, and the fever is at the breaking point. God, my very own God, slay me breath by breath, torture me body and soul as You please, but *let me bring the world to Your feet.*"

Nor in Teresa's case is there anything resembling the Little Flower's "Little Way," which is hardly more than a commentary on Our Lord's "Except ye become as little children, ye shall not enter into the kingdom of heaven." In the same way there is nothing particularly new in the statement that Teresa gives: "As I understand it, God's purpose in my life is this in general: to teach men that Our Lord's promise 'If any man love Me, he will keep My word; and my Father will love him, and We will come to him and make Our abode with him' is held out to every single soul regardless of calling; and is the perfect realization of His prayers and ours: Thy kingdom come." Surely nobody can object to Teresa's declaring that to be the purpose of her life, and the doctrine she advances can never be stated often enough. What has aroused criticism, however, is what immediately follows as a corollary: "The immediate object is to help sanctify this Community (and all His spouses engaged in the active life) by bringing home to them by force of example and word that God desires with desire to become one spirit with them; and that this life of union, far from being incompatible with their state, is the one thing necessary, for upon it depends the fruitfulness of action." Against this two objections have been brought: that a novice should have been so lacking in humility (so it is alleged) as to set out to teach those with long years in the religious life, and that the work of the Sisters of Charity is definitely active.

None of Teresa's critics would deny that the contemplative mode is higher than the active; and they would be reasonable in saying that not everybody is called to extraordinary mystical states. Teresa's basic contention was that all are called to the contemplater's mode, that a vocation to the active life need not exclude contemplation, and in fact can do so only to the impoverishment of that vocation. That is why in one of her conferences she warned Sisters against being so "absorbed in striving to become excellent teachers, nurses, bookkeepers, cooks, what not, that the affairs of the soul are relegated to a minor level, and eventually almost to oblivion." In no sense could she be said to have presumed to have suggested a new vocation to her Community; she merely indicated that their existing vocation was larger and deeper than many had supposed.

People with too keen an awareness of having a mission are often not liked, and may even be insufferable. This is because a suspicion may arise that their mission is self-conferred and due to their vanity. Christians cannot but recall Christ's ironic remarks about first casting out the beam from one's own eye before trying to cast out the mote in our neighbour's. But Teresa began with herself, and she never gave the faintest hint that she was out to reform anyone. What she did was only under inspiration from God, and even so was attempted only after her spiritual director had assured her that this inspiration was, in his firm conviction, perfectly genuine. As to what she herself believed about her mission, we have letter after letter to Father Benedict, from which this may be extracted as a typical passage: "Father, I've been thinking too that this double purpose—the secular and religious appeal—is also evident in the fact that He in His wonderful mercy gifted me with the grace of union while I was still a secular. I've always felt that He gave me the experience of the mystic phenomena only . . . that I might be of help to others." With which we come again to St. Thomas Aquinas's classic *tradere contemplata.*

There is another passage about her mission which should be quoted. She says that she thinks it was about five weeks after she entered, and while she was, of course, still a postulant, that Christ asked her to sacrifice her life for the immediate end, to help sanctify her own community. Until then, she says, "I did what I was told, giving it no further thought than when I had been ordered to sweep the novitiate or scrub the corridor. But a day came when I saw things in their real value, and realized that what I am now doing is His work marked out for me, and for which He has prepared me all my life."

Finally there are these two passages from letters to Father Benedict, the one written on June 26, 1926, and the other on July 6th of the same year: "During my adoration the truth of these words in my regard struck home, 'For them do I sanctify myself.' Really, love for my own soul would never be sufficiently strong to impel me to do the things I daily do for others. I can say in all sincerity I love them better than myself. They are in very truth my children—hence the necessity of spiritual travail." The other is: "Light is never wanting for others. And since I must be about my Father's business, it suffices—what a wonderful mercy of His—that my will is securely established in Him . . . God has been very good to me, treating me like a spoiled child (not that He ever spoils anybody) in so completely absorbing all the faculties of my soul in Him during prayer, both the inferior and superior parts, that anything short of this is really painful." And these spiritual "children" of hers were not only her fellow novices but all the nuns of her community—including her superiors Sister Mary Ellen and Mother Alexandrine, though probably this last logical implication did not occur to her.

From all this it becomes evident that Father Benedict did not, so to speak, "invent" Teresa, though there were some who believed she was "mesmerised" by him—that was the word actually, but no doubt loosely used—as though he were a kind of Svengali and she a Trilby. What might not be far from the truth, however, (and this also was advanced with more seriousness than "mesmerism"), was that Father Benedict had hoped to induce a more contemplative spirit in the community and that he was overjoyed at finding in Teresa an instrument for this purpose. He cooperated with her, advising her as a priest and experienced director of souls, at the same time being somewhat awed at having at his disposal one whom he regarded as a saint. After she told him about her mission, he would have felt that to have acted in any other way than he did would have been the gravest neglect of duty. He did not for an instant imagine that he was himself a saint. And as a spiritual director he took what has to be admitted was a very long chance with Teresa, for she might have turned out to be an impostor. But to the end he remained unshaken in his certainty both as to her personal holiness and as to the work she had been brought to do at St. Elizabeth's.

It speaks volumes for Teresa's humility that the influence she found she was exercising—for though her main influence was exercised by her posthumously published conferences, she became more and more aware of what she was accomplishing—did not turn her head. No doubt it was part of the divine plan that an instrument was used who did not have much physical attractiveness, nor even any great degree of charm, though her deficiencies in these respects should not be exaggerated. Had the matter been left to Father Benedict— that is, had he proceeded according to a preconceived plan of his own—he would presumably have selected somebody else as more apt for his purposes. But when he encountered Teresa, he accepted her as God's gift—first as a soul whom he might direct to still higher flights of sanctity, and then as one who might inspire others. He *had* to accept at his own grave peril.

Chapter Fourteen

Misunderstandings

AFTER Teresa's death Father Benedict wrote, "For her own sanctification [God] permitted her to be terribly misunderstood, and this proved the heaviest cross of her life." She doubtless would have been misunderstood even had Father Benedict not appeared upon the scene, and he certainly had no intention of causing any misunderstanding, for he expressed compunction if he had contributed to it. But there can be no doubt that he was to a considerable extent responsible. Teresa once told him that even if he decided against the reality of the mission she felt she had, she would continue to believe in it, but would not try to exercise it against his judgment. As he was strongly of the opinion that her mission was very real, she confidently proceeded. It is in this that she was misunderstood—as she still is.

Those who criticise Teresa by implication condemn Father Benedict's judgment. But the reverse need not be true; it must be understood that, though Sister Mary Ellen, the novice-mistress, was not always fair to Teresa, such unfairness was due to an understandable exasperation, and the exasperation itself arose from her feeling that she was being interfered with in her own province, in which she should have had a free hand. This interference concerned only minor matters, and in fact she herself gave Teresa the permission to do certain things that were not permitted to other novices. But this was at the request of Mother Alexandrine, who was acting under Father Benedict's request, or at a request that Father Benedict made to Sister Mary Ellen personally. While she could have stood upon her rights and refused, it was not easy to do so; therefore she could not but consider that rather unwarrantable pressure had been brought to bear on her.

One may cite the matter of the correspondence that took place between Teresa and her spiritual director. It is the custom in all novitiates for the novice-master or mistress to have all outgoing letters given to them in unsealed envelopes and to open incoming letters to their charges—in all instances having the right to read them. It is true that ordinarily this right is not exercised, unless to the extent of tearing off a corner of an envelope to remind the novice that the right exists but also to show that the letter has not been read. Teresa, however, was given permission to mail her letters to Father Benedict herself, and to receive letters from him freely. These letters were written only during the summers of 1925 and 1926, when Father Benedict did not go to St. Elizabeth's; but during those periods Teresa wrote often and at great length, because Father Benedict wished to be kept fully informed. He himself did not write to her very often, and Teresa promptly destroyed all his letters—as soon as they had been read—so as not to gratify herself by having them in her possession. Sister Mary Ellen could not but suspect that there was information in the correspondence that she felt might better have been imparted to herself, and she did not at all like the privilege that Teresa enjoyed.

On Teresa the situation put a great strain—so great a

strain that it undoubtedly had much to do with the sudden breakdown of what had hitherto been a robust constitution. Despite the vow of obedience she had made to Father Benedict, under which she was strictly enjoined not to talk to the novice-mistress about her spiritual condition, she once partially disobeyed it. She had written to Father Benedict begging him to allow her to speak, but before his reply arrived, still holding her to silence, she could not stand it when (as she afterwards confessed to Father Benedict) Sister Mary Ellen "began to talk about the hurt she had experienced, and she didn't blame me, but in all the years, etc. etc. such a thing had never happened to her that Mother interfered with her authority." Therefore, Teresa argued to herself, "If Father knew all the circumstances at present, he'd surely, without any doubt, give his permission." Using what she called "the devil's logic," she reminded herself that the obedience she had vowed to Father Benedict bound her "only if nothing is commanded contrary to the rule or the commands of superiors," and now Sister Mary Ellen had given what was virtually a command. "And besides," she continued arguing to herself, "your vow of perfection takes precedence over the vow of obedience—why, you're quite free to act as you think fit. Your vow doesn't tie you down at all, not nearly as much as you think."

Accordingly Teresa went to the novice-mistress, and had begun to tell her something of what was on her mind when she broke down crying, and was literally "saved by the bell"—the bell that rang for some community duty. By the time the talk was resumed, Father Benedict's letter forbidding her to speak had arrived, so Teresa had to tell Sister Mary Ellen that she had made a big mistake. She got a studiously careless, "Oh, that's all perfectly all right—don't bother your head about it. Indeed, I'd rather you wouldn't. I've heard many things in my life (I don't doubt it) and this will go with the rest."

Father Benedict's firm attitude was not without reason: he well understood that if Sister Mary Ellen did know even a little of what was transpiring in Teresa's soul, she would have been confirmed in her opinion that this novice should be with the Carmelites and not with the Sisters of Charity. In this way, while he unquestionably made things hard for Teresa, he was also protecting her. His attitude also served to place the novice-mistress in a false position; but that probably did not unduly worry him, as he would have thought that a woman who had been fifty years in religion ought to be capable of looking after herself, whereas Teresa's position was delicate and precarious.

Yet one must sympathise with Sister Mary Ellen's point of view. She had been during two terms of office novice-mistress for over thirty years, and after that time might be presumed to know what she was doing. Now she was being overridden by Father Benedict on the one hand and, to some extent, by Mother Alexandrine on the other. She had a right to consider that she was paramount in her own department but that her jurisdiction was being interfered with, if not undermined. Though she seriously misjudged Teresa, she could hardly do otherwise, so completely was she kept in the dark.

Another of her grievances was that Teresa had been given free access to the room of one of the professed, Sister Marie Dolores, her Spanish teacher in college. The novices themselves knew that this was an infraction of the rule, and some of them may have resented it as much as their mistress that such an unheard-of privilege had been given to one of them. Here I confess that Father Benedict's order (which of course had to be confirmed by Mother Alexandrine) seems to me not altogether judicious, as it was hardly necessary. Teresa went to her former professor with the

novices' minds to considerations that were too exalted for them she could console herself with the thought that in a year or two perhaps another spiritual director would replace him, probably a man of a rather different sort.

Teresa wrote her conferences in longhand, for her one experiment with the typewriter was not successful, and then she would give Father Benedict what she had written when he next came to St. Elizabeth's. But as he had up to that time spoken only from notes, in a somewhat discursive fashion, he announced, when reading Teresa's first conference, that he was going to change his method and stick to a prepared address. He continued, however, to supply running comments, which Teresa encouraged him to make in order to conceal what she had supplied.

Father Benedict always typed out what Teresa had given him, and this script was handed over to Mother Alexandrine, who got some of the novices to make mimeographed copies, as these were being sent out to other convents of the Sisters of Charity and, through them (though this Teresa did not know), to such convents as asked for them. By this means copies went to some of the most distant parts of the world.

Teresa once came rather close to giving herself away. This was when she went to the office where the mimeograph machine was and asked that she might see the original, her intention being to make some slight change in it. The novice who was doing the mimeographing said: "You seem to be very much interested in these conferences, Sister. If you like, I'll give you a copy each week." Teresa, who did not wish to do anything that might seem to deny her authorship, smiled and said that that was not necessary.

Sister Zita tells me that Father Benedict had advised her one day after confession to discuss the conferences with Teresa—which again was a little risky, if the secret was to be kept. But Teresa merely asked her if she thought that the conference on baptism was "over their heads." Sister Zita said: "No, I think most of them understood. But why do you ask?" To this Teresa returned, "Oh, I heard somebody say that," with which the matter was dropped. The secret remained safe.

Yet not altogether was the truth unsuspected, but only by two. One of these was Sister Marie Dolores, and it is perhaps hardly surprising that, in view of her weekly spiritual conversations with Teresa, she should recognise that what was said in them and in the conferences ran on somewhat similar lines. But when she ventured to question Teresa, she was put off with the kind of evasive answer which only confirmed her suspicions. If she kept her counsel about this, a novice did not, though she really had nothing to go on except a familiarity with Teresa's prose style. They had been at college together, and had graduated in the same class, and it was rather clever of her to divine what she did. But when she mentioned her suspicions to a few friends, she was laughed down as suggesting something quite impossible, and so dropped the subject. If I do not mention her name, it is only because she was one of the few novices who returned to the world.

There were also a few professed Sisters who wondered whether Father Benedict had really written the conferences. Perhaps there was only one, for of only one do I know for a surety, and this was my old friend Sister Mary Vincent, who had been Teresa's professor of English. She remarked one day, "Well, Father Benedict's literary style seems to have suddenly improved!" But this went no closer to the truth than a vague surmise that perhaps one of the monks of St. Mary's Abbey at Newark, to which Father Benedict was attached, may have taken the job on his shoulders, or had polished up what Father Benedict had written. And during the summer of 1926, when the spiritual director was away on vacation and sent a circular letter to the novices (that also written by Teresa), Sister Mary Ellen, no literary critic but not without shrewdness, remarked upon reading it, "That does not sound like Father to me." But except for the two mentioned in the previous paragraph, not a soul thought of Teresa's being Father Benedict's "ghost writer."

Some of the older Sisters were a little uneasy about the wide distribution of the mimeographed copies of the conferences. Everybody acknowledged that they were good, but considered that this made them all the more unsuitable for Sisters of Charity, because of the strong mystical tendencies that were so apparent. Father Benedict wrote afterwards, "Many sisters refused to read them and some tore them up." But there were others who greatly admired them and did their best to see that friends they had in other convents should see papers that were so excellent. Because of this, the gathering of the conferences into a book—to be published under a nom de plume—was already being thought of, and was once mentioned by Father Benedict in a conference. It never seems to have occurred to anybody that, if he were the author, he would have had no reason for avoiding the use of his own name.

But if no suspicions were aroused, one person was told, but kept the secret. That person was Mother Mary St. Francis Xavier, the Visitator of the Good Shepherd nuns, when she was in this country. She had had many extraordinary privileges in her religious life, among them that of having the famous Jesuit Father Willie Doyle as her spiritual director; it was to her that most of the letters used in his biography were written. She considered the conferences very remarkable but was pledged to silence. It is not at all clear why Father Benedict should have taken her into his confidence, though he must be presumed to have had reasons of his own.

During the summer of 1926, as has been remarked,

Teresa was so troubled in mind that she wrote to Father Benedict, begging him to allow her to impart at least something to Sister Mary Ellen. "Father," she wrote, "I think the time has come for me to let the Mistress know more of me than heretofore, because it does not help matters to have us really perfect strangers. I'll do whatever you say in this regard. Only I think the way has been broken to tear down the barrier of reserve and misunderstanding, and if it's not torn down now the misunderstanding will rise doubly high and trebly thick. And don't you think she should know everything about the conferences she has given me permission to write?" Actually, of course, she had only given permission that Teresa should do some work—she did not have any idea what—for Mother Alexandrine. Yet the novice-mistress was often accusing Teresa of a lack of frankness. And perhaps even more ominous was the conversation Teresa reports: "Are you perfectly happy and contented? No regrets? It's a wonder to me that you never entered Carmel." This was all the more disturbing for being so frequently harped upon. Teresa was in real fear of being asked to leave. And though the decision would not have been made by the novice-mistress alone but by the Community Council, Sister Mary Ellen's opinion would have weighed for much, especially as many of the members of that Council, including Mother Alexandrine herself, had at one time or another been her subjects or her novices.

Father Benedict has left an account of how the conferences came to be written. He says: "At the beginning of June, 1926, the thought came to me that Sister Miriam Teresa might be able to write excellent instructions for the novices. I believed that she enjoyed extraordinary lights, and I knew that she was living an exemplary life. Moreover, I felt that she had an experimental knowledge of the science of the saints. Besides this, I thought that one day she would be ranked among the saints of God, and I felt that it was incumbent upon me to utilize whatever might contribute to an appreciation of her merits after her death. For this reason in particular did I oblige her to write the conferences." Though for over a year Teresa had known that her mission was to be that of leading her community to lay a great stress upon contemplation, she had had no very clear idea as to how she was to effect this. It was Father Benedict who discovered the means.

From nobody did she get any help. And writing was painful to her because of her eyes and because she rather impatiently gave up the use of the typewriter after a single experiment, though blind people have been able to manage the machine. Hitherto none of her compositions had been very long, except for her two plays (about which more later) and her poem on Mother Xavier. To these must be added her letters to Father Benedict, some of which are voluminous. Even apart from the handicap of poor vision, she said that she composed slowly; but in this instance she had little difficulty, as she felt that she was inspired by the Holy Ghost and was merely a pen held in God's hand.

When her first conference was given to Father Benedict, his criticism was that it was too "flowery," so he advised her to take the style of the Gospels as her model. The advice is good, if it can be carried out, but I confess that her first conference (which appears as the last in her book *Greater Perfection*) does not seem to me very different from the rest. Of course Teresa could not begin to approach the literary style of Christ—who ever could?—so she continued to write like herself. My own criticism of her as a writer would be that, while she is generally good, she has a tendency to swing between the stilted and the colloquial, though at her best she is pungent and even humourous, and always is practical and to the point.

She explained her methods in a letter to Father Benedict,

saying: "Whatever has been written has been done under obedience, and though the commands may not have been to my natural liking, and I haven't an idea of what I should say or where I should begin, a prayer to the Holy Ghost straightens out every difficulty, and what to other minds may seem a detailed plan, logically and deliberately thought out in advance, has really been nothing of the kind. I write what is in my mind at the moment, not knowing what is coming next, though when I am in Chapel, I see clearly how it is going to end up. So I never know how long a dissertation I may produce. Now the point I wish to make is this: no matter what has been commanded, or how short the time, God provides. In fact, the more I have to do, the more I accomplish, at least so it appeared all my life." She had not read widely, but she was saturated with the Bible and the Missal. She had read Abbot Marmion too, and her method is similar to his, a closely woven tissue of the Scriptures and the Liturgy, which is itself so largely scriptural. One must not expect to find in her the same degree of Marmion's scholarly familiarity with his sources, and indeed it is probable that a good many of Teresa's citations— not that she makes a large number of quotations—are taken from him at secondhand. Her favorite quotation was St. Augustine's, "God became man that man might become God."

In all this Teresa may be considered as a forerunner in America of the Liturgical Movement of our time. Nor is this in the least fanciful, for we know that she had read Father Virgil Michel, who did more than any other one man to give an impetus to this movement. This does not mean of course that it was anything new in itself, but merely that, under Benedictine influence (especially in the Middle West, where Benedictine abbeys are more numerous than in the East) the Liturgical Movement has come to play a prominent and fruitful part in American Catholic life. It was under a Benedictine spiritual director that Teresa took part in this, but it should also be remembered that the Catholics of the Eastern Rite, among whom Teresa had been brought up, are more elaborately liturgical than their Latin Rite brethren.

Sister Mary Ellen must be admitted to have been right in thinking that conferences of this sort—good though she acknowledged them to be—did not very closely accord with the vocation of a Sister of Charity as she understood it. The formation of the novices was something that had been entrusted to her, and while she was working in one direction it could not but seem to her that Father Benedict was working in another. She knew of Teresa's inclination for the contemplative life; and she feared, not without reason, that there was a similar inclination among Teresa's intimates in the novitiate that would end by unfitting them all for the work they would be called upon to do in the community. It must be granted that things were being made difficult for her.

She in her turn made things difficult for Teresa. Yet Teresa never really complained to Father Benedict about this, though acting under his explicit instructions she had to tell him about the state of affairs as far as the novice-mistress was concerned. She did so guardedly, referring to Sister Mary Ellen as "somebody," and still continuing to hope that she would be permitted to explain things to her. "Father," she wrote to him, "when I entered religion, I never intended to be anything other than open and frank with my superiors because I did not know how to be anything else. And I think I have been so. . . . I never look for flaws in anyone, and to admit even to myself what was so very evident, or I should say, what was making itself evident, seemed to me disloyalty to those to whom I owed obedience. . . . I suffered in silence, accepting everything that was told me with the sincerity of an infant even when certain inviolable rights were attacked. And after listening for a year and a half to the refrain drummed on continually: 'You're not a bit simple and open, but closed and secret. I don't like that attitude at all; that's not the way a novice should act,' I suppose I began *unconsciously* to believe that I was lacking in simplicity. I know now only too well what somebody's idea of simplicity is and that she's lost *everything* thereby. . . . The whole rub was the idea that I was talking to you, and it was stated very plainly."*

In another letter she told Father Benedict that all the signs pointed to the likelihood that her name would be crossed off the list of the novices preparing for their vows. Now Teresa says: "I do not impute base motives to anyone. The argument will be that my vocation is not to the active but the contemplative life. And always, too, I am not like ordinary novices. I get that in season and out of season. And again I'm not simple. And even the very fact of my writing to you is held against me—novices generally don't act that way. Somebody has a good deal less confidence in you than she used to have. And somebody was, times past, the superior of the Mother, and I shouldn't wonder a bit, but what the current will change, time enough given, someone else being forced to action."

All this is very painful. But Father Benedict, grieving though he did over the situation, nevertheless held to his injunction of silence. As for Sister Mary Ellen, when shortly before her death she was asked how she felt about Teresa, she could answer, "All that I did, I did in the presence of God." But a little later she said, "God permitted that I should not understand the child, for her own

*This is the closest she ever came to saying that undue pressure was being brought to bear by the novice-mistress, an infringement of Canon Law of which Teresa would certainly have been ignorant had Father Benedict not informed her. A fair statement of the situation might be that, while the novice-mistress was not meaning to force confidences, she was *encouraging* Teresa to make them voluntarily—a fine but real line of distinction.

sanctification and my humiliation." Father Benedict for his part said, "The mystery of it has always been: why should [God] choose a miserable sinner like me for a work so holy?" How strange and diverse are the crosses of circumstance upon which the victims of God are crucified!

CHAPTER FIFTEEN

✧

The Conferences

THE title *Greater Perfection* was chosen by the late Louis
Kenedy of the firm of P. J. Kenedy & Sons, the publishers
of the book. This, however, presumably was in the light of
the information he was furnished about Teresa's private
vows, and yet applies to Teresa herself rather than to her
book, where greater perfection is not so much as mentioned. That is to say, it is not *explicitly* mentioned, for of
course it is frequently implied.

The sources upon which she drew were virtually restricted to the Bible and the Liturgy, for though she does
make an occasional quotation these are only incidental to
her main theme. Early in the course of the project she
wrote to Father Benedict: "What do you think of giving
the necessary instructions in connection with the liturgical
spirit of the Church, living the interior life as it should be
lived in her and with her? What I mean is to get the main
thought of the discourse from the proper of the Sunday or
some special feast, and develop it according to the wants of
the ones in mind. It would simplify matters for them and
make them realize the *oneness* of things. Multiplicity in
devotion is a great drawback, and a mass of even very good

the only essential—until the sugar-plum of consolation is withdrawn, and then the tide turns. Oh, what is the use in praying? My prayers are never heard anyway. And besides, I am no better for it. In fact I am worse. I used to be able to pray, and to keep my thoughts from running around, but now—I might as well give up as try to remain in God's presence only to show Him irreverence." On the next page we find: "If you knew that without work, and hard work at that, you cannot acquire a thimbleful of secular knowledge—a great deal of which you will sooner or later forget—and yet spend an enormous effort in so doing; why argue differently because the knowledge to be gained is spiritual? Nothing really worth anything is ever acquired without an effort; and ordinarily the more we prize the object we wish to attain, the greater and more earnest the effort we put forth. Now it is hardly necessary to mention that of all things worth striving for, God, the one Supreme Good, the First Cause and Final End of all created beings, should hold chief place. If men in the world do not begrudge sacrifice and struggle in order to gain a miserable bauble, we, who are religious, should certainly stop at nothing in order to attain God Himself. . . . Do you know why we give up? Because we are not humble. We feel that our service is not pleasing to God, whereas, the truth of the matter is that it is not pleasing to ourselves; and since it is hard—and nature does not like hard things —we yield to nature."

It must already have been noticed that in much of this there was an undercurrent of sarcasm, and perhaps it was this that made one of the novices suspect that Teresa was the real author. Be this as it may, such a passage as the following is characteristic: "With regard to interior conquests, you may apply it always, without any harm, and the oftener the better; with regard to exterior mortifications, common sense and wisdom are necessary. Since all of us have the most uncommon common sense in the world, and the lion's share of its wisdom, we are by this very superiority incapable of judging for ourselves—hence prudent direction is of supreme necessity." That was Teresa's own experience, nor had she failed to observe the situation she describes in the passage about those who meet with misunderstanding in their superior: "They may be worried about affairs at home and abroad—and quite often these are of their own and the devil's creation under the widespreading cloak of a misdirected charity. These and a hundred things may harass and vex them, and how do these religious, who have professed to follow the Master, then act? Very much like worldlings, I fear. If they do not openly refuse the repugnant commands, they obey exteriorly only, inwardly fussing and fuming, and making no attempt to bring their wills into submission to the will of God. Obedience such as this is no obedience at all."

In the previous chapter a letter from Teresa to Father Benedict has been quoted, in which she gives an account of her method of composition. This too is worth quoting, for it will have interest to all those who have ever tried to do any writing, though few people are likely to follow Teresa's system, or would be well advised to do so. She tells him of one of her conferences:

"I honestly had no notion of what I was going to say or how I was going to say it, before I started. And that's nearly always true. The 'nearly' stands for the few instances when I know in a general way what is the end in view. And yet, nothing that I say is new to me. But God gives me wonderful light (and how wonderful He was last Sunday) to understand in a way that others can grasp—maybe not just now, though. And, Father, as to the diction, well, I just can't help it. Since I realized the mistake when I wrote that first paper* on the

*This was the conference that Father Benedict considered too flowery.

knowledge alone is not so much valueless as dangerous; it is dangerous because one knows what is required, and yet acts unconformably to that knowledge. It serves only to increase guilt." But of course the key word there is "alone," and this Teresa makes plain by immediately afterwards quoting from the *Imitation*: "Never read anything in order that thou mayst appear learned or more wise—for the kingdom of God consisteth not in speech but in virtue." If Father Benedict asked her to quote some Benedictine author now and then—and she did this by citing Blosius once and Marmion more frequently—probably his object was that of throwing people off the scent with regard to the composition of the conferences.

Teresa's mode of approach was more practical than speculative. The whole of her life—especially her spiritual life, which was almost wholly nourished by personal experience, to which whatever reading she did was no more than corroborative—had been little touched by theory. And her home training had served further to develop her practicality, for since childhood she had many household chores and for two periods managed the household. She was therefore disposed to place no very high value upon book learning; therefore when she composed her conferences she set out only such ideas as would be of practical service. It is so, for example, with her explanation of the three states of prayer: "A sharp and distinct division is not implied. One does not leave the purgative stage to enter the illuminative, as one would pass from one room to another, and close the door after entering. No. The mortifications of the purgative way are carried on to the end with increasing intensity; the lights of the illuminative path burn at white heat only in the unitive. And union and enlightenment are not wanting in purgation. . . . The three-fold division simply refers to the predominating movements of grace in the soul in its progress toward perfection."

Nothing could be more clearly or simply expounded. Nor

could anything be more to the point than this warning against too great a hurry in the spiritual life: "Hurry is born of the devil, and is one of his choicest tools for injuring souls. God is never in a hurry. He works only in peace and quietness. We cannot perfect ourselves—God's grace understood—overnight; we have the whole day of life to achieve this end. Precipitation has been the ruin of many a possible saint. It arises from secret self-love, and causes disgust and discouragement and ultimately a positive distaste for spiritual exercises; all because of an uncontrolled disquietude over one's spiritual advancement. As long as we *try* we need never fear or worry, for we *are* advancing. Only when we give up trying have we cause to feel anxiety about our progress, but that is just the time when none is evident, for we feel secure. But it is a false security, in which a proud self and a prouder devil have steeped us." Again she says: "Our failings are not a hindrance to holiness; they are positive helps, if we employ them to our advantage. It is only in the conquest of these faults that we are sanctified."

All this ought to be helpful by giving encouragement. But it should be noticed that few such writers have insisted more on the absolute necessity of mortification, not of extraordinary physical austerities, but of mortifications of the kind that are at once simpler and more efficacious. Nor is the "infallible test" she offers that of the time spent in prayer, even of the most exalted type, but the advance made in virtue, which is unattainable without the mortification and humiliation of the senses. And mortification, Teresa reminds us, "will inevitably lead to humility, and humility to charity. . . . When the mortification gets to the point where we in truth love our neighbor as ourselves, we shall also love God with our whole heart and mind and soul. . . . We shall then have begun to keep the *one* commandment perfectly."

With this we come to the core of her doctrine. "How," she asks, "is this continuous spiritual breathing, prayer, to be

This understanding of the human heart is sometimes edged
with sarcasm, as when Teresa comments: "We acknowledge
our sins and confess their share in Christ's expiation, but
only in a vague general way. We are really not honestly sin-
cere. We say 'mea culpa,' but rather from a sense that it is
the proper thing to do at certain times, than from a realization of our guilt."

Not infrequently Teresa uses some humour, and though
this is often rather deliberate and "contrived," no doubt what
will follow was well adapted to an audience most of whom
had only recently been at college or high school: "Heaven is
the post-graduate course; death the commencement. This
degree is given for one course only—a science course. It is a
Master's degree in the science of the Master. The signature
that makes it valid is written in the blood of the Lamb, on the
living substance of our soul, and the seal is a gory cross. . . .
Only *one* entrance examination is allowed." I cannot say that
I relish that very much, but it carries out its purpose, as is
also true of the extended series of comparisons to the dentist's
chair, where the soul must pull the teeth, even to probing
about for some chipped pieces that may still be left, and
where God is the mirror and supplies the surgical instruments and medicine. I prefer the other "college humour" bit
about the Alpha Omega fraternity of the saints, though I
wince a little at the description of the "initiation" and the
"frat-pin": "A cross shaped of a sprig of thorn, becomes only
in eternity an ornament revealed in its true splendor, formed
of the gold of charity, encrusted with the diamond of faith,
the emblem of hope, the pearl of purity, the amethyst of sor-
row and mortification, the ruby of courage, the bloodstone
of desire, the turquoise of watchfulness." At least it is not
so appalling as the "cuteness" the Little Flower displayed in
her famous invitation cards (much admired by some people,
I am afraid) to the wedding of "Jesus, King of Kings and
Lord of Lords, with little Thérèse Martin." At least our

Teresa's quaintness, though equally remorseless, is less distressing.

What follows has sometimes been taken to be a foreshadowing of Teresa's early death, Father Charles Demjanovich seeing in it a presentiment close to prophecy. It is true that her death was less than a year away, but that there was so much as a presentiment of this seems to me definitely discounted by the phrase with which it opens, for this says no more than that death will come to all some day: "Some day, and very soon, no matter how far distant, time for me will cease, and eternity begin. I shall die. Some day, and very soon, curious eyes will pause before a little gravestone in God's acre and read:

HERE LIES

YOURS TRULY

BORN: IT MATTERS NOT WHEN.

DIED: YESTERDAY IN THE LORD.

WHILE IN THE WORLD HE FILLED A

PLACE, NOW FILLED A LITTLE BETTER

THAN JUST AS WELL BY ANOTHER.

R. I. P.

Teresa recognised that Father Benedict's command made more distinct the nature of the mission which, some time before this, she knew to have been entrusted to her. She also knew that he wanted her letters as a complete record for his guidance in the task of directing her. He himself says: "In her letters she speaks plainly, concealing nothing. The things she had to suffer are recorded only because she was acting under obedience. She realized it as a matter of obligation that I should know all, in order that I might safely advise her. From the beginning of her noviceship, she was under obedience to tell me, week by week, of all supposedly extraordinary manifestations of grace in her soul, and this she did with the greatest aversion (natural). This weekly manifestation included her temptations and trials of every kind, her triumphs, and what appeared to her as visions, ecstasies, raptures, locutions, and inspirations. As a rule she placed these apparent mystical phenomena in their respective classes, distinguishing between what affected the imaginary faculties, and what affected the intellectual faculties, her intellectual lights. What I term her visions, were generally of the intellectual kind, that is, as I understand it, a clear perception of that which is normal, in ordinary thoughts, even under the influence of extraordinary grace." Yet in her conferences Teresa, in common with most of the best writers on the mystical life, tended to dismiss the phenomena of mysticism as of no great importance in themselves, though it is clear from some passages of her letters, as also from the statements made later by Father Benedict, that a large part of her material was given to her in what may be described as at least a supernormal way.

But though it is clear that Teresa believed herself to be inspired when writing her conferences, that term must not be taken in other than a very general sense. The human instrument was fallible, and the personal characteristics and limitations of the author were by no means obliterated. For that matter some of the Fathers and the greatest Doctors of the Church have said things which are not to be taken as the official doctrine of the Church, and in some instances they have had to be corrected by more complete and carefully considered pronouncements as to what the full doctrine of the Church actually is. One must not therefore expect that a young woman who had never had any formal theological training, and who knew little about philosophy, should always give perfectly accurate presentations of the truth. Thus when she writes, "Nature is another name for the animal part of us," she was not correct, except in the sense (which is what she is trying to convey) that the animal part of our nature is its lower part. Again, when she says: "Why is [Christ] suffering? What does it all mean? For all mankind? No." the words could be taken in a Jansenistic connotation that we may be sure was far from her mind. And again, this is not accurately put: "If we aspire to be saints in heaven, we must strive to be saints on earth; and if we wish to be devils hereafter, no effort is needed on earth," for of course the lost in hell remain human beings for all eternity, whereas the devils are entirely spiritual beings. Yet these slight slips are innocuous if looked upon, as they should be, as merely a fashion of speaking: if they had been more than that Father Benedict would have edited and changed the material she supplied.

What is wonderful is that, being as untrained as she was, she should have done so well. Often she put things in a way that could hardly have been bettered by the most consummate theologian, of which the following passage may be taken as an example: "Since man is lord of creation, his homage to God must be and is superior to the combined glory given to God by all other living but unintelligent beings. Each individual act of worship on man's part incomparably outweighs the combined worship of sentient and inanimate nature. Yet the homage of nature to the Author of nature is invariable, perpetual, entire. And the homage of man, finite intelligence, is changeable, fleeting, incomplete. . . . Just the same, man by his reason and free will is almost as highly exalted above nature as God is above man. Therefore God, in exacting from us the work of our sanctification, is only asking us to return Him in justice what He receives from insensible creatures according to their capacity."

If in the previous paragraphs there were some small defects in Teresa's mode of expression—things to be regarded as hardly more than slips of the pen—all these were corrected and balanced, at least by implication, by Teresa herself in the page that has just been cited.

CHAPTER SIXTEEN

Other Writings

IT will be remembered that Francis de Sales never imagined that his letters to his mother and Madame de Charmoissy would be made into a book, and that he explained, after its immense success and while he was writing his *Treatise on the Love of God,* that he did not think of himself as an author at all. So Teresa, when she undertook to write some conferences for Father Benedict Bradley, never supposed that they would appear in book form as *Greater Perfection,* or that the poems she had composed from time to time would be gathered up and published after her death. Yet she has to be treated as an author, the author of one remarkable work and, because of the interest that this aroused, the author of the otherwise not very important bits of writing that must be briefly touched on in this chapter.

To begin with her letters. Except to Father Benedict she wrote few, and those rather brief. If she wrote to her college friends Agatha Spinella and Margaret Conklin during vacations, it was only on Charles Lamb's principle that one should "keep one's friendships in repair," but without a particle of the enjoyment that Lamb showed in what was, with him, a rich, delicate, and joyous art. Even to her brother

Charles, dear as he was to her, she wrote only rarely while he was at college and the seminary (or he did not preserve her letters); and the best touch in these appeared after the seminary had been transferred to another location, so that she could address him as "Dear darling of Darlington."

Aileen Flynn tells me of having received two letters from Teresa while she was in the novitiate, one sent to her while she was on a summer vacation in the holiday resort conducted by the Dominican Sisters in the Catskills, the other shortly before Teresa's death; but as neither these nor the letters she presumably wrote now and then to her sisters appear in the voluminous dossier of documents made available to me they were evidently not considered worth preservation. A voluminous correspondence might have been of some assistance to her biographer, yet such a correspondence could only have been produced had Teresa been an altogether different kind of person from the one she was; then there would probably be no biography. Upon the whole it is a convenience that the correspondence should have been virtually confined to one person, Father Benedict; and though none of her letters to him has been reproduced here in full, the citations from them have been copious. Their value lies in what they reveal of Teresa's spiritual life, not in their literary merit. She showed nothing of the *cacoëthes scribendi*.

There are several other letters written during the novitiate period to Alice Pratt, her friend in Bayonne, when she joined the Benedictines, and these will be dealt with in a later chapter. But the items listed comprise all that she apparently wrote. She herself kept none of the letters she received; it was a mode of mortification. Even a minor opportunity of this sort she would not allow to escape.

There are a few things other than the posthumously published *Greater Perfection* which were composed with sufficient deliberation as to be described as literary production, though none of them was written with publication in mind—

not even the one poem that found its way into a magazine or the two that were included in an anthology of college poetry during her lifetime. They, together with a few other items, will be considered here.

It may be, however, that when Father Benedict suggested that she write her autobiography he was thinking of a book that would be eventually printed, and one suspects that he had in mind something similar to the autobiography of the Little Flower. She wrote half a dozen pages of this when she was stopped by her last illness; those pages are given in full by Sister Zita and have been drawn upon already. What soon becomes clear is that she had no narrative gift, and almost at once the autobiography becomes a series of spiritual reflections.

After all, Teresa had much less of a story to relate than Thérèse. The Little Flower's account of the Martin family, in their pious, comfortable, bourgeois household, while it exhibits a social milieu which many people (including myself) do not find very attractive, certainly paints a picture that is perfect of its kind. Other French writers have drawn something of the same sort (almost always with the piety left out, unless piety of a stuffy, routine brand), but, so far as I can recall, always with savage distaste, whereas Thérèse tells about it with artless simplicity, without ever once suspecting that there might be anything saccharine or suffocating about it. I should like to have had from our Teresa a description of the Demjanovich household and the religious and social circles in which she was brought up, but perhaps Teresa was too close to all this to perceive that there might be anything specially interesting about it. In any event her temperamental reticences would have forbidden her striking anything remotely resembling the attitudes of Marie Bashkirtsev.

Though Teresa tells us on the fourth page of the fragment she did write that her powers of observation were never more acute, she gives no proof of this, but stops after giving a few reminiscences of her childhood. It is rather staggering to read: "This narrative is truly autobiographical, being the actual life history of the author; truly biographical, also—being the actual life history of one whose existence began on the twenty-sixth of March, 1901, and ended on the eighth day of December, 1924. Since that day, 'I live, now not I, but Christ liveth in me.' I am no longer myself, though I still inhabit the same body—no, not the same, but very much changed. Still it is precisely because I am not myself that I am really myself, that I have at last found myself . . . which means I am now living in eternity—in God." The hyperbole may be allowed to pass, but it cannot be literally true of anyone before death. To paraphrase very simply that difficult passage, apparently what Teresa means is that she has come to view all things *sub specie aeternitatis*. It is at least obvious that on such terms the autobiography would never have got very far in any sense in which the word is ordinarily understood.

Another assignment given her by Father Benedict was to write a series of formal meditations, point by point, according to the manner in use among the Sisters and many other communities. They appear as an appendix to Sister Zita's book. About them Teresa wrote to her spiritual director asking for further instructions: "Shall I rewrite and make them all uniform—three points—or restrict all to two—or simply write them as they seem naturally to develop? I'm afraid that if I set myself to task to develop them all according to a set formula, I may have to force myself in the doing. However, I'll do whatever you think best." Though we do not have Father Benedict's answer, he must have told her that it did not matter much whether she had two points or three; apart from this, she kept rather closely to a formula, and always concluded with an aspiration and resolution. Everything is somewhat cut and dried, as is perhaps hardly avoidable in the case of a bare skeleton which each person making the meditation might clothe with his own reflections. Only once, it seems to me, does she attain a certain amount of freedom, when she used what the Jesuits call the "composition of place" in her meditation for the Feast of St. Stephen, though to some extent this is true of the meditation immediately preceding it, that on the Nativity of Our Lord. She writes: "Philip and James have been torn from us in the mad rush upon Stephen. He has been kicked and buffeted, spat upon and mocked, he has been sneered at and cursed; his clothing has been shredded by the angry claws of the insane populace; his hair has been torn out in handfuls. They have tied rope tightly under his armpits and, shrieking and hooting, have dragged him, half-naked, down the uneven street, through dirt and mud and stones, here, outside the gates.

"But Stephen has uttered neither cry nor groan. 'Jesus, Master, help him,' we breathe. How like the Master on that awful night is Stephen! The blood is streaming from countless cuts and bruises, and, momentarily, caked by mud and dirt, bursts forth again under the sand-papering action of the gravel, like glowing lava over the quaking earth. . . .

"Stephen's hour now is. Mine may come tomorrow,—today. If I could only bear the sneers and taunts and buffets of those who condemn my Faith with the marvelous fortitude and Christ-like charity he has shown! 'Lord, lay not this sin to their charge.' The cry rings out loud and clear above the dull thud of the rock that is hurled at him by Saul, the leader. It has just grazed his head, but broken his shoulder. The echoes of memory awake at the call, and repeat another: 'Father, forgive them for they know not what they do.' A hailstorm of rocks, pieces of broken bottles and jugs, huge fragments of jagged marble riddle the poor trembling flesh of the first Christian martyr."

That should not be subjected to literary criticism, for its primary intention was not literary. Yet as Teresa has permitted herself to be carried away, it should be noticed that some of the details of her description (the bit about Saul's casting a stone that breaks Stephen's shoulder, for instance) are not quite justifiable. Even as description, if it is judged strictly as that, it is not very successful, for it states rather than describes. The words chosen, and the rhythm in which we hear them, do not heighten the mood or suggest anything beyond themselves; nor do we find here much of the genuine eloquence that Teresa sometimes displays in her conferences.

These meditations were seen by nobody except Father Benedict and Mother Alexandrine. It was different with the two long letters that Teresa wrote for Father Benedict to send the novices in his own name while he was on vacation. They occupy pages 172–188 in Sister Zita's book, in which they may be consulted by those who wish to study them in their entirety. To a great extent they took the place of conferences at a time when conferences could not be given. The tone of Teresa's voice might have been detected in them were it not for the fact that they were written in the same style as the conferences, and those were accepted as the work of Father Benedict. Nobody was made suspicious even by so "Teresian" a passage as this: "If feelings of devotion are present, well, thank God for them Who is giving us the lollypop of sweetness to coax us along and make things easier. If feelings are absent, well, thank God just the same, and do not make a fuss because the lollypop is gone and you have only the stick to chew on." Once again she escaped detection.

Also to be mentioned is the "Litany of Love," which appears as an appendix in Sister Zita's book. It stands almost alone among the things that Teresa wrote after entering the novitiate in that it was not written under Father Benedict's instructions. She sent it to him during the early fall of 1926,* saying: "I'm enclosing a conference, two meditations and a litany. It was composed—or rather burned into my soul—

*Teresa had the all too common fault of omitting the date from most of her letters, or, if the day and month are given, of omitting the year.

during an ecstatic prayer in May, 1925. I wrote it in the book I gave to Mother but I felt urged to send you a copy. Perhaps I should have done so before. I have three other meditations finished and am on the fourth, but you'll have to wait since Mother wants them too and they're done in longhand." She added: "By the way, Mother hasn't seen the first two conferences for September and you have the originals," which seems to indicate that, at least sometimes, Mother Alexandrine saw the conferences composed by Teresa before they were handed to Father Benedict.

Teresa's litany was quite short—only about thirty lines—and is addressed throughout to Christ, with a doxology in conclusion. It was used by Teresa for her private devotions, as others are free to use it; but it is not, of course, an "approved" prayer. In the Eastern Rite litanies are freely used, being a part of the Mass and also of the ceremonies for baptism and confirmation. Here, as in several other respects, the East remains more medieval than the West, for though the Latin Rite retains its litanies they are now relatively rarely used, even at Benediction something shorter being usually substituted for the Litany of Loretto.

When one comes to what were nearer to being, according to our concepts, the literary efforts produced by Teresa, one finds a short story, "Love's Hate," apparently the sole piece of that kind at which she ever tried her hand. Whether she submitted it to an editor or not I do not know, but if she did it was returned. However, in 1931 her brother sent it to *Extension Magazine,* as it was sponsoring a competition for discovering hidden talent, and it won the first prize.

This clears the ground for a consideration of her poems as gathered and edited in 1931 by Father Charles and privately printed. Some of these poems have been quoted as illustrative of biographical points, but as I felt constrained by honesty to say of them, I do not feel they have much poetic merit. They have been praised for their "technique," yet even as to that I must offer the reservation that, though most of the lines are correct enough, and here and there a fine line or two appears, her versification was usually wooden and common-place. All the best things she had to say were said in prose.

It may be argued that she might have developed had she lived longer. Yes, but not, I feel sure, along poetic lines. Her prose itself, as we have seen, was not the product of very care-ful composition. The result is that, while *Greater Perfection* was remarkable in its content, and sometimes is powerfully phrased, it sometimes uneasily alternates between the racy and the stilted in style. Her idea seems to have been to fol-low Lewis Carroll's dictum, "Take care of the sense and the sounds will take care of themselves," which is not always a safe method to follow if one is aiming at an artistic effect. One has to have an ear finely attuned to the movement and color of words to use that dictum at all, and though something of a biblical roll comes into the work of one who read the Bible so assiduously Teresa was not greatly interested in the craft of letters but only in the science of the saints.

This is very evident in her verse. Some of her lines limp painfully, and even when they are "correct" they do not often contain the music and magic that constitute poetry. I conclude that she would not have improved much, for poets almost always approach their maturity by their middle twen-ties, and Teresa had been writing verse since her high-school days. Though it is obvious that, except for a few assignments, she wrote only when she felt genuinely moved, unfortunately emotion, even genuine poetic emotion, is not enough, unless it is accompanied by the power to give it utterance. We can always see what it is she wants to say; we can also see that she was not able to say it. The meaning is plain but the incanta-tion is lacking.

What she did have, in my estimation, was a dramatic gift, had she been given an adequate chance of using it. The verse play which gives its title to *The Seventieth Week,* written in

blank verse, and the shorter play "The Leper Colony"—
partly in prose and partly in a kind of "biblical" verse—both
have power. The second of these, covering only a dozen
pages, is divided into two acts, each of which has two scenes.
It has been produced by the Jesuit scholastics at Pough-
keepsie. "The Seventieth Week" was performed by the postulants at St. Elizabeth's at Christmas, 1925, for as they were
not yet in their habits they could wear costumes and even
beards, when these were called for; and it has been staged
elsewhere, in convents and seminaries. "The Leper Colony"
has as its theme the healing of a leper by Christ, though with
both tact and skill Teresa avoids introducing Our Lord as a
character, or even very definitely alluding to Him. The characters are all invented but are more than pasteboard.

"The Seventieth Week" is also short, though rather longer
than the other play by Teresa. Its title is explained by a reference to Daniel 9: 24–25, and by the lines:

Know thou, therefore, and take notice; that from the going
forth of the word, to build up Jerusalem again, unto Christ the
prince, there shall be seven weeks and sixty-two weeks; and the
streets shall be built again, and the walls in straitness of times.

Similar biblical references are given throughout, but were
not of course actually spoken when the postulants produced
the play. Even the Martyrology, when drawn upon, is exactly cited, but such scrupulous accuracy hampers the play
itself. (Incidentally, this shows that Teresa had the scholarly
temperament, though her poor eyesight would have been a
barrier to her attaining all that scholarship demands.) The
scene of the cave at Bethlehem is shown in tableau, with no
word spoken; and when the Holy Family appear again, again
it is in tableau, as is true of the appearance of the Magi, when
they arrive with their gifts, and of the angels who stand
around. After all, their song, "Glory to God in the highest!"
was on Christmas night, not the Epiphany. Though the play
has faults—for who but a supremely great dramatist could do

justice to this theme?—it is moving to read and was, one would imagine, effective, even when presented by postulants.

The most impressive of the poems is the one on Mother Xavier, the Foundress of the New Jersey Sisters of Charity, and this was recited at her centenary celebration in 1925. It is about eighty lines long, and is in hexameters, a measure well-nigh impossible to use in English. A more consummate Latinist than Teresa would have been aware of this and have avoided it, but perhaps she was beguiled by the fact that Longfellow ventured upon this form of verse in his *Evangeline,* freely and very skilfully adapting it to his purposes. It is in this measure that Teresa, blithely sailing in, salutes Mother Xavier:

The light that illumines the mind unto brightness majestic,
The meat that envigors the spirit to conquest continued,
The fire that consumes the soul with vehement yearnings,
These are the riches inlaid upon which thou hast builded
The towering house of thy works, whether seen or invisible,
This was thy crown and thy cross, thy reward and thy anguish.

With the poem that might be regarded as Teresa's next best, her class ode of 1923, I have dealt in an earlier chapter. Some consider it the best of all, and in this they may be right. But in any case it obviously derives much from Oliver Wendell Holmes and Lowell.

The purely personal poems—such as those addressed to her mother and her brother Charles and her friend Elizabeth Szabo—I have mentioned elsewhere and so need say no more about them here. But one more remains to touch on, a poem written on February 27, 1925, that is, just two weeks after she had entered the novitiate as a postulant. Taken literally, it would mean that Teresa had, instead of the stigmata, the actual marks of Christ's crown of thorns on her own brow. About whether this was actually so or not I shall have something to say later, but at least she meant that figuratively she

felt that her head wore that crown, which would explain why
when she allowed a fellow novice, Sister Catherine Patricia,
to read the notebook in which she had copied out her poems,
she gave her the strict injunction, "Don't read the last poem."
This novice must have had an iron self-control to resist her
curiosity, but she was older than most of those in Nazareth
and had entered there after having filled an executive position in the world.

Our Teresa has often been compared to the Little Flower,
and a point of similarity has been found in the fact that both
of them wrote verses. But that, of course, means nothing. If
we must compare them in this particular, it should be said
that Thérèse's poetry, though nothing very wonderful, with
its patterns patently derived from Chateaubriand, was more
"accomplished" than Teresa's. On the other hand, I should be
inclined to say that Teresa put more of herself into her verses
than Thérèse did, rough in texture and commonplace in sentiment though many of her poems are. I am aware after a
careful study of the Little Flower's letters—only recently
published as a whole—that she was not quite so simple and
uncomplicated a soul as she is generally supposed to be. But
she was simplicity itself when compared with our troubled,
aloof, and (dare I say?) rather "difficult" Teresa. The Carmelite's message to the world was that of what she called her
Little Way—a stony way full of brambles, as will be discovered by anyone who tries it. The novice of the Sisters of
Charity also had a message: that there was no incompatibility
between the active and the contemplative life; but what she
offered was the system of classical asceticism, moderate, it is
true, so far as physical austerities are concerned, but as she
exemplified it, about as drastic a system as can be imagined.
The curious fact is that the young Carmelite nun experienced
few of the concomitants of mysticism, whereas her American counterpart (if she *is* a counterpart) had a life filled with
such marvels. In the case of neither young poet does this come

out in the poetry they wrote—possibly because, with each, verse was a mere side-line, hardly more than an occasional diversion. Their real significance must be looked for elsewhere.

This is not intended to be a cavalier dismissal of the versifying of either Teresa or Thérèse. With both of them the writing of verse, with the intellectual discipline entailed, undoubtedly was an excellent training for the writing of prose, as has been found by many good prose writers who began as poets. Such time is never wasted; to want to be a poet, to try to be a poet is always good. In our Teresa's case, while the immediate results of her poetry did not, from the strictly literary point of view, result in much, her efforts in this direction unquestionably helped her to a command of expression, as they also provide us with biographical material for which we may be grateful.

CHAPTER SEVENTEEN

✐

Deepening Spiritual Life

I WRITE the title for this chapter with some misgivings, for of course the only person competent to speak was Father Benedict, but it is evident from the statements he made about Teresa that she had long enjoyed union with God. However, as such a union must be progressive, unless it is to wither away, we may safely conclude that it became more and more complete, even when we are unable to trace her spiritual growth.

Father Benedict has this astonishing thing to relate of Teresa: "Among the most remarkable of the passive unions of which some of God's saints have had experience is the Vision of the Trinity. According to her own admission, Sister Miriam Teresa had enjoyed this privilege. The purpose and fruit of this grace are a marvellous strengthening of the faith. The intellect is illuminated and the will is strengthened by the light received in this vision of the greatest of all mysteries and the soul is established in God." What Teresa herself related about it (if this is what she is referring to) is this: "It is remarkable [that] although I seem for the most part insensible of His presence, yet penetrated with it always, and that He holds from me the embraces of His love, still, when others are in want, He supplies their deficiencies through me in an extraordinary manner. Since I must be about my Father's business, it suffices—and what a wonderful mercy of His!—that my will is securely established in Him."

Regarding this point, it might be best to go to one of the great writers on mysticism. Teresa of Ávila says in *The Interior Castle*: "By some mysterious manifestation of the truth, the three persons of the Blessed Trinity reveal themselves, preceded by an illumination which shines on the spirit like a most dazzling cloud of light. The Three Persons are distinct from one another; a sublime knowledge is infused into the soul, imbuing it with a certainty that the Three are of one substance, power and knowledge, and are one God. Thus that which we hold as a doctrine of faith, the soul now, so to speak, understands by sight, though it beholds the Blessed Trinity neither by the eyes of the body nor of the soul, this being no imaginary vision." Put in other words, what had formerly been of faith now has almost the force of an axiom and, as our Teresa's great namesake expresses it, *"so to speak,"* understands as though the mystery had been unveiled, as indeed is the case, even if the manner of this is beyond our comprehension. It was at this time, as Teresa told her spiritual director, that her great devotion to the Trinity began, and especially to God the Father.

It must be noted that Teresa, while attaining to the grace of union, affirms most positively that this is possible to all Christian souls. She writes: "Union with God is the spiritual height God calls everyone to achieve—'anyone,' not only religious, but 'any one' who chooses, who wills to seek this pearl of great price, who specializes in the traffic of eternal goods, who says 'yes' constantly to God the Holy Ghost. Witness Catherine of Siena, the ecstatic household drudge*; and

---

*Not quite accurate of Catherine, except for a brief period in her early life, when her family were trying to knock what they considered sense into her head. Later she did occasionally undertake the washing in her parents' large household, but this was entirely voluntary. For the most part she lived as free as the air.

Joan of Arc, the unlettered soldier-heroine, the saviour of her
people; Elizabeth of Hungary, the contemplative of the royal
court; and countless others—beggars and peasants, and mer-
chants and princes. If those out in the world have attained
this exalted degree of friendship with God, with what greater
reason does He not expect the same of us who are especially
consecrated for this one end, and no matter what the external
form our service may be." Over and over again she declares
that her graces are given her for the benefit of others and that
similar graces are within the reach of those who seek them. At
the same time she told Sister Marie Dolores, who kept careful
notes about her conversations with Teresa, "We must be satisfied with what Our Lord gives and desire no other degree of
perfection than what He intends we should reach." This, however, is by no means inconsistent with her insistence upon the
universal availability of grace. "Ask and you shall receive;
knock and it shall be opened unto you," must always be understood as referring primarily to spiritual goods, though it by
no means need deter us from asking also for our material
needs. These, however, will not always be met in the form we
expect, for we do not really know what those needs are, and
often ask for things that are unnecessary and even foolish.

    Several times in these pages a protest has been made against
making too much of accidental resemblances as existed between Teresa and Thérèse of Lisieux. Yet unlike as they were,
they were friends in a very real fashion. Sister Marie Dolores
tells of how one evening, just before six, Teresa came to her
room and, taking up the picture of the Little Flower from her
table, kissed it many times. This surprised Sister Marie
Dolores, for she knew how reserved Teresa was. The only explanation she received—for a moment or two later the supper
bell rang—was that Teresa was late because Sister Mary Ellen
had told her to go for a walk in the "park," as she had missed
the walk with the other novices. To this Sister Marie Dolores

had just time to ask, "In the dark?" (It was winter). "Why didn't you ask me to go with you?"

No answer came just then, but later Teresa explained that, as she had been afraid to go out alone in the dark, she had asked the Little Flower to be her companion. And precisely that had happened. After Teresa's death Father Benedict spoke of the same incident in one of his conferences, showing that she had told him about it. But while taking a keen natural pleasure in such an occurrence, she would have been the last person to give it undue supernatural importance. Even manifestations of a much higher order she valued not so much for themselves as for the grace that went with them. Rather, as she explained in a letter to her spiritual director: "My comfort is to be without comfort; my consolation, without consolation; my delight, without delight. After all, it is He who is suffering for me and in me and with me."

Perhaps this will serve to account for Teresa's saying, "It has been my experience all my life to derive more consolation from the Sacrament of Penance than from Communion," which she follows with the somewhat enigmatic comment, "but then, the confessions have cost so much—and the Communions even more."

In another note—this bears the date of March 6, 1926— Father Benedict records: "Some months ago she asked permission to pray that God would take from her spiritual life all the comforts and consolations with which He was accustomed for years to visit her, with the result that she did suffer great desolation and even temptations against the Faith." Yet he says that it was at this time that Teresa told him that "the metal crucifix she wears over her breast is so hot that it seems on fire. The crystal of the little watch she wears is at such times covered with drops of water, caused by the heat that pours from her heart. The watch under these conditions often stops, but when she finds it necessary to know the time, it points exactly at the right place." This sounds contradictory, but perhaps is so only to people less spiritual than Teresa. One would gather that it is perfectly possible to be without spiritual consolations and yet to have an intense unconscious fervor. It would be rash and presumptuous for anyone like me to say more.

Our knowledge about the graces Teresa received must be derived from her letters to Father Benedict and the statements he made after her death. There were, of course, things which he was not free to divulge; but the mere observance of her private vows—many of which one would think it virtually impossible to perform, but which we know, from Father Benedict's testimony she performed perfectly—would have immensely advanced her in grace, and this grace steadily increased.

All these vows helped to sustain her, but perhaps none more than that of perfect abandonment to the will of God. Yet this did not save Teresa from fears—mostly it would seem panic fears—that she would be asked to leave, in spite of which she never deviated from her confidence that she was fulfilling a mission entrusted to her. She was human, and therefore she often shed tears; but the definition of bravery is not the absence of fear, but steadfastness in spite of fear. Real courage is dour and not brilliant.

One of her rewards is indicated in a letter she wrote to Father Benedict on July 6, 1926. "Sometimes," she says, "not often, during my reading, my memory is completely, or nearly so, absorbed in Him, for I read without remembering what I have read (but most of the things come back when needed); and the understanding the same way, for I can read without understanding, yet understand everything." This strikes me as an extremely interesting passage, but I think it calls for an interpretation from a better psychologist than I can pretend to be.

Let it be stressed again that Teresa, in common with almost all mystics, deprecated the seeking of what are generally considered the manifestations of mysticism. St. Philip Neri, one of the most extraordinary of ecstatics—a man who had to bring himself down to earth by reading a joke book before he could say Mass—severely reproved those who set too much store on the incidental phenomena of mysticism. So Teresa in one of her conferences wrote: "A word of warning. Don't confuse revelations and locutions and ecstasies and the gift of tears with the essential part of perfection. All these things mentioned are accidental to the state of perfection; that is, they are not necessary." So far as I am aware none of the other Sisters had her experiences, but there was always the possibility that if they looked for them they might bring them on by a process of autosuggestion. It is to be feared that some of the cases of the stigmata have been due not so much to holiness as to hysteria, and some have no doubt been fraudulent. This is why the Church is most cautious in such matters. It speaks much for Teresa's honesty that she uttered frequent warnings.

One of her brother Charles's names for her was "Impetuosity," a side of her which still remained under her restrained external demeanor. While at college she had offered God the gift of her sight for her brother John that he might have spiritual sight. After being discharged from the army in 1918, he had been more or less of an invalid. Perhaps army life had a bad effect on him spiritually, also. He had not exactly lost his faith, but like so many people he made no great effort to practice his religion. In May, 1923, the day after his brother's first Mass, John made his peace with God and remained a practicing Catholic until his death from tuberculosis at Saranac Lake in 1932. When Teresa asked Father Benedict for permission to make the sacrifice of her eyesight "in favor of one who needs sight more than I do"—meaning spiritual sight —he absolutely forbade Teresa's doing anything of the kind. I do not know for whom she wanted to make the sacrifice this time. Perhaps she was thinking of her brother's final perseverance. I confess that I find it hard to believe that God has to be propitiated in such a way, but at least it shows how generous—how extravagantly generous—Teresa could be. Also, it shows a lack of judgment: if she went blind she would have been of no further use to the community, or of so little use that she would almost certainly have been dismissed—to be a burden on her sister Mary. "Impetuosity" is surely the right word.

Teresa's visions, whether physical or intellectual, have been noted. Father Benedict tells us that her association with her guardian angel "seems to have been most intimate." But he also mentions satanic apparitions; and about these something must be said.

In the first place, though Satan can appear as an angel of light, or even as Christ Himself, he may delude God's children, but he has absolutely no power over their will's basic freedom. Personally I long ago made up my mind that if the devil should ever appear to me (which I do not expect to happen) I would go straight up to him and without the slightest hesitation tweak his nose. But he did appear to Teresa several times, always under the image of Christ. Once he told her that she was a big fraud, and she almost believed him; at another time he tempted her to pride, saying that she would one day be canonized; at still another that she would be ranked among the great theologians of the Church.* But he failed in all his assaults; these were only passing incidents in her life which did not affect the imperturbable calm of her soul.

Some of the saints have been subjected to diabolical apparitions, as well as many people who will never be canonized. To this class belonged that humble disciple of St. Philip Neri, Tomaso, the Sicilian floor-sweeper of St. Peter's. When one night the devil appeared to him in the form of a Negro,

---

*One would think that the devil would be more clever than to make such a suggestion. But perhaps his intellectual powers have been diminished by sin.

Tomaso went straight up to him with his fist clenched for a blow, whereupon the devil vanished. St. Philip himself, in his youth, put three devils to flight by deriding them, finding it true, as St. Thomas More said, that what the proud spirit can least endure is to be mocked. Don Bosco, who on one occasion had the devil try to frighten him, dealt with him by making the sign of the cross, and the Curé of Ars patiently, and rather humorously, put up with the devil—the *grappin* as he called him—never once seeing him but often being dragged out of bed and still more often hearing the high thin voice crying, "Vianney, potato-eater, we're going to get you!" Compared with these, Teresa did not suffer much, though the apparition under the form of Christ is the most dangerous of all.

In all matters relating to visions and locutions it is very easy to be deceived. There are fraudulent visionaries, and there are also those who, though in good faith, are led astray by their own imaginations. Therefore it is good to have Father Benedict's unequivocal assurance: "The lights she received in her mystical experience appear so unerring since childhood that, as far as I can judge, she had never once been subject to an illusion." He adds: "It is only after entering the novitiate that she became aware of the many dangers she had escaped, and she was deeply grateful to Our Lord for His mercy." Father Benedict means that, as until then she had had no spiritual direction, she naturally would not have been able to distinguish between what was physical, intellectual, or imaginative.* But she escaped safely, and Father Benedict pronounces: "I believe that the light Sister received from the vision . . . of the Holy Trinity—which I think is genuine—shines forth in many places in the conferences." Father Bene-

---

*The word that he and Teresa herself used was "imaginary." It can bear the meaning of imaginative, but it seems to me an unfortunate usage, for it suggests to most people something unreal. If I have used it, this is only because I found it in the documents supplied me.

dict was, after all, the only person competent to pass an opinion.

There was a secondary part of Teresa's mission which should be considered, though it manifested itself in a form that not everybody will think attractive; it was the guidance she gave to others, whether by means of conversation or letters, regarding the spiritual life. What must be remembered, however, is that she was acting under Father Benedict's orders, and that she had made a private vow of obedience to him. If she found the writing of the conferences much to her distaste, it may be presumed that these minor obligations were also distasteful.

Her private letters were pitched in a lower key. Thus to Margaret Conklin she wrote encouragingly when she was encountering some opposition because of the bigotry prevalent in her community; but it is a little amusing to find Teresa, who was not a very successful teacher, telling her friend, "You have probably hit the hardest stumbling block of the first year's teaching—discouragement." She sensibly advises her not to undervalue her gifts because they have not been as yet recognized: "True humility," she says, "is not blind to its talents and powers; it must, if it be real, recognise its possibilities—but—and this is the essence—it ascribes the power and the action and the result to the actual doer and amplifier—God. And you must have confidence in yourself, which, you know, is not synonymous with self-esteem, if you are to succeed." Excellent advice, and certainly not showing a particle of presumption.

There was an unnamed novice whom Teresa was asked to help by Father Benedict, but this—rather strangely—she seems to have done mainly by notes, possibly because their duties did not often permit a personal meeting. One finds Teresa in one of these notes advising her to drink milk instead of tea, but what of course is more important is that Teresa tried to pull her out of the scrupulosity into which she was in danger

of falling. Yet Teresa was at times rather short with her, as appears in the note: "I can't see you at 5.30. Impossible. I'm sorry. Use your will power and stop the moaning. Tell Our Lord everything for the present." I am afraid the poor girl was pushed deeper into the dumps after that; it is evident that Teresa could be very brusque. In a longer note she tells this novice: "I know I added to your pain yesterday. It was very necessary. You've got to beat the devil at his own game and you must do as you're told. You have been doing faithfully— but when you're told a thing is *not* your fault . . . you *must not* go on repeating, even if it be vaguely, that you don't know whether it is or not." Here it seems to me that Father Benedict acted ill-advisedly—for he was in effect making Teresa, so far as this girl was concerned, a kind of deputy spiritual director—but Teresa's curtness may be taken as measuring the vast distaste with which she looked upon the assignment.

Then there was an academy student whom it is not necessary to identify except with the name of Marie. As such she would have had nothing to do with Father Benedict, but it may be that Sister Marie Dolores or Teresa herself consulted him about the case. She was what is called a problem child and did not get along very well with her parents, whose neglect of her (or what she believed to be that) had been replaced by the almost excessive attention she had been receiving at St. Elizabeth's, perhaps because she had joined the Catholic Church while there. One of the Sisters who had her in charge apparently had talked so much about the manifestations that sometimes go with mysticism—raptures, heavenly voices, visions, and so forth—that the poor child began to imagine that she was experiencing these things herself.

Teresa had to try to knock all this out of Marie's head—no very easy task, for the girl was woefully lacking in humility, or, as Teresa put it, had a "cocksureness as to her absolute certainty with regard to her interior." She further reported, "The child has quite a high idea of her own goodness."

Adolescent conceit almost always wears off, but Teresa, as the youngest of her family, did not know that, so she took Marie seriously. I do not know enough about the case to say that her judgment was faulty, but obviously she was exhibiting charity, even if this was penetrated (which is all right, so far as I am concerned) with a certain acidity.

A case of a very different sort was that of Alice Pratt, whom Teresa had known in the Sodality of the Blessed Virgin at St. Vincent's Church at Bayonne and who now entered religion under the name of Sister Marie de Lourdes. That she joined the Benedictine order made me surmise that Father Benedict had something to do with the matter, but she assures me that this was not the case and that she never met him. It was therefore only as a friend that Teresa gave her some advice, knowing that the novitiate might be somewhat strange to Alice. She wrote to her friend congratulating her, and it is perhaps worth noting that the first of her letters (dated June 27, 1926) was addressed to "My dear Alice" but that afterwards, when Alice had received the habit, she became "My dear Sister," such being Teresa's punctilious formality.

In the first letter Teresa says: "May I suggest a thought? It is this: be the real thing. A religious by halves mocks God and is an abomination in His sight. To be a religious, not a religious habit, requires hard labor, persevering labor, long-suffering labor *on ourselves*—the inside. Take care of the interior and the exterior must inevitably fall into line. Being clothed with the habit means that we must *aim* at sanctity because we have contracted an engagement with Sanctity Itself." The whole of the letter is an exposition of the old saw (found even in Shakespeare) that the cowl does not make the monk.

In her second letter Teresa points out "something of a coincidence. You became a daughter of St. Benedict on the Feast of St. Vincent de Paul; I entered on the Feast of Our

Lady of Lourdes . . . to become a daughter of St. Vincent.*
And we both received the habit alone. It seems that Our Lady
and St. Vincent have a special interest in two somebodies we
both know. . . . Mary is always our model. Her vow of
chastity was prompted by a humility which, if we cannot begin to fathom, we can and must begin to imitate." The same
idea is expounded in a wonderful sermon by the greatest of
St. Benedict's sons, the Cistercian St. Bernard. In it, while
hymning her virginity, he points out that virginity (good
though it is) is not necessary to salvation, whereas none but
the humble of heart may enter the kingdom of God. Though
it is almost certain that Teresa never read this passage, St.
Bernard's thought came to her by her own reflections, which
is the better way.

Probably the most remarkable instance of Teresa's influence appears in her relations with Sister Marie Dolores, a
woman who must have been at least twenty years older than
herself and who had been Teresa's professor of Spanish in
college. Now the teacher became the disciple, and it speaks
volumes for Sister Marie Dolores's humility that she grate-
fully accepted this, as it also proves the obedience with which
the otherwise complicated Teresa fell in with so strange an
arrangement. To this Sister, at Father Benedict's bidding,
Teresa went once a week, much to the mystification and the
understandable annoyance of Sister Mary Ellen.

In this, too, Father Benedict accepted a considerable risk—
that of getting Teresa puffed up. For she naturally supposed
when she started that she was intended to benefit from her
former teacher's experience in religion. Sister Marie Dolores
exclaimed to Father Benedict after the first meeting: "Father,
did you mean me to help her? Why, I cannot hold a candle to
her—*she* helps *me*." Possibly Father Benedict hoped they

*The dates of these two feasts might be noted here; the one is on
February 11th and the other on July 19th.

would help each other; if so, he soon discovered that the untaught Teresa was to be the teacher.

Of these conversations Sister Marie Dolores kept a rather detailed record, as it soon dawned on her that she might become a sort of witness to Teresa's sanctity, as she expressed it in a manuscript she has given me for my use. In an article she contributed to the *Sister Miriam Teresa League of Prayer Bulletin,* she transcribed several of these conversations. One quotation must suffice:

"In speaking to me of the indwelling of the Holy Trinity, Sister Miriam Teresa asked me one day, 'Where is God within you?' and I pointed to my heart.

" 'No,' she said, 'He is not there.' As I looked at her in great surprise, she continued, 'The heart is the seat of the affections, of the feelings, the lower part of the soul. The three faculties, memory, understanding and will are in the upper part of the soul. Point to where they are.'

"I placed my hand on my head. 'That's right,' she said approvingly, 'in the centre of the soul the Blessed Trinity resides. Every soul in the state of grace has God within her, but unfortunately we never give a thought to that presence.' "

This, of course, was pedagogical simplification, and may be misleading. It goes without saying that both sisters understood that the soul informs the entire body. In speaking as she did, Teresa merely wanted to emphasise the intellectual nature of God's presence, as against the too common idea which attributes so much to the feelings.

The conversations were a good deal more than formal instructions. And it must be remembered that the one doing the teaching had been Sister Marie Dolores's student at college; yet here she was sent to direct her in the spiritual life. These talks, like the writing of her conferences, were undertaken only under orders from her spiritual director. Sister Marie Dolores therefore knew more than anybody except Father Benedict himself about her relations with God, though even she probably could no more than surmise the apostolic intensity that was expressed in the prayer: "I'll never be satisfied, never, because my desire is infinite. That is why You, Father, God my own, thirst and thirst and thirst for love—the love of souls that bear Your image. Only when the whole is one in You will I rest and be satiated. . . . My whole soul would spend itself in giving testimony to the Word that dwells within it, that *is* itself, *God*."

CHAPTER EIGHTEEN

Signals for Departure

It would be to cut that rather fatuous figure—one who is wise after the event—to say that by now Teresa had accomplished her work and had nothing further to live for; but that others thought so too is evident from several sources, in particular a letter written in 1929, soon after the publication of *Greater Perfection*. "In different novitiates," so one appreciative reader said, "the book is already being made the subject of the study of the spiritual life. Our Lord had given her the great privilege of continuing her mission after her death. She is more active today than she was during life. Personally I have always believed that her death was opportune. She might have written more, but otherwise I think her usefulness was at an end." Other conferences might, in fact, have been produced, but Father Benedict, as he was soon to retire from his position, would not have been able to read them, and his successor might have disapproved. Moreover, one could not expect this kind of a secret to be kept indefinitely, so had Teresa continued to write it would no doubt have been books of a somewhat different type.

All this, however, is beside the point: she had worked hard and had been suffering so intensely that she was gradually being worn down and was approaching the breaking point. In one of her letters she tells Father Benedict: "For the past two days especially—no it's more, maybe three or four or five—I've felt a terrifically powerful urge to work and work and work. The point is that I felt a violent need to finish up everything without delay. I haven't experienced this feeling for about nineteen months (even when I was teaching, and writing, and producing the Christmas play). . . . The thing to be noticed is that twice, once yesterday and once today, I've had to hold myself in good check to keep from being impatient because an unexpected delay prevented me from doing what I had intended at the time I had planned. And I've been realizing, too, since my last letter, that I've been wounding Our Lord by a lack of confidence which quite frequently manifested itself in mental anxiety over trifles." But perhaps Father Benedict set this down merely to the fact that she had been working under pressure; it should not have meant too much in the case of a woman of twenty-six who had hitherto always enjoyed good health.

What might have been more disturbing is the constant references Teresa was now making to her great weariness—at least in her letters to Father Benedict, for she knew that Sister Mary Ellen would only have been impatient with this and set it down as imaginary. Even Father Benedict probably did not quite understand, as he was such a vigorous man himself.

Yet the letter Teresa wrote to him on July 6, 1926, should have been a warning: "In proportion as God withholds the consolation of prayer, my physical strength decreases until what with the heat, and the weariness, and the sleepiness, and the mosquitoes, and the incessant strain of doing what I naturally don't want to do, I wonder that I can take another step or even keep standing upright. I know that at times only a very slight push would be sufficient to topple me over. And how anybody can sleep as soundly as I do, and yet awaken feeling as though he had been pounded all night, and hardly able to keep his eyes open, being almost too tired to dress, is as much a natural enigma as my falling asleep at my bedside years ago in the cold nights and getting up without feeling a bit cramped or shivering, with a zest for work which could have cleaned up the world if needed."

That was written, it should be observed, during the summer, when Teresa's tasks were lightened because she was freed from her distasteful work in the academy. Yet it was at this time, when she ought to have been able to get some rest, that she speaks of being always exhausted. Three weeks later she writes in the same strain, and a few days later again tells Father Benedict: "During morning prayers and meditation and Mass I can scarcely keep awake, and I'm so tired that I can hardly kneel upright. The sleepiness wears off after Mass (the devil has a hand in it) but the weariness persists." Even at meals—she says she knows this sounds silly—but even at meals she almost falls asleep in the act of eating.

By August she felt somewhat better—so the rest of the summer had done some good—and on the 25th of that month she tells Father Benedict, "I am not nearly so tired out as formerly, though the sleepiness persists." She attributes this to a vacation from the practice of mortification he had ordered. But she adds that "the relaxation means that I have to fight harder to get down to work—the fiddle string is loosened. It seems almost as if the will had lost what the body has gained." Three days later she tells him: "I have a physical pain in my heart—not severe, dull and not continuous—perhaps three or four times a day. The first time I experienced any trouble with it was the day my father died. The pain then was quite sharp and lasted several hours. Also of late when very tired, and especially during the rainy season just passed, I have found breathing rather difficult—as though a heavy weight were compressing my chest. No pain, however. I'm fine on the whole."

It would be foolish for me to make any diagnosis except

to say that it is evident from these letters that Teresa was not at all well. And probably Father Benedict would have suggested to Mother Alexandrine that she send Teresa to a doctor were it not that she spoke of her health as being better than it had been in July. If he did speak, Mother Alexandrine would no doubt have consulted Sister Mary Ellen, and she no doubt would have suggested that there was nothing the matter except that her novice was a bit run down but that as there was still another month before the academy reopened the time would suffice to set everything to rights.

But Father Benedict remained uneasy. For he believed that Teresa was not mistaken in the intimation she had received about her early death, and not being able to take her vows with the others. However, he may have detected the streak of melancholy that underlay her usual cheerfulness, and of course he did not take this intimation as an article of faith.

Looking back upon the situation, he somewhat changed his opinion. In fact, after Teresa's death he told Sister Zita that he did not see how she could last. It was then that he said, "Appendicitis may have been the occasion of her death but not the cause; she could not live long, so consumed was she by the love of God." Teresa, Sister Zita is sure, did not expect death; what she had in mind when she said she would not take the vows with the other novices was that she would be asked to leave. It was, in my opinion, the constant preying of this fear upon her mind that was at the bottom of her illness, which otherwise seems to have been very mysterious. It is hard to see how the love of God could cause death; rather it should induce serenity and security.

Now we come to her two hardly separated illnesses, neither of which was in itself a serious matter, but which were more serious than anybody imagined because of the general debility which made her unable to withstand more than a very little. Early in December, after a stay in the Sisters' infirmary, a quinsy sore throat called for Teresa's removal to the Sisters' hospital at Paterson. As this was only an inflammation of the tonsils, which a single snip can remove, it cannot be considered more than a very minor operation.

Even so, the operation was not performed at once, the doctors no doubt hoping that treatment would suffice. On the 23rd of the month we find Teresa writing to Father Benedict, telling him that she had been in St. Joseph's Hospital for two weeks and that she is now sitting up in bed for the first time since her tonsils were removed. She gives him a full account of herself, saying that the quinsy sore throat "hurt much less than the abscesses I had a month ago, which in turn were not so painful as the one I had had previously." The most disturbing part of the letter reads: "Really my heaviest physical cross has been to force myself around and work when I have wanted to drop dozens of times daily. I've been going on my will power alone (not mine, either, it would never have supported me) for many, many months. My one ambition from the day I got the habit has been to go to bed and sleep for a week without getting up. And here when I've had the opportunity I haven't been able to do it. But now that my nerves are more quiet I guess it won't be quite so necessary. But the physical pain is most acute."

Earlier in the letter she mentions the soreness in her throat and the back of her neck—which are, of course, only to be expected after a tonsillectomy—but she also says, more significantly: "From my waist down I guess I'm made of paper. But that's not to be wondered at considering the past few days. This morning I was actually a little hungry. My nerves are a good deal steadier and my eyes don't jig as much as they did last week." She could report some improvement, though she knew she had been very sick, and told Father Benedict, "It was almost a requiem instead of Christmas carols." It is evident from her wry jest that she quite expected to get well. (The fact that the hospital report shows that she had turned cyanotic during the operation seems to indicate a weak heart.)

What did distress her was what she took to be lack of sympathy from the doctors and nurses, who found it hard to believe that a case of tonsillitis was to be taken very seriously. Teresa once heard a nurse in the hall say, "There is nothing wrong with that little Sister except her imagination." And the doctor asked her (she considered gruffly), "Where'd you get that squeaky little voice?" As for Sister Mary Ellen, who was constitutionally almost incapable of believing that any of her novices were ever ill, she never visited Teresa, either during this stay in the hospital or the next (from which she was carried out dead), and even expressed her "disgust" with the whole situation. She was by no means an unkind woman, but she failed to understand, yet was given to expressing in an unnecessarily forthright way the opinions she happened to hold.

One of the strange features of Teresa's case was that when her temperature was taken, as recorded on the hospital charts I have before me, it was normal or not much above. Yet we are told that she often knew that she had a high fever. The only suggestion that I can offer is that this must be similar to the supernormal manifestation of heat that some of her friends noticed in her college days after she returned to her place after receiving Holy Communion. Sister Marie Dolores and Agatha Spinella now testify to this condition prevailing in the hospital. If it was not, strictly speaking, physical, it would not register on the thermometer. St. Philip Neri exhibited the same phenomenon, and used to walk about in wintry weather with his cloak thrown over his shoulder and laughing at his younger companions who were shivering in the cold. It is abundantly clear that his was not a "pathological" condition, but what it was it would be hard, if not impossible, to say.

The tonsillectomy was on December 20th, and eleven days

later, which should have been ample time for recuperation, Teresa returned to Convent. But she was so far from being recovered that she had to cling to the walls to support herself, and had to be helped up the stairs to the dormitory. Yet we find her going to Mass the next morning, after having participated in the community prayers the day before, and even making private visits to the Blessed Sacrament. But it was all so much of an effort that she wrote to Father Benedict: "I have been crying a good deal today, and I don't know that I'm through yet. . . . The tears are a weakness I know; and yet they are a mercy and a relief, otherwise something inside of me must have snapped." She began this letter on January 18th but did not mail it until the 24th, when she added: "Father, I don't know what's happening, but it's happening fast. Yesterday the Principal [of the academy] asked me for an outline for all my English work for the second semester, having obtained one of the former graduates to take my place, and I was fully expecting to be told to go right on duty, because Saturday Mother asked me if I didn't think I could take the English. And since I felt it to be her desire, and since the Mistress had said a week previously that if I had the right spirit and a good will I would go and offer to take the class—I said 'Yes.' " From which it would seem that Sister Mary Ellen considered that Teresa's convalescence had lasted long enough, and that Mother Alexandrine had agreed with her until, after she had seen Teresa, she recognized that she was in no condition to go back to the classroom.

Teresa's nervous condition was much worse than most people imagined. Thus the outbursts, "Oh, how I hate, hate everything!" and "I feel like tearing anything and everybody to pieces," are all too evident an indication of her nervous condition, and as such should be considered very excusable. She continued: "Most of all I hate this continual watchfulness over myself that doesn't give me a moment's breathing space. But fidelity is the price of the souls I must bring forth, and everything has to be paid for in advance. If you wonder at the sublimity of some of the things God has inspired me to write, try to fathom the depths of the corresponding anguish which, if I dare to say it, forced God's hand. So long as I am suffering, I know there is nothing to fear. I must labor in travail of spirit for the life of my spiritual children. He gives me the grace to sing *Te Deum laudate et superexaltate eum in saecula.*"

In that passage she had recovered her calm. Yet she confesses to Father Benedict that while she had been talking to Mother Alexandrine she had been crying—not, she explains, because of the work she had very inconsiderately been asked to do at the academy but because she had been "very rude to the Principal." She adds, "I apologized, but Father, honestly I'd rather take a thousand digs than give one unmeaningly." She even suggests that he give her a "good penance" for this. But that she had much to put up with appears from what she relates: "I heard almost incessantly in one form or another, 'Don't give in to yourself!' " Sister Mary Ellen had told her: "Stop that nonsense and behave yourself. Don't be forever giving in to yourself." Even Mother Alexandrine had said, "Pull yourself together." Teresa can only exclaim pitifully, "But, Father, for a long time there has been nothing to pull." Perhaps even more pitifully she says that when she saw Mother Alexandrine, she was asked, "Don't you intend to teach?" About which Teresa comments, *Intend?* I did not know that I was supposed to have any intentions. I know I left mine outside the convent gate before I came in. I'm here to do what I'm told. . . . I have an idea that she also thinks I don't want to get better." Yet on top of all these admissions she can say: "I am feeling much better and getting to be myself. I don't get tired out nearly as soon as I did when I first came home." She has forgotten for how many months she has been speaking of her utter exhaustion. She was trying to pull herself together; she was even engaged in the futile performance of trying to pull herself up by the boot-straps.

The word had gone around (and can we wonder?) that "It was only tonsillitis," and that she had been discharged from the hospital after a period a good deal longer than tonsillitis requires. It was New Year's Eve when she returned to the novitiate. What else was the matter with her was not guessed, except by her brother Charles (who always believed that she was going to die) and by Father Benedict, who had some inkling of this. Now, if Teresa "forced" God's hand, as she put it, her sister Anne forced Mother Alexandrine's. It seems that Father Benedict called Father Charles and asked him if he knew that his sister was really ill. "Why, no," he said, "I thought she was better when they brought her home from the hospital." "She is worse than ever," was Father's reply. It was then that Father Charles got in touch with his sister Anne, who was now a nurse at St. Elizabeth's Hospital in Elizabeth. Anne went to see Teresa, interviewed Mother Alexandrine, and more or less insisted that her sister must be sent to the hospital, where she could keep an eye on her. Mother agreed, and the following day two Sisters took Teresa to St. Elizabeth's Hospital.

Sister Zita relates how Teresa came, rather unexpectedly, to say goodbye in the novitiate classroom where she was preparing for her classes in the academy. She asked at the same time, "I've come to get that book I lent you, if you have finished with it—and also to say good-bye." It was Kramp's *Liturgical Sacrifice*. She explained that she was going back to the hospital that day, in saying which she seemed rather depressed.

"Do you really *have* to go?" her friend asked.

"Yes; I know there's something very wrong with me, but I don't know what it is."

Sister Zita now said, "Of course I know you only want what God wants."

At this Teresa smiled through her tears as she said, "Yes, of course that is all I want." Then she "swept her friend off her feet" with a good-bye embrace and kiss, saying: "When you return to the novitiate at noon after class, I'll be gone. Pray for me."

This happened, so I read in the hospital chart, on January 24, 1927. At first nothing was done except to keep her under observation, but the diagnosis read, "Physical and nervous exhaustion with myocarditis and acute appendicitis," but the chief symptoms were put down as "Exhaustion, shortness of breath on exertion, palpitation and precardial pain." This, however, was the case as surveyed in its whole history, after Teresa's death, for the daily report at first was not particularly alarming, indicating improvement rather than otherwise, though with some variations. Not until March 26th was it thought that an appendectomy might be necessary. But that passed off, and things went on much the same as before.

To Father Benedict she wrote a few days after her arrival, "It might be the better part of prudence to make your visits here as infrequent as possible." This must be because they aroused some criticism, as had always been true, to some extent, of her relations with him. It may be that the community guessed (and this may have had some truth in it) that she was where she was because of his declaring that she was far more sick than was supposed. But with all due prudence he did go to see her fairly frequently, and so did Agatha Spinella and Sister Marie Dolores. This Sister took her some ice-cream and was delighted when she ate it with evident enjoyment. Later she thought there could have been no enjoyment, for she had heard that Teresa had lost the sense of taste. But the Sister was mistaken, for Teresa had told Father Benedict on January 24th that her sense of taste had returned. To her friend in Bayonne, Aileen Flynn, she sent as a birthday present on April 26th a little meditation book and an Agnus Dei. This was probably the last gift she gave to anyone.

Though Sister Mary Ellen refused to visit Teresa, Mother Alexandrine did so several times, and she had really remained her friend all through the novitiate, though she was herself put in a rather difficult position sometimes, just as her protection of Teresa put the novice-mistress in a difficult position. The day before Teresa left the convent, the Mother-General had said to her, "You are just beginning to realize that you are human," by which one gathers that she wished to convey to the novice that her strength was not inexhaustible. Teresa's terse comment to Father Benedict was, "I've only been too painfully aware of the fact." But even Mother Alexandrine did not understand how very ill Teresa really was.

To Agatha Spinella she wrote: "They don't think I'm sick but I am; this is the beginning of the end." During the last visit Spin paid her, Teresa said, "I know what's on that chart but the nurses tell me the opposite of what's there." This, however, need not be taken literally. While Teresa was aware that her condition was worse than they knew, if Teresa imagined that they were recording ominous things with the glib assurance, "Oh, you are so much better today," she was in error; the chart records improvement upon the whole, though there are some setbacks. Thus for February 28th the chart reads, "Very weak, was cyanotic twice"; for the next day, the patient was "much weaker"; for March 2nd, "condition unchanged"; for the 3rd, "Patient was cyanotic this morning." But these were her worst days. It was an undue sensitiveness that made her take casual comments from the nurses as sarcasm.

Now I must record two unusual stories, in both of which crucifixes figure. One, a small crucifix with a relic of the true cross in a sliding case at the back, had been loaned to Teresa by Father Benedict on Holy Thursday, and of this I will say more a little later.

The other is a cheap wooden cross about eight inches high, with a figure of lead. This belonged to Mother Alexandrine, who brought it to the hospital for Teresa; it is now in the possession of Sister Marie Dolores, who permitted me to hold it in my hands while she told me the following story. It seems that while holding it Teresa received, or believed that she received, an embrace from our Lord such as we hear of St. Bernard's receiving.

Father Benedict, when he called to see her, was calmly told of this incident. He was himself matter-of-fact about it, for when she pointed to the crucifix hanging on the wall he noticed that one of its arms was broken at the wrist and that the figure was attached to the cross by a bit of string. He merely remarked that she should get it fixed. This, however, was not done.

Without exhibiting undue scepticism, it seems to me that if anything is going to cause doubt it would be that Christ should need to break the wrist of His figure, as hanging on a crucifix, to be able to give this embrace. Then, too, the possibility cannot be excluded that the fracture may have occurred while Teresa was holding it—perhaps in a half-awake condition—and that the falling of the arm upon her neck may have roused her from sleep by *seeming* to be an embrace. In mentioning these possibilities—possibilities that might have occurred to anyone—I should in no sense be understood as trying to cast doubt upon what has been recorded, but merely as expressing uncertainty about some of the circumstances surrounding the matter. Father Benedict and Father Charles and Mother Alexandrine all made enquiries about the miraculous crucifix, and Father Benedict has left a long statement, without, however, so far as I can see, putting this beyond all question. Such being the case, I have presented the matter according to the best of my understanding of what may have happened.

The other crucifix story has come to me from several sources, and as again some confusion was left in my mind, I consulted Sister Emeline of the hospital in Elizabeth. She answers that she cannot vouch for it, for she heard it only a few years ago. But it would, she thinks, have been Sister Regina Carmel who would have been concerned, for she was in charge of the floor where Teresa was. As this Sister died in 1930, she cannot be asked about it. So with some question in my mind as to whether all the details about to be given are perfectly accurate, I tell the story as it has been told to me.

It seems that when Teresa entered the hospital, her feet were put in a cast because she could not hold them upright on account of her extreme weakness. Therefore she could not walk so much as a step.* But now notice what happened. She was holding Father Benedict's crucifix in her hands until Sister Regina Carmel, apparently thinking it too heavy for her weak fingers, took it away and put it on the bureau. A few minutes later, having occasion to return, she saw the crucifix back in Teresa's hands, though she had not noticed anyone enter the room who could have given it to her. Again she removed it, and this time she left the door ajar and stood outside. She was absolutely certain, therefore, that no one entered the room and that Teresa did not leave her bed— even on the supposition that she would have been capable of doing so. Yet when Sister Regina Carmel entered a third time, Teresa was again holding the crucifix.

Anne Demjanovich had wanted Teresa brought to St. Elizabeth's Hospital, and she may well have told her brother

---

*Teresa herself said they were strapped together; Father Charles says it is all news to him. But as the nurse, Sister Emeline, is positive about the cast, I will describe Teresa's feet as fastened in that way, though whether it was a cast or a strapping does not seem material.

that Teresa was more ill than was supposed. But he alone was sure after seeing her this time that she was not going to recover, which was not what the doctors said (though it may have been what they feared) but which appears to have been divined by him "psychically" because of the exceptionally close sympathy which existed between him and his "twin" sister. So firmly was he possessed of this idea that he asked Mother Alexandrine in April to allow Teresa to take her vows *in articulo mortis.* Though this was a rather strange request, in view of there being no expectation of death at that time, Mother Alexandrine asked Father Benedict to attend to the matter, giving him for the purpose her own copy of the formula of profession. She added that she had not yet obtained the concurrence of her council, and made the proviso, "If you do not receive a telephone call from me at the hospital, go ahead with the ceremony." As no such call came, Father Benedict took it for granted that the conditional permission she had given him might be presumed to have been confirmed.

In his statement on the subject he says that this happened "about a month" before Teresa died. He also says that he believes the last day he saw her was on Holy Thursday. Further he tells us that it was April 1st that Father Charles asked that Teresa be allowed to be professed.* But though appendicitis appears on the hospital chart for March 27th as suspected, the reports for the next month indicate some improvement, though this may have been brought about by Teresa's joy in having, in spite of all her panic fears, taken her vows as a

---

*Though again, while there is not an absolute certainty about dates (something hardly possible in view of the uncertainty of human memory), it would seem clear that the Community Records of St. Elizabeth's have made a mistake. The profession is put down on page 137 as occurring in May, but without any closer date being assigned. Sister Maria Liberata, the Assistant Mother who wrote this page, was undoubtedly a bit vague and therefore obliged to do a little guessing. Her record is dated September 10, 1939, more than twelve years after the event.

Sister of Charity on the second Saturday of April. Possibly it may have been because of this that the doctors decided that an operation could perhaps, after all, be avoided. At least they were trying to build her up in case it could not be avoided.

A sharp turn for the worse came in early May, and an emergency operation was found to be necessary, to which Teresa's brother Charles and her sister Anne gave their permission. The operation, which took place on Friday, came too late; peritonitis set in, and on Sunday morning, the 8th, Teresa died. It was the third Sunday after Easter.

It was all so unexpected and sudden that none of the members of Teresa's family, or any of her close friends, could be summoned in time. A telephone call reached Father Charles at the Darlington Seminary that his sister was sinking. Monsignor McLaughlin, who was about to say the eight o'clock Mass for the laity at the parish church, let Father Charles say it, so that he could go to the hospital. Monsignor, then Rector of the seminary and afterwards Bishop of Paterson, offered the solemn High Mass at nine thirty, which had been assigned to Father Charles. In spite of the expert driving of the seminary chauffeur, Father Charles arrived at the hospital ten minutes too late. At about the same time there arrived Father Benedict, Mother Alexandrine, and Sister Mary Ellen, the last of these apparently having received a belated conviction that Teresa's illness was really serious.

I have done my best to piece together the various (and slightly discrepant) accounts of Teresa's last moments. In fact, the witnesses do not always agree with themselves, for Sister Emeline writes in the *Sister Miriam Bulletin of Prayer* for May 8, 1947, of Sister Grata, the superior of the hospital and afterwards superior-general, being present at the death-bed, whereas in a letter to me she says positively that Sister Grata was absent because of being obliged to make a number of telephone calls. She mentions as being present Sister

Theresa Mary, Eliza Kelly—her own sister, who is now Mrs. Lowther—Anne Demjanovich, and herself, adding that there were a few others "whom I cannot recall." Anne Demjanovich, consulted on the same point by her brother at my request, answered "that for the life of her she could not remember."

Teresa had received the Last Sacraments a few days before. On the morning of the 8th, just after the community Mass (which would be about seven forty-five), word was telephoned from the floor to Sister Grata that "Sister Miriam Teresa is going." Father (now Monsignor) Brady, who was then the hospital chaplain, was summoned, but as Teresa was already unconscious all that could be done was anoint her, after which those around her bed knelt and said the Prayers for the Dying. It all happened very quietly, without pain of any kind, and Teresa's passing was marked by no more than a slightly perceptible sigh. This is down in the hospital chart as taking place at ten-thirty.

Whatever discrepancies there are in the various reports of Teresa's death that I have seen are of slight importance. One of the best accounts was written for the *Elizabeth Daily Journal* for July 6, 1951, by Dorothea M. Wingert. She does not mention Anne's being present. In all likelihood not all these people were in Teresa's room from the moment that she was known to be dying, but all went in and out, some at one time and some at another. It seems probable that Sister Grata was there at the last moment, just after everything was over, which would account for her sometimes being included and sometimes omitted. It is hardly correct to say of Teresa, as Father Benedict did, that she died, like Christ, in dereliction, for she was not alone, even if several of those she would have wished to see before she expired arrived just too late. Even Christ had His mother and two of His greatest friends standing at the foot of the Cross. His abandonment by God was of a unique and incomprehensible nature, at which theologians can do no more than darkly guess; all the others of God's children can reach out their hand to that of their heavenly Father, if they choose, and die upon His bosom.

CHAPTER NINETEEN

Afterwards

IMMEDIATELY afterwards there began the long series of marvels—many speak of them as miracles—which we hear of in connection with Teresa. On the very day of her death, after Teresa's body was taken to the room where it was to wait for the undertaker, a patient suffering from the very painful tic douloureux asked to be taken there. She went escorted by Sister Emeline, and the moment she placed Teresa's hand on her face she was cured. This is something that would not be accepted as a miracle by the Congregation of Rites, even were there medical testimony on the point, for the disease can be cured by natural causes, or may simply pass away. Furthermore, I am in no position to vouch personally for this or for any of the things about to be recorded, but can merely set down what has been told me, with having felt it at all incumbent upon me to do any cross-examination to arrive at truth. My informants have all struck me as perfectly honest people, so I let it go at that.

A word, however, should be said about miracles in general. Though the term has a popular connotation, strictly speaking it should be restricted only to such wonders as are declared miracles by the Church after she has been asked to pass judgment on them. Those accepted for beatification and canonization are usually instantaneous and permanent cures of some physical condition that is beyond medical help, and must be satisfactorily certified to by doctors. Miracles of grace are not susceptible of this kind of proof, but are of much greater value and occur far more frequently. In addition there are many so-called favours, which while they may be due to the intercession of a saint—things such as finding a lost article or obtaining a position—cannot be recognised officially, as they might in any event have happened. So also with regard to the recovery from a dangerous illness; that may be due to prayer, but it may not. There is no doubt that thousands of such minor miracles happen, but even when they happen as a direct answer to prayer (and who can say with any absolute certainty that this is the case?), they are classified as "favors." The Catholic lives in the spiritual climate in which he takes the miraculous for granted, but whether the miracles of which he knows actually are such can only be a matter of pious opinion. Even should this opinion, in a particular instance, be without solid foundation, no harm is done, but rather a great deal of good if it results in the quickening of faith; what does immense harm is the ruling out on a priori grounds of the possibility of miracles. One is not obliged to believe all that is related of the saints; what one must believe, as a Catholic, is that the intercession of a saint may mightily avail with an omnipotent God.

These provisos having been made, we come to what seem some very remarkable happenings. One of these was that when Teresa's body was taken from the undertaker's to St. Elizabeth's and laid out in the reception parlor of the convent, Sister Marie Dolores asked Mother Alexandrine's permission to put one of her own caps on Teresa's head. She had arrived there wearing one of Mother Alexandrine's caps (for she was now entitled to the cap of a professed Sister), but

Sister Marie Dolores hoped that she would be buried in something that belonged to her. Therefore while the community were at supper, Teresa's old friend went with Sister Jane Teresa (since dead) to make the change.

Sister Marie Dolores had another object in mind. She took a pair of scissors with her to cut off some of Teresa's hair as a relic. Again strictly speaking, it is not correct to speak of "relics" in connection with one not yet beatified but only of "mementos," but the expression is often used and may pass. What are called first-class relics are relatively rare, as only what was an actual part of the body is considered as such; but anything that has ever touched the body of a saint is held to be a relic of the second class. The hair belongs to this category, for as it may grow in the grave, it is not considered a part of the body; but the usual second-class relic is a minute fragment of something worn by one canonized or beatified. However, of relics of this sort, the hair is very personal, and therefore very precious, so Sister Marie Dolores naturally wished to get some of Teresa's hair.

It was in cutting this off that she felt a depression or indentation on Teresa's head, and when she read, as she did later, Teresa's poem "To the Most Holy Crown of Thorns," she was certain that Teresa, though she did not have the stigmata, bore other marks of Christ upon her body. This was the one poem, it will be remembered, that Teresa would not allow her fellow novice Sister Catherine Patricia to read when she let her see the notebook in which she copied out her verses. It opens and concludes with the stanza:

> Thrice-holy thorns, encircling with thy fire
> The pain-racked brow and agonizing Head
> Of Sin's redeeming Victim, anguish bled,
>   Thou art my sole desire.

The poem is not very good, but its sentiment is striking, and even more so is the startling deduction made from it.

That deduction may be quite correct; but while one might gather from a statement left by Father Benedict that Teresa actually did have the marks of the Crown of Thorns, Sister Zita tells me that he really went no further than saying that she suffered the mystical pain of this Crown occasionally from 1925 to 1927. That is not quite the same thing, though of course it could have resulted in the appearance upon her brow of the physical manifestation that Sister Marie Dolores believes she found.

It must be added that some of the other members of the community remain sceptical, and as they have offered me a natural explanation of the matter this must be considered. It is that the kind of stiff fluted cap they wear, and the headband of equally stiff linen press so close that marks are often left on the forehead and the cheeks. Against this, however, it must be remembered that when they are in hospital the Sisters do not wear their ordinary headdress, but a soft kerchief of muslin (something that is much more nearly what people understand by the word "cap"), and that this is loose-fitting for the sake of comfort. The other kind of headdress was put on Teresa only for her journey in the hearse to the convent. I do not believe that any mark of this sort could have been made in the way that has been suggested on the face or head of a dead body. So without maintaining that we have here a demonstrated fact, the evidence seems to indicate that Teresa did have the physical marks of the Crown of Thorns. At the same time, though Teresa was clearly writing about herself, the poem may be symbolical rather than literal, as, for example, may be the case with this typical stanza:

> O sanctifying circlet, tight-compressed,
> Thou boring band, thou sharp death-dealing vise,
> Thou prodigy of mental sacrifice,
>   With thee I am caressed.

On the day of the funeral, May 11, feast of the Solemnity of St. Joseph, Father Benedict pinned on the bulletin board in the main corridor a notice. It read, "The conferences which I have been giving to the Sisters were written by Sister Miriam Teresa." He had always known of course that such a confession would eventually have to be made. One day he had said to Teresa, "The conferences are making me famous, but my day of humiliation is coming when I shall have to acknowledge that I did not write them." To this she countered with a wry smile, "You do not object to the humiliation, do you, Father?" Yet the secret had been kept until Teresa's death; he had put off making the disclosure, perhaps not so much to avoid the "humiliation" as in hope that, if Teresa lived, she would write some more conferences. Now there was no point in preserving silence any longer.

It will be imagined what astonishment the notice caused. And when Father Benedict arrived for his conference on Friday—that is, five days after Teresa's death—everybody was most anxious to know what he would say. After a long pause, as though he did not know how to begin, he at last forced the words out: "Sisters, you have lost a companion who is a saint. It frequently happens when a religious dies that people say, 'She was a saint.' I do not mean that. I mean that you have lost one who will, perhaps, be canonized one day." And as though that were not explicit enough, he put the same idea more fully in several of his written statements, giving the reasons for his belief.

In the convent there were a number who at once began to pray to Teresa instead of for her, and among these were some of the novices who had been critical of her, though some among them still maintained that she was an extremist, as some do to this day. But after it was known that she had written the conferences, it was acknowledged on all hands that she must have lived on a very high spiritual plane, as those who knew her—including those who did not particularly like her—could not but admit that she had been a model religious. Even Sister Mary Ellen, in an instruction she gave her charges, pronounced Teresa a saint, but a little strangely singled out for special praise what she called her "religious" politeness, giving a hint that she hoped would be taken to heart, by saying, "She never left the novitiate without turning at the door and inclining her head to me. She never passed in front of this desk without turning to me." Years later, when she was asked by a member of the community who was about to leave as a missionary to China what she really thought about her former novice, she answered simply, "She was right and I was wrong." At another time she confessed, "God permitted me to misunderstand the child, to my humiliation and her sanctification." This was beautiful humility, though the truth obliged her also to say, "Everything that I did I did in the sight of God."

Perhaps the bit about religious politeness deserves a word of comment. This is something inculcated in all convents and monasteries, and is indeed part of the Liturgy itself. The rules followed at St. Elizabeth's give a couple of pages to the matter, the gist of which is this paragraph: "Religious, the most charitable, the most mortified, are capable of committing serious faults as to politeness and courtesy, either through the want of discernment, to see what may wound or displease others, or else being often so abstracted and careful in the practice of recollection, as to give no attention whatever to what is passing around them." The praise is all the higher when its significance is understood: Sister Mary Ellen was declaring that Teresa never allowed herself to become so lost in recollection as to fail to show consideration to others. She may have been intending a rebuke to those of the novices who had not been very polite to Teresa, and in this rebuke I believe Sister Mary Ellen intended to include herself.

At the Requiem the celebrant was Monsignor McLaughlin, the Rector of the seminary at Darlington, with Father Dolan of St. Vincent's in Bayonne as Deacon and Father Benedict as Subdeacon. The Monsignor declared that the Mass should be the one known as *Dilexisti* from the first word of the Introit; it is the "common" for a virgin not a martyr. Father Benedict, however, thought that it should be that for a virgin and martyr. It need hardly be said that none of this could have been quite seriously meant, and of course it was not attempted. Even when Pope Innocent IV, who happened to be in Assisi on the day in 1253 when St. Clare was buried, was on the point of stopping the Requiem and ordering that the *Dilexisti* be sung instead, he allowed himself to be persuaded by his cardinals to let Clare's process follow the ordinary course and not canonize her then and there. It goes without saying that the clerics present at Teresa's funeral well understood that in her case anything that might have been regarded as "a public cult," would have destroyed her chance of canonization completely. What was said was intended only to express a private and personal conviction that she was a saint, and that of course was harmless enough, so long as it is understood that the decree of Urban VIII is borne in mind.

At this requiem Agatha Spinella, like others of Teresa's college friends, was present. It seems that she had some sort of skin trouble at this time—as she describes it, a bleeding— for which she had received medical treatment without any success. She also says that she had "a kind of depression" in her side, but though it is hard to make out just what this could have been, she definitely says that it was not a tumor, as has been reported. After the priest had pronounced the last blessing, and the coffin was turned around to be wheeled out of the chapel, Agatha prayed to her friend, "Treat, if you are a saint, prove it now." Instantly, she says, her skin infection and the "depression" went. It was just as though she heard "click" and knew herself well again. I asked her whether she had gone to her doctor to let him know what had happened, but this had not occurred to her, as the introduction of Teresa's cause for beatification had not so far been thought of by anybody. Moreover, Agatha is a very diffident person, and usually when she speaks of anything in which she has played a part is inclined to minimize matters to such a degree that she omits salient facts. This has been tantalizing to me, for I have not felt that I had any right to cross-examine her. Yet precisely because her testimony is given so reluctantly, it is all the more convincing. Here was what would seem to be a real miracle, though perhaps not one that could be presented in furtherance of Teresa's cause, for, although an immediate and complete cure was effected where medical treatment had failed, one would gather that further medical treatment might have been capable of reaching the same result.

An even more remarkable story Agatha Spinella had to tell was this. Some years later she had been praying to Teresa—or, as she put it, "talking to Treat; I do not 'pray' to her"—to help a friend who was in hospital. Then, at about five in the morning, Teresa appeared to her—Agatha does not know whether as an actual vision or in a dream at the moment of awakening. She was as Agatha had known her in college, not garbed as a Sister.* She told her to go to the seven o'clock Mass at Paterson cathedral, and in the seventh pew from the Grand Street door she would find a sister of her friend who was ill. To her she was to give a little statue of the Little Flower (which Teresa had given to Agatha) and tell her to put it "where the pain is," and that the vomiting the friend had had for several days would stop at noon exactly. To do this Agatha was obliged to dress in a great hurry to catch the bus, but she reached the cathedral in time, found her friend's sister, and everything happened just as Teresa said it would. The friend recovered but died a year or two later.

The fame of such happenings spread, and now when re-

*Several other times Teresa appeared to her friend again, and again Agatha is unable to say whether in a dream or as an actual apparition, and in these later cases she was wearing her habit. I was unable to draw from her more about these incidents.

ports of other favors, or what seem to be miracles, come in, as they constantly do, they are passed on to Father Stephen Findlay, headmaster of Delbarton, the Benedictine preparatory school at Morristown, who is in charge of Teresa's cause; he makes further investigations, so as to gather securely established data for the Congregation of Rites. I do not know whether or not he has obtained the kind of information necessary, though some reports include the signatures of reputable physicians, but it is clear that a good many people seek Teresa's intercession and that they believe that they obtain answers to their prayers. Some of the manifestations of this enthusiasm are, in fact, a considerable nuisance, for twice the marble cross over Teresa's grave (identical with all the others in the convent cemetery) has had to be replaced, because of people chipping off pieces for "relics." Even the present cross, of the hardest granite that could be found, is being chipped at.

With the publication of *Greater Perfection,* fame of another kind arrived. Teresa's conferences were edited by Father Charles Demjanovich, who at first could find no publisher because, as he was told, "These were not written by any young novice but by a priest noted for his ascetic tendencies, or at least by a religious of many years' standing." To charge Father Charles with trying to perpetrate a hoax was not very complimentary to him, but it was a great compliment to his sister. We have seen what the true story was, and it may be added that the original papers—along with all the other documents of the case—repose for safekeeping in the Chancery Office at Paterson.

The book was an immense success and sold about 40,000 copies, which is very remarkable for a work of this character. It won the Catholic Press Association first prize in 1928, its closest runners-up being books by Father James M. Gillis and Father Joseph Husslein. Hundreds of letters about it poured in, most of them extremely laudatory, almost too much so for me to venture to introduce here. But one from a Carthusian in Italy, a man who should be an expert in the contemplative life, pronounced *Greater Perfection* "a great book," adding, "It is astonishing to find such deep psychological insight, such a knowledge of human nature and such pure and lofty views of the spiritual life in a writer so young in years and younger still in conventual training." A nun in Ireland, however, was much more reserved, but so acute as to be worth quoting. She says that she liked three or four of the conferences, "the mild ones," and goes on to say: "On the whole . . . I would not agree with her sense of values. . . . Most probably postulants would find her conferences stimulating, but, it seems to me, the average novice would be discouraged by them. We had a lively discussion at recreation about her, but most of us came to the conclusion that she was a most promising novice who needed a life's experience to tone her down. She seemed to have a lot in common with St. Thérèse, so earnest, so vigorous, and, at times, so sarcastic." No doubt Teresa would have mellowed in time (and to her personal advantage), but perhaps the effectiveness of her conferences is all the greater because she wrote them when she was still young, intense, plain-spoken, and a bit tart in her tone.

To return to the "favors," many of these are of a trivial character—the landing of a job, the finding of a suitable apartment, the passing of an examination, the curing of a relative from his alcoholism, all of which, it need not be said, might have come about without anybody's intercession. However, even here there are some striking things. Thus the case of a Mrs. G. is related at length. She had obtained her law degree from Fordham but was not able to give the time to serving a year in a law office before being admitted to the bar, which is what the New York State law requires. She carefully avoided bringing any political influence to bear but left the whole matter in Teresa's hands. However, the

Court of Appeals emphatically denied her appeal, at which point she invoked Teresa again. Then the impossible happened: the Court of Appeals took the unprecedented action of reversing itself. Usually, however, the favors announced are such things as: "October, 1927, umbrella found"; "August, 1928, auto started, Huntington, L.I."; "October, 1928, lost library book found." The *Bulletin* for December, 1950, makes the sensible statement that though such reports are welcomed, "They do not bear any weight with the members of the Ecclesiastical Tribunal, who must look for genuine miracles as testimony of God's sanction and approval of the progress of the cause of the candidate for beatification."

There is, nevertheless, one happening that would presumably count as a miracle, provided that it is backed with medical attestation. This is that a Sister Alice Marie of a convent in Connecticut—not a member of Teresa's community—reports that her brother broke both his legs on October 13, 1938. She says that Teresa cured him, as was shown by the X-rays and still more by the fact that he was out of the hospital the week before Christmas and walking without crutches. Of course the term "broken leg" may mean many different things, from a mere dislocation of a joint to a fracture, and about this the report is not very clear.

Sister Anne Lucille has herself told me of what seems to be a miracle of grace—something of greater value than a cure, but of no use, as has been said, to a process for beatification. It seems that there was a young novice who suddenly announced to everybody's astonishment that she was leaving. Her friends in the novitiate begged her to reconsider, but she said: "No, it's too late; I've already told Mother. It's all settled." The best that they could do was to ask her to go with them to Teresa's grave, and she told them, "Well, I'll do it, but everything is arranged. I'm leaving." Then, as they prayed at the grave, what her friends considered her unaccountable spiritual blindness seemed to leave her, and she remained happily in the community.

Once again I must make it clear that in setting down such matters as these I do not vouch for their truth. The furthest I can go is to express my belief that my informants are perfectly honest; in fact, I have been struck forcibly over and over again with their candor and their willingness to recognise that views clean contrary to their own may be those that are correct. It is also, of course, possible to be perfectly honest and yet be mistaken, or to draw a false inference from the most solidly established fact.

The Sisters of Charity are divided in opinion regarding Teresa, though in religious communities there is, as there should be, an *esprit de corps*. Yet this can be a bad thing if pushed to excess, so as to be exclusive. I can at least testify that though no doubt Teresa's own community would be pleased if any of their deceased members were put forward for the highest honors the Church has to bestow, many of them would prefer to see such honors conferred on somebody other than Teresa. As it was rather quaintly put to me, "Now if the Sisters want to canonize somebody, why don't they canonize Mother Xavier?" To this one can only make the mild rejoinder that the Sisters themselves can have nothing to do with the matter, the introduction of the cause falling within the province of the bishop of the diocese, with the final decision resting upon the Holy See. But so far from trying through this book to further her cause, I have studiously avoided anything like partizanship to such a degree that I shall be lucky if some of those who might be described as her partizans do not think that I have done part of the spadework for the *advocatus diaboli*.

But to indicate what the proper ecclesiastical authorities have done, the present condition of affairs is this: On December 11, 1945, Bishop Thomas H. McLaughlin of Paterson opened what is called the ordinary or informative process, and on May 11th of the following year ordered that all the faithful under his jurisdiction should send whatever writings of Teresa's they had—published or unpublished, including discourses, letters, diaries, autobiographies—to him by the end of the year. Notarially attested copies of these were sent to Rome (the originals remaining in his Chancery Office), and another set of copies has been the basis of this book. The Bishop also approved the founding in the same year of the Sister Miriam Teresa League of Prayer, which since October, 1946, has issued a quarterly *Bulletin*. At the first meeting of its directors it was declared that "the primary object of the League is the sanctification of souls, and that although we do want to see Sister Miriam Teresa raised to sainthood, yet we must not forget that her mission is the all-important consideration." Since Bishop McLaughlin's death on March 17, 1947, this work has been backed by his successor, Bishop Thomas A. Boland. Matters relating to the informative process have been delegated to Father Stephen Findlay as Procurator, matters having not yet progressed far enough to call for the appointment of a Postulator of the cause in Rome, with a Vice-Postulator for this country. But while everything apparently is progressing very satisfactorily, nobody is in a position to predict the final outcome.

The introduction of Teresa's cause for beatification took place less than a couple of weeks before Father Bradley's death at the age of nearly eighty. As he had steadily believed for twenty years that she would one day be canonized, and though he perfectly understood that such things take time, at least a start had been made, so he could sing his *Nunc Dimittis.*

And here I might insert the account Sister Zita has given me about her last interview with him. On December 18, 1945, she received word that he was dying in St. Michael's Hospital, Newark, and would like to have her come to see him on the following day. She could not go until after school, and it happened that a blizzard arose and she was not able to get to the hospital until about four thirty in the afternoon. She found Father Benedict fully conscious but so weak that he was hardly able to talk. "I'm so glad that you were able to get here. Everything that I had hoped for regarding Sister Miriam Teresa is at last coming to pass."

Having in mind the importance of the message of Teresa rather than the messenger, Sister Zita said to the dying monk: "Don't you think, Father, that if Sister Miriam Teresa is ever canonized it will be because of her mission?"

"Yes, of course," came the answer faintly, "the mission— that is the all-important thing."

"But, Father, do you really think now that she will ever be canonized?"

"Yes, I believe God will bring this about. It will do much good for souls."

There was a pause. Then Sister Zita spoke about the consolation which comes from trying to do God's will perfectly.

"Yes," answered Father Benedict, "that is the only consolation I have now. Everything I did regarding Sister Miriam Teresa, I did because I was convinced that it was God's Will."

After every few words Father Benedict had to stop, as though trying to get his breath. "I wish that Father Stephen, Father Francis,* you, and Agatha Spinella would have a little talk before you leave the hospital about what I have said. Father Stephen has just been appointed procurator of Sister's cause and will give some plans for the carrying out of the ordinary process. And now I will give you my blessing."

Sister Zita knelt down and the old monk raised his hand, almost inaudibly pronouncing the words of the priestly blessing. She then arose and expressed her gratitude for all his kindness, promising that she would come to see him again in

---

*This was another Benedictine monk, who has not figured in Teresa's story. But he happened to be present because he was from youth a close friend of the elderly monk.

a few days, though in reality she was very doubtful whether she would ever see him again. His eyes followed her as she went out the door, and he murmured a last "God bless you!"

In the corridor she found Agatha Spinella waiting for her interview with Father Benedict. Father Stephen and Father Francis and Sister Zita talked in a small parlor until Agatha joined them. Then they had their little conference as Father Benedict suggested, all agreeing that they should try to follow the will of God as indicated by providential circumstances. It was six o'clock when Sister Zita and her companion left the hospital, and though the storm had subsided it took a long time to get home. The next day, after she had finished her morning's classes, she rang up the hospital to ask how Father Benedict was. She was told that he had died at about ten thirty that morning.

As to whether Teresa Demjanovich will ever be beatified, I express no opinion, except to say that I hope and pray for it, and believe that it would be for the good of the Church. But my business with her ends with the writing of this book, and it would horrify me if anybody looked upon me as a kind of publicity agent for her cause. Many a cause is introduced that does not get very far, or, after making rapid progress at first, comes to a standstill. I have touched upon marvels which apparently have occurred, and these are of great importance, though greater still is the question of the degree to which the candidate for beatification possessed heroic virtue. That he or she may have had faults does not matter very much if such faults are what one might expect to encounter in a human being subject to human frailties. That Teresa had such faults has been made clear, but I hope her spirituality will also be evident. Yet it is not for me to assess such matters. I will go no further than to say that *Greater Perfection* is a work that has already been of considerable influence and that its influence, so far as I can judge, seems likely to increase. If her doctrine is not new, so much the better; she might justifiably be brought under suspicion did she inculcate novelties. She has merely reiterated something that can never be said too often: that the life of contemplation is not reserved solely for mystics withdrawn from all mundane occupations but that, at least to some degree, it is intended to be shared by all of us. We realize, of course, that if we achieve heaven we shall practice there a joyful intensity of uninterrupted contemplation that is impossible, and even inconceivable, to any while still on earth; yet even now, to our poor mortal intelligence may come a gleam of the Radiance beyond our grasp—but not beyond our reach.